First World War
and Army of Occupation
War Diary
France, Belgium and Germany

24 DIVISION
Divisional Troops
106 Brigade Royal Field Artillery
29 September 1915 - 31 May 1919

WO95/2197/3

The Naval & Military Press Ltd
www.nmarchive.com
Published in association with The National Archives

Published by

The Naval & Military Press Ltd

Unit 10 Ridgewood Industrial Park,

Uckfield, East Sussex,

TN22 5QE England

Tel: +44 (0) 1825 749494

www.naval-military-press.com

www.nmarchive.com

This diary has been reprinted in facsimile from the original. Any imperfections are inevitably reproduced and the quality may fall short of modern type and cartographic standards.

© **Crown Copyright**
Images reproduced by permission of The National Archives, London, England, 2015.

Contents

Document type	Place/Title	Date From	Date To
Heading	WO95/2197-3		
Heading	106th Brigade R.F.A. Sep 1915-May 1919		
Heading	Defence Scheme Centre Group 24th Div. Arty. To Accompany War Diary.		
Miscellaneous	Centre Group 24th Divisional Artillery Defence Scheme		
Miscellaneous	Contents		
Miscellaneous	Dispositions		
Miscellaneous	Locations		
Miscellaneous	Instruction "A"		
Miscellaneous	Instruction "B"		
Miscellaneous	Instruction "C"		
Miscellaneous	Instruction "D". "S. O. S".		
Map			
Miscellaneous	Instruction "E".		
Map			
Miscellaneous	Instruction "F".		
Miscellaneous	Instruction "G"		
Miscellaneous	Instruction "H".		
Map	106 Bde. R.F.A. Visual Communications		
Miscellaneous	Instruction "K"		
Miscellaneous	Instruction "L"		
Miscellaneous	Instruction "M".		
Miscellaneous	Instruction "N". Alternative Positions.		
Miscellaneous	Instruction "O"		
Miscellaneous	Instruction "P"		
Miscellaneous	Instruction "Q"		
Miscellaneous	Instruction "R" Counter Attack Scheme.		
Miscellaneous	Counter Attack K.B.O.		
Miscellaneous	Instruction "S"		
Heading	A Battery, 106th Brigade, R.F.A. (24th Division) September (29.8.15 To 30.9.15) 1915		
Miscellaneous	War Diary A. Battery 106 Brigade R.F.A.		
Heading	24th Division "A" Battery 106th Bde R.F.A. Vol I Oct 15		
Miscellaneous		01/11/1915	01/11/1915
War Diary	Isbergues	01/10/1915	01/10/1915
War Diary	Lynde	02/10/1915	02/10/1915
War Diary	Proven	03/10/1915	08/10/1915
War Diary	Reninghelst	09/10/1915	31/10/1915
Heading	24th Division A/106 Battery R.F.A. Vol: 2 Nov 15		
War Diary	Dickebusch	01/11/1915	24/11/1915
War Diary	St Silvestre Cappell	25/11/1915	26/11/1915
War Diary	Broxeele	27/11/1915	28/11/1915
War Diary	Heuringhem	28/11/1915	28/11/1915
War Diary	Tattinghem	29/11/1915	30/11/1915
Miscellaneous	24th 106th Bde: R.F.A. Vols: 41		
War Diary	Tatinghem	01/12/1915	31/12/1915
War Diary	Noordpeene	31/12/1915	31/12/1915
Miscellaneous	2Q. 106th F.A. Bde: Vol: 6		
Miscellaneous	24 A/106 Battery Vol: 4		

Type	Location/Description	Start	End
Miscellaneous		06/02/1916	06/02/1916
War Diary	Tatinghem Noordepene	01/01/1916	01/01/1916
War Diary	Steenvoorde	02/01/1916	02/01/1916
War Diary	Ypres	03/01/1916	31/01/1916
Miscellaneous	106 RFA Vol 67		
War Diary	16 Rue De Cassel Poperinghe	01/02/1916	29/02/1916
Miscellaneous	Officer To A.G's Office At The Base.	23/03/1916	23/03/1916
War Diary	Ypres	01/03/1916	12/03/1916
Miscellaneous	24th Div 106th Bde: R.F.A. Vols 2&3 Sep 15 To May 19		
War Diary	Novelles Lez Vermelles	29/09/1915	30/09/1915
War Diary	Isebeurgues	01/10/1915	01/10/1915
War Diary	Lynde	02/10/1915	02/10/1915
War Diary	1 1/2 Miles N Of Watou	03/10/1915	09/10/1915
Miscellaneous	1 Mile E Of Reninghelst	10/10/1915	18/10/1915
Miscellaneous	H.29.C.2.6	19/10/1915	25/11/1915
War Diary	St Sylvestre Cappel	26/11/1915	26/11/1915
War Diary	Broxeele	27/11/1915	27/11/1915
War Diary	Heuringhem	28/11/1915	28/11/1915
War Diary	Tatinghem	29/11/1915	02/12/1915
War Diary	Noordpeene	01/01/1916	01/01/1916
War Diary	Steenvoorde	02/01/1916	03/01/1916
War Diary	16 Rue de Cassel Poperinghe	04/01/1916	31/01/1916
Miscellaneous	A/106 Battery Vol: 5 24		
War Diary	Ypres	01/02/1916	29/02/1916
Miscellaneous	O. i/c A.G.s. Office Base	06/04/1916	06/04/1916
War Diary	16 Rue de Cassel Poperinghe	01/03/1916	14/03/1916
War Diary	Ramparts Ypres	15/03/1916	18/03/1916
War Diary	Ypres	19/03/1916	31/03/1916
Miscellaneous	O. i/c, A.G's Office Base.	02/05/1916	02/05/1916
War Diary	T20.C8.9 (Sheet 28)	01/04/1916	18/04/1916
War Diary	T.20.C 8.9	19/04/1916	30/04/1916
War Diary	Ploegsteert	01/05/1916	31/05/1916
Miscellaneous	Appendix I. New Organization of 24th Divisional Artillery.	13/05/1916	13/05/1916
Miscellaneous	Appendix II. Temporary Tactical Grouping of 24th Divisional Artillery.	13/05/1916	13/05/1916
War Diary	Ploegsteert	01/06/1916	05/07/1916
War Diary	Kemmel	06/07/1916	08/07/1916
War Diary	Ploegsteert	09/07/1916	11/07/1916
War Diary	Romarin	12/07/1916	22/07/1916
War Diary	Ecke	23/07/1916	25/07/1916
War Diary	Longueau	26/07/1916	26/07/1916
War Diary	Hangest-S-Somme	27/07/1916	31/07/1916
Heading	106th Brigade Royal Field Artillery August 1916		
War Diary	Vicquemont	01/08/1916	04/08/1916
War Diary	Bois-De-Tailles	05/08/1916	12/08/1916
War Diary	Maricourt	13/08/1916	31/08/1916
Heading	106th Brigade R.F.A. September 1916		
Miscellaneous	Head Qrs (Q) 24th Division	09/10/1916	09/10/1916
War Diary	Briquetrie	01/09/1916	06/09/1916
War Diary	Bois-De Tailles	07/09/1916	12/09/1916
War Diary	Maltze Horn Ravine	13/09/1916	21/09/1916
War Diary	Leuze Wood	22/09/1916	28/09/1916
War Diary	Bois De Tailles	29/09/1916	29/09/1916
War Diary	Pierregot	30/09/1916	30/09/1916

War Diary	Authieute	01/10/1916	01/10/1916
War Diary	Vacquirie Le Bourcq	02/10/1916	02/10/1916
War Diary	Bours	03/10/1916	03/10/1916
War Diary	Verdrel	04/10/1916	05/10/1916
War Diary	Berthonvale	06/10/1916	31/10/1916
War Diary		01/11/1916	30/11/1916
War Diary		01/12/1916	31/12/1916
War Diary		01/01/1917	31/01/1917
War Diary	Philosophe	01/02/1917	13/02/1917
War Diary	Ecquedecques	14/02/1917	28/02/1917
War Diary		01/03/1917	31/03/1917
Heading	106th Brigade R.F.A. 24th Division April 1917		
War Diary	Field	01/04/1917	30/04/1917
Miscellaneous	Appendix I.		
War Diary	Matringhem	01/05/1917	31/05/1917
War Diary	In the Field	01/06/1917	31/08/1917
Heading	106 Bde R.F.A. Sept 1917 Vol 25		
War Diary	In the Field	01/09/1917	30/09/1917
Heading	War Diary for October 1917 106 Bde R.F.A. Vol 26		
War Diary	Field	01/10/1917	31/10/1917
Heading	24 Div War Diary 106th Bde R.F.A. From Nov 1st to Nov 30th 1917.		
War Diary		01/11/1917	30/11/1917
War Diary	In the Field	01/12/1917	31/12/1917
War Diary		01/01/1918	31/01/1918
War Diary		01/02/1918	28/02/1918
War Diary	Georges	01/03/1918	01/03/1918
War Diary	Copse near Templeux	02/03/1918	04/03/1918
War Diary	Montecourt	05/03/1918	12/03/1918
War Diary	Trefcon	13/03/1918	14/03/1918
War Diary	Vendelles	14/03/1918	22/03/1918
War Diary	Briost	23/03/1918	25/03/1918
War Diary	Meharicourt	25/03/1918	29/03/1918
War Diary	Rouvrel	29/03/1918	31/03/1918
Heading	Headquarters, 106th Brigade, R.F.A. April 1918		
War Diary	Rouvrel	01/04/1918	02/04/1918
War Diary	Fouencamps	03/04/1918	06/04/1918
War Diary	St. Fuscien	07/04/1918	07/04/1918
War Diary	Revelles	08/04/1918	08/04/1918
War Diary	Andainville	09/04/1918	10/04/1918
War Diary	Sorel	11/04/1918	16/04/1918
War Diary	Bellancourt	17/04/1918	17/04/1918
War Diary	Beauvoir-Riviere	18/04/1918	18/04/1918
War Diary	Hernicourt	19/04/1918	20/04/1918
War Diary	Etree Wamin	21/04/1918	04/05/1918
War Diary	Hoxton Post M.15 b.1090	05/05/1918	04/06/1918
War Diary	Maroc	05/06/1918	30/06/1918
Heading	War Diary of 106th. Brigade, R.F.A. From 1st July, 1918. To 31st July, 1918. Vol 35		
War Diary	Maroc	01/07/1918	31/07/1918
Heading	War Diary. of 106th Brigade, Royal Field Artillery. From:- 1st August 1918. To:- 30th August 1918. Vol 36		
War Diary	Maroc	01/08/1918	06/08/1918
War Diary	Fosse 10. Sans en-Gohelle	07/08/1918	17/08/1918
War Diary	Maroc	18/08/1918	01/10/1918
War Diary	Quarries M.6.a.80.30.	02/10/1918	02/10/1918

War Diary	Hythe Tunnels	03/10/1918	12/10/1918
War Diary	Maroc	13/10/1918	13/10/1918
War Diary	Ecurie	14/10/1918	14/10/1918
War Diary	Guemappe	15/10/1918	15/10/1918
War Diary	Cambrai	16/10/1918	18/10/1918
War Diary	Avesnes	19/10/1918	19/10/1918
War Diary	St. Aubert	20/10/1918	20/10/1918
War Diary	Haussy	21/10/1918	25/10/1918
War Diary	Bermerain	26/10/1918	01/11/1918
War Diary	La Justice	02/11/1918	02/11/1918
War Diary	Sepmeries	03/11/1918	03/11/1918
War Diary	Jenlain	04/11/1918	04/11/1918
War Diary	La Bois Crette	05/11/1918	06/11/1918
War Diary	La Bois	07/11/1918	07/11/1918
War Diary	Le Louvion	08/11/1918	08/11/1918
War Diary	Les Gueulards (Feignies)	09/11/1918	09/11/1918
War Diary	Leveau (Feignies)	10/11/1918	11/11/1918
War Diary	Feignies. (Guislan Bray)	12/11/1918	16/11/1918
War Diary	Eth	17/11/1918	17/11/1918
War Diary	Escaudain	18/11/1918	18/11/1918
War Diary	Lewarde	19/11/1918	26/11/1918
War Diary	Bertinquesme (Rosult)	27/11/1918	30/11/1918
War Diary	Bertinquesme Rosult.	01/12/1918	31/12/1918
War Diary	Antoing	01/01/1919	31/01/1919
Miscellaneous	Appendix To War Diary of 106th Brigade, R.F.A., For Month Ending 31st January, 1919.	31/01/1919	31/01/1919
Miscellaneous	Appendix to War Diary of 106th Brigade, R.F.A. For Month of January, 1919.		
War Diary	Antoing	01/02/1919	25/03/1919
War Diary	Templeuve	26/03/1919	31/03/1919
War Diary	Templeuve (Belgium)	01/04/1919	31/05/1919

W0 05/21/07/13

24TH DIVISION
DIVL ARTILLERY

106TH BRIGADE R.F.A.
SEP 1915 - MAY 1919

COPY No. 11.

SECRET

DEFENCE SCHEME
CENTRE GROUP
24TH DIV. ARTY.

To accompany War Diary.

SECRET

CENTRE GROUP
24TH DIVISIONAL ARTILLERY
DEFENCE SCHEME

Copies to :-

1. 24th Divisional Artillery.
2. 17th Infantry Brigade.
3. Right Group 24th Div. Arty.
4. Left Group 24th Dov. Arty.
5. Centre Group Commander.
6. ~~52nd Army~~ HQ/106 Brigade R.F.A.
7. A/106th Brigade R.F.A.
8. B/106th Brigade R.F.A.
9. C/106th Brigade R.F.A.
10. D/106th Brigade R.F.A.
11. War Diary.
12. FILE

CONTENTS

DISPOSITIONS

LOCATIONS

INSTRUCTION
- A. Artillery Policy.
- B. O. P's.
- C. Liaison.
- D. S. O. S.
- E. Counter Preparation. + ARTILLERY ATTACK
- F. Gas.
- G. Anti-Tank Defence.
- H. Mutual Support.
- J. Visual Communications.
- K. Harassing Fire.
- L. Local Defence.
- M. Arrangements in case of Retirement.
- N. Alternative Positions.
- O. Ammunition.
- P. Retaliation Schemes.
- Q. Zone calls, LL calls and S.O.S. Aeroplane
- R. Counter attack scheme.
- S. PREPARE FOR ACTION and MAN BATTLE STATIONS

DISPOSITIONS

1. The Divisional front extends from N.13.b.6.0. to H.25.d.25.85.
   [handwritten: N 14 c 45 15]

2. It is divided into Brigade fronts as follows:-

   Northern Bde. 73rd.Inf.Bde. H.25.d.25.85. to H.32.d.3.4.
   Centre   Bde. 17th.Inf.Bde. H.32.d.3.4.   to N.8.b.55.60.
   Southern Bde. 72nd.Inf.Bde. N.8.b.55.60. to N.13.b.6.0.
   [handwritten: N 14 c 45 15]

3. <u>Inter-Brigade Boundaries are as follows:-</u>
   <u>Between 73rd and 17th Inf.Bdes.</u> - Front line at H.32.d.3.4.-
   HYTHE ALLEY (inclusive to 73rd I.B.)-H.31.d.05.35.-G.36.d.30.30.-
   along Southern outskirts of LOOS. - Cross Roads G.34.d.8.5. -thence
   due West to MAROC (inclusive to 17th I.B.)
   <u>Between 17th and 72nd I.B.s.</u> - Front line N.8.b.55.60. -CARFAX -
   junction CARFAX and DOUGLAS both inclusive to 72nd I.B. - N.7.a.9.5.-
   COUNTER ALLEY (inclusive to 17th I.B.)-N.7.a.00.35.-M.12.a.00.85.-
   M.11.a.8.8. -VILLAGE LINE M.9.b.6.8.-MAROC (inclusive to 17th I.B.)-
   M.8.d.35.80. -thence along Railway to BULLY GRENAY (inclusive to
   72nd I.B.).

4. <u>SYSTEM OF DEFENCE</u>
   The system of defence is divided into two main zones.
       (a) OUTPOST Zone.
       (b) BATTLE Zone.
   (a) OUTPOST Zone consists of a series of trenches and posts held
   in sufficient strength to repel anything but a determined and
   organised attack. In the event of reliable information being received
   that an enemy attack is iminent, the order "PREPARE for ACTION" will
   be sent out, when the OUTPOST Zone will be thinnedout, leaving
   fighting and observation posts.
   (b) BATTLE Zone is the Zone in which the enemy is to be fought
   to the last and is organized in depth, consisting of a chain of
   inter-supporting defended localities, distributed checker-wise.

DISPOSITIONS (Cont.)

4. (Cont.

The front of the BATTLE Zone is known as the BLACK Line and is the main general line of defence with various switch lines and defences in rear.

On receipt of the order "MAN BATTLE STATIONS" all other troops not already in their BATTLE positions will occupy them.

In rear of the BATTLE Zone are lines of defence known as the GREEN Line, BULLY Switch, ARMY Line and G.H.Q. Line.

5. **ARTILLERY DISPOSITIONS.**

The Centre Group, 24th D.A. covering the Centre Infantry Brigade front consists of :-

18 - 18pdrs. and 6 - 4.5" Hows. 106th Brigade, R.F.A.
~~6 - 18pdrs. and 6 - 4.5" Hows. 52nd Army Bde. R.F.A.~~

LOCATIONS

CENTRE INFANTRY BDE.(17th I.B.)	M.3.b.20.50.
RIGHT do do (72nd I.B.)	FOSSE 11 de BETHUNE
LEFT do do (73rd I.B.)	G.34.d.95.30.
CENTRE GROUP (& H.Q.106th.Bde.RFA)	M.3.b.00.45.(with 17th.I.B.H.Q.
RIGHT GROUP	M.11.a.60.10(with 72nd.I.B.H.Q.
LEFT GROUP (& H.Q.48th Army Bde.RFA)	G.34.d.95.30(with 73rd I.B.H.Q.
~~58ND ARMY BDE. R.F.A.~~	~~M.14.d.X.X~~
RIGHT BATTN- CENTRE INF.BDE.	M.6.c.1.6.
LEFT BATTN. do do do	M.6.a.9.2.

PRESENT POSITIONS OF BATTERIES

Battery	No. of guns	Location	Arc of fire true bearing	Wagon Lines
A/106	2	M.11.c.30.00.	38 to 80	R.2.b.5.9.
	4	M.9.c.93.16.	51 to 105	PETIT SAINS
B/106	4	M.9.b.70.75.	52 to 124	R.2.c.2.5.
	2	M.12.a.20.25.	47 to 97	SAINS EN GOHELLE
			57 to 87	
C/106	4	M.2.d.60.78.	54 to 106	R.26.b.5.7.
	2	M.10.d.35.90.	65 to 90	MARQUEFFLES
D/106	4	M.3.d.10.30.	55 to 114	R.1.d.6.3.
	2	M.10.a.62.25.	48 to 103	SAINS EN GOHELLE
~~A/52~~	~~6~~	~~M.10.a.75.75.~~	~~48 to 103~~	)
~~122nd~~	~~6~~	~~M.2.b.23.58.~~	~~72 to 107~~	) ~~R.31.d.~~
~~C/52~~	~~6~~	~~M.10.a.55.85.~~	~~50 to 105~~	)
~~D/52~~	~~6~~	~~M.14.d.18.88.~~	~~57 to 98~~	) ~~FOSSE 10~~

INSTRUCTION "A"

ARTILLERY POLICY

1. The Artillery policy is to keep the main battery positions silent (after registration) and to push forward single guns and sections to carry on harassing fire by night and on misty days. During the day, shooting to be confined principally to firing on all movement seen in enemy lines and carrying out the necessary registration and calibration.

2. The guns covering the Centre Inf.Bde.front are divided up as follows:-

(a) Forward guns.	(b) Intermediate Batteries and Sections.	(c) Rear Btys.
A/106 1 gun	A/106 5 guns (1 detached)	C/106 4 guns
B/106 2 guns	B/106 4 guns	D/106 4 Hows.
	C/106 2 guns	~~52nd. Army Bde.~~
	D/106 2 Hows.	~~6 guns & 6 Hows.~~

Of the above only the forward guns and detached sections are active

3. In case of attack when "PREPARE FOR ACTION" or "MAN BATTLE STATIONS" has been received the forward guns will not be withdrawn but will take part in Counter-preparation and S.O.S. barrages until all ammunition is used up. Attempt will then be made to withdraw them or they will be destroyed according to circumstances.

4. Should a retirement from main battery positions become necessary this will be carried out by XXXXXXXXXXXX sections or whole batteries according to the situation, the retirement being so arranged that continuous fire on the enemy is maintained.

INSTRUCTION "B"

O. P's.
----

1. Each battery of the ~~46th Bde.~~ will man an O.P. for the OBSERVATION LINE daily from 9 am till dusk and in addition the two batteries finding the Liaison parties will man their O.P's. until dark and again from dawn until 9 am. the next morning. Liaison Officers may be used for this purpose.

2. O.P. parties will consist of:-
   One Officer
   One N.C.O.
   Two Telephonists.

3. O.P's. for the OBSERVATION and BLACK LINES are as follows:-

For	Name	Location	Allotted to	Arc of view true bearings
OBSERVATION LINE	CONSTANCE	N.1.d.90.10.	A/106	70 to 140
	RAILWAY	N.1.d.3.5.	B/106	86 to 90
	AURORA	N.2.a.21.83.	C/106	65 to 145
	HAWK	N.1.a.78.88.	D/106	89 to 140
BLACK LINE	SONIA.	M.6.d.6.6.	E/106	
	JAMPOT	M.6.d.15.75.	B/106	
	MOUND	M.12.a.43.90.	DC/106	
	TOWER	M.11.b.75.60.	AB/106	
	JERRY	M.13.2.?		

4. JAMPOT O.P. will be manned ~~day and~~ night by the 52nd Army Bde.RFA. as a GROUP O.P. and S.O.S. Rocket repeating station.

INSTRUCTION "B" (cont).

5. On the receipt of the order "PREPARE FOR ACTION or MAN BATTLE STATIONS:-

All batteries will at once man their BLACK Line O.P's.
Outpost Line OP parties except that at HAWK will withdraw to thar their batteries.
The party at HAWK will remain there until the attack by the enemy infantry commences. The Officer will then fire the OBSERVATION LINE S.O.S.Signal and withdraw his party to his battery.
If there is a party at JAMPOT when the above orders are given, that party will remain until relieved by the party from B/106.
Officers manning BLACK LINE O.Ps. will watch the situation and if they consider it advisable, may take two of their battery guns ~~temporarily~~ temporarily off the pre-arranged barrage in order to engage important targets. For this reason the BLACK LINE O.Ps. will be manned by responsible Officers.

INSTRUCTION "C"

LIAISON
----

1. Group Headquarters adjoins the Headquarters of the Centre Inf. Bde.

2. Batteries of the 106th Bde. take it in turns to find a Liaison party to be at each Battalion Headquarters in the line at night, A ~~B/106~~ ~~D~~ 6/106 finding the party with the Eight Battalion, ~~B and~~ C & D finding that with the Left.

   A Liaison party consists of:-
   One Officer
   Two Telephonists.

3. Battery Commanders will visit Battalion Headquarters at frequent intervals. Also Battery Officers will constantly visit Company Commanders and Officers in the line.

4. If the order "MAN BATTLE STATIONS" is issued at night, Liaison parties will remain at Battalion Headquarters until daylight and will then rejoin their Batteries.

INSTRUCTION "D".
"S. O. S".

1. The S.O.S. Signal or message is the call for Artillery fire to be opened at once on pre-arranged S.O.S. Lines.

2. There are two S.O.S. Barrages prepared on the Centre Infantry Brigade front, one for the OUTPOST and one for the BLACK Line. (See para. 7).

3. OUTPOST S.O.S.
   (a) The S.O.S. Signal for the OUTPOST Line is a number 32 Grenade bursting into 3 GREEN lights, closely followed by a No. 31 Rifle Grenade giving out BLUE SMOKE.
   (b) OUTPOST S.O.S. on the Centre Brigade front will be repeated by all O.Ps. that are manned at the time, and will also be sent back by telephone, visual or other means.
   (c) On receipt of OUTPOST S.O.S. the forward sections of batteries will open fire at once on their S.O.S. Lines without waiting for further orders. Main Battery Positions will "stand to" but will not open fire unless previous bombardment or other sources of information have led to the expectation od an attack on a large scale. In the event of communications being cut Battery Commanders will use their own discretion about this.
   (d) Subsequent procedure will be as follows:-
   Guns and Howitzers will search and sweep:-
       18-pdrs. back to a depth of 300 yards from <u>our</u> front line, 4.5" Hows. from 200 to 400 yards.
   On reaching the limit of the zone to be searched, barrages will jump back to their starting line, on which they will remain for a few minutes, the process being continued as long as the situation demands, but this procedure will be varied.
   Normal rate of lifts - 100 yards every 2 minutes.

INSTRUCTION "D" (contd)

3. **OUTPOST S.O.S.(contd)**
   Rates of fire:-   5 minutes INTENSE.
                      5 minutes RAPID
                      5 minutes NORMAL

   If after 5 minutes the Infantry consider that a quicker rate should be maintained, or, after 15 minutes, that they require the barrage to be repeated, a second S.O.S. Signal will be given, whereupon all batteries will revert to INTENSE rate of fire, and repeat the same process

INSTRUCTION "D" (contd)

4. Concentrations for Raids.

The following concentrations have been arranged for dealing with hostile raids on the Group front:-

CODE CALL	Battery	Guns	Barrage
BARRAGE HILL 70	C/106	2	H.32.d.38.30. - H.32.d.40.11.
	B/106	2	H.32.d.40.11. - N.2.b.50.95.
	A/106	2	N.2.b.50.95. - N.2.b.52.75.
	D/106	2	Sweep H.32.d.38.30. - N.2.b.52.75.
	18-pdr) Rt.Grp.)	2	NOGGIN TRENCH from N.2.b.52.75. - N.2.b.10.30.
BARRAGE NETLEY	C/106	2	N.2.b.20.42. - N.2.b.08.30.
	B/106	2	N.2.b.08.30. - N.2.b.15.10.
	A/106	2	N.2.b.15.10. - N.2.d.20.90.
	D/106	2	Sweep N.2.b.20.42. - N.2.d.20.90.
BARRAGE NESTOR	C/106	2	N.2.d.20.90. - N.2.d.34.85.
	B/106	2	N.2.d.34.85. - N.2.d.35.70.
	A/106	2	N.2.d.35.70. - N.2.d.44.50.
	D/106	2	Sweep N.2.d.20.90. - N.2.d.44.50.
BARRAGE COSY	C/106	2	N.2.d.44.38. - N.2.d.44.18.
	B/106	2	N.2.d.44.18. - N.2.d.54.04.
	A/106	2	N.2.d.54.04. - N.2.b.60.85.
	D/106	2	Sweep N.2.d.44.38. - N.2.b.60.85.

On receipt of one of the above calls the forward sections will switch on to our front trench as detailed above for 15 minutes at OUTPOST S.O.S. rates.

4.5" Hows. will sweep the whole extent of the target.

AMMUNITION:- 18-pdrs. - 75% AX. 106 fuze (if available)
18-pdrs. - 25% A.
4.5" Hows. - 100% BX.

BARRAGE HILL 70 and BARRAGE COSY may also be called for in support of the Left and Right Groups respectively. For details see Instruction "H".

INSTRUCTION "D" (contd)

5. BLACK Line S.O.S.
The barrage on the 24th Divisional front may be brought back to the BLACK Line in 3 ways:-
   (1) On the whole Divisional front.
   (2) On the combined fronts of Left and Centre Inf.Bdes.
   (3) On the Right Bde. front.

The signal for bringing back the barrage is a Mortar Signal bursting into RED GREEN closely followed by a Mortar Signal giving out RED SMOKE. RED

The only post forward of Bde.H.Q. from which this signal will be fired on the Left and Centre Bde. fronts is HARTS CRATER, or if this is impossible, the QUARRY M.6.a.9.5.

This signal will be repeated from both Inf.Bde.H.Q.(M.3.b.20.60.) & G.34.d.95.30.) and from the Centre Group Rocket Station M.3.b.05.85.

Batteries will bring their barrage back to cover the BLACK Line either on receipt of orders from Group H.Q. or on seeing the signal go up from any of the above stations.

The same procedure will be employed for S.O.S. barrages on the BLACK Line as for the OUTPOST Line (see para.2 above) except that the rates of fire for the BLACK Line barrage will be:-
   10 minutes - INTENSE.
   10 minutes - RAPID.
   10 minutes - NORMAL.

When the attack has been repulsed, the fire of batteries should work slowly forward up to their maximum range.

6. In the event of the barrage on the combined Left and Centre Inf.Bde. fronts being brought back before that on the Right Inf.Bde.front, the following barrage will be placed on the exposed flank of the Right Inf. Bde. until such time as their barrage is brought back also:-
   A/106 (2 guns) N.7.b.96.50. - N.8.a.70.60.

The Code Word to be used to call for this Barrage will be "HELP CANTEEN".

I N S T R U C T I O N "D" (contd)

7. S.O.S.Lines on the OUTPOST and BLACK Lines are as follows:-

OUTPOST S.O.S. BARRAGE.

A/106 - N.2.d.73.00. - N.2.d.xx 73.56.
B/106 - N.2.b.55.45. - N.2.b.63.70.- N.2.b.62.92.
C/106 - N.2.b.62.92. - H.32.d.58.40.
D/106 - N.2.d.72.62.
        N.2.d.70.70.
        N.2.d.70.80.
        N.2.d.70.90.
        N.2.b.80.90.
        H.32.d.75.05.

BLACK LINE S.O.S. BARRAGE.

A/106   -   N.7.b.65.88.- N.1.d.60.42.
B/106 (4 guns) N.1.d.60.52.- N.1.d.54.90.
      (2 guns) N.1.b.28.50.- N.1.b.25.70.
C/106   -   N.1.b.25.70.- H.31.d.10.30.
D/106   -   N.7.b.68.40.
                        N.7.b.60.58.
                        N.7.b.65.70.
                        N.7.b.68.80.
                        H.31.d.20.10.
                        H.31.d.18.25.

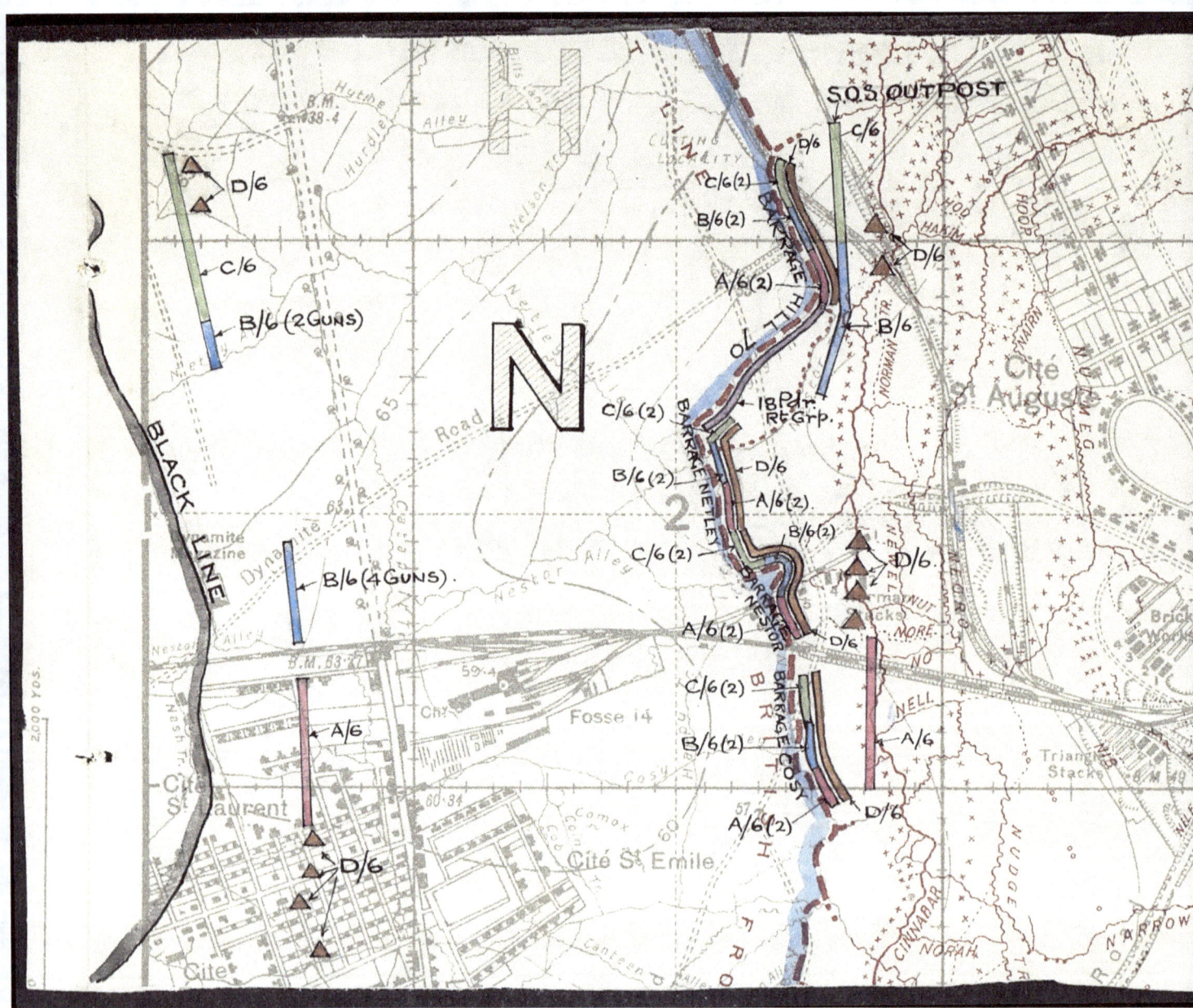

INSTRUCTION "E".

ARTILLERY ATTACKS and COUNTER PREPARATION.

1. Artillery Attacks are a modified form of Counter Preparation and will be employed during periods in which an attack on a large scale is considered improbable. They will take the form of short concentrations of Heavy Artillery on the most suitable areas, principally with 6" Hows., combined with searching fire by Field Artillery (using forward sections and guns) on approaches.

2. Counter preparation will be employed when a general attack by the enemy is considered probable. All natures of guns and hows. will be employed.

Owing to weakness of Artillery on the front of the 24th Division, areas (lettered A, B & C) will be successively concentrated on.

Artillery action will be as follows:-

<u>Field Artillery</u>. All available 18-prs. will be used to form frequent barrages at irregular intervals, rolling backwards and forwards over the enemy's front line, and extending beyond it to about 500 or 600 yards. 4.5" Hows. will fire on M.G. and T.M. emplacements, trench junctions & communication trenches.

<u>Heavy Artillery</u> will fire on T.M. positions reserve lines & possible assembly places.

If wind is favourable 4.5" Hows. will use gas shells.

Should Counter Preparation continue for a long time the rate of fire will be controlled by Group H.Q. or by Batteries if communications are cut, to avoid exhaustion of personnel & undue expenditure of ammunition.

A zero hour will be given with the order for Counter Preparation.

Should the OBSERVATION Line S.O.S. Signal go up during Counter Preparation it will be at once responded to by all batteries.

INSTRUCTION "E" (cont).

3. **Artillery Attack.**
Tasks for 18-prs. & 4.5" Hows. are allotted as follows:-
Area K.

    A/106   PURDY road from N.4.c.5.5. to N.5.a.90.15.
    B/106   Roads from N.4.b.00.65. to N.5.a.00.95 and
                N.4.b.95.00. to N.5.a.9.4.
    C/106   Road from N.4.c.9.8. to N.4.b.9.7.
    D/106   Track junctions N.4.b.95.90. and N.4.c.00.75.

The time of zero hour will be given, also duration of concentration.

Rates of fire will be:-
    Zero to zero plus 5 mins.   Rapid.
    Zero plus 5 onwards.   Normal with bursts of rapid fire at irregular intervals.

These "Artillery Attack" Schemes will be varied from time to time and may be carried out by night at likely times of relief as well as by day.

INSTRUCTION "E" (cont).

4. **Counter preparation.**

Zones for 18-prs. & targets for 4.5" Hows. are allotted as follows:-

Area A.
    18-prs. Roll backwards & forwards at irregular intervals from enemy front line to a depth of 500 to 600 yards.

        A/106. (2 guns). From H.32.b.70.00. to H.32.b.60.25.
        B/106. (6 guns). From H.32.b.60.25. to H.26.d.30.00.
        D/106. (3 Hows). Shell holes H.32.b.70.76 T.J. H.32.b.94.66.,
                H.Q. H.33.a.60.10.

Area B.
    18-prs. Roll as above from enemy front line
        A/106. (6 guns). From N.2.d.85.00. to N.2.d.75.60.
        B/106. (6 guns). From N.2.d.75.60. to N.2.b.7.2.
        C/106. (6 guns). From N.2.b.7.3. to N.2.b.7.8.
        D/106. (6 Hows). T.M. N.2.b.94.12., T.M. N.3.a.2.0. T.Ms. N.3.c.
                20.45. T.M. N.3.a.ØYYEX 98.36., T.Ms. N.3.a.7400
                T.M. N.3.a.66.24.

Area C.
    18-prs. Roll as above from enemy front line.
        A/106. (6 guns). From N.14.b.0.8. to N.8.d.2.2.
        B/106. (4 guns). From N.8.d.2.2. to N.8.d.5.6.
        D/106. (3 Hows). T.M. N.9.c.16.62. T.M. N.8.d.8.1. Trench
                N.14.b.14.66. to 30.36.

Concentrate on Area "B" ZERO to ZERO plus 15 mins.
    do. on Areas "A & C" Zero plus 15 to zero plus 35 mins.
    do. on Area "B" Zero plus 35 mins. to zero plus 65 mins.
    do. on Areas "A & C" Zero plus 65 mins. to zero plus 90 mins.

INSTRUCTION "E" (cont).

4. (cont).
   If Counter-preparation lasts more than 1½ hours, repeat as above for every period of 1½ hours till S.O.S. goes up.

   Rates of Fire   Zero to zero plus 5.   RAPID.
                      Zero plus 5½ onward.   NORMAL with bursts
                                                                  of Rapid fire at
                                                                  irregular intervals

INSTRUCTION "F".
G A S.

In the event of CLOUD GAS or PROJECTOR attacks the message "GAS" will be sent at once by F.O.O's. and Liaison Officers to all concerned.

Procedure will *then* be as follows:-

(a) GAS CLOUD.

FORWARD SECTIONS OF Forward Sections of 18-pdrs. will search communications. 4.5" Hows. ~~will open fire on~~ will open fire on enemy front line with H.E.

Rates of fire NORMAL. All guns and hows. searching and sweeping until receipt of further orders from Group H.Q. *other battery positions "Stand to" prepared to open fire on S.O.S lines.*

(b) PROJECTORS.

FORWARD SECTIONS OF 4.5" Hows. will open fire at NORMAL rate on trenches from which gas is being projected.

18-pdrs. will "Stand to" prepared to open fire on S.O.S. lines.

Reference S.S. 534 "Defence against Gas" (Appendix 1V).
The following are the GAS ZONES in and in neighbourhood of the 24th Divisional Area.

(1) The "ALERT ZONE"

The country East of a line drawn between the following places, SOUCHEZ (exclusive), ANGRES (inclusive), ORMEAU (inclusive), MAZINGARBE (exclusive), SAILLY-LABOURSE,(exclusive).

(2) The "READY ZONE"

The country between Western limits of the "Alert Zone" and the following points, VILLERS AU BOIS (exclusive) GOUY SERVINS (exclusive) Bouvigny (inclusive), HERSIN (inclusive) BARLIN (exclusive)

INSTRUCTION "G"

Anti Tank Defence.

1.   There is one 18-pr. A.T. gun on the Centre Group front. This
gun (BILLY) is located at M.6d.65.75. with an arc of fire from 30
to 132 degrees T.E.

2.   The detachment consists of an N.C.O. not below the rank of Cpl
and 3 men. This detachment has orders to fire on hostile tanks by
direct laying without any regard to any infantry action that may be
going on.

3.   In the event of an enemy attack developing without the assist-
ance of tanks, they will fire on the enemy infantry by direct laying
and will not withdraw until all ammunition has been used up or their
gun has been put out of action by the enemy.

4.   In the event of an enemy attack developing during mist or fog
the detachment will have little chance of seeing Tanks or the
attacking Infantry. In that case they will fire on a definite line
after the BLACK LINE S.O.S. Signal has gone up. This line will be
called the MIST LINE, and is at present the line S.1.b.65.65. to
H.35.c.6.1.   It will be marked by two aiming posts and the gun
will be kept laid on it.
       When our barrage has been brought back to in front of the
BLACK LINE the N.C.O. will open fire as laid down in the special
MIST LINE orders, a copy of which is attached.

5.   The complete detachment will be found by batteries in turn
and will be relieved once a fortnight, no two men on the same day.
Charge of the gun will pass on from one battery to the next on
alternate Sundays (the day on which the N.C.O. is relieved).

INSTRUCTION "G" (cont)

5. (cont).

The remainder of the detachment will be relieved on the two days before and one after the relief of the N.C.O. Reliefs will be in alphabetical order commencing with C/106 on the 16th, 17th, 18th and 19th August.

6. Every member of the detachment will be armed with a rifle.

7. The detachment will be rationed by the battery whose N.C.O. is in charge, the relieving battery supplying rations for the day after their N.C.O. takes over.

8. An Officer of the responsible Battery will visit the gun at least every second day, and will
    (a) Inspect the gun for cleanliness
    (b) Inspect all rifles
    (c) Inspect the ammunition
    (d) See that all Maps, Instructions etc. ordered to be hung up in the gun pit are actually there, and that the N.C.O. understands his duties, knows the country and ranges to the various range boards.

9. On taking over the gun, batteries will report to Centre Group H.Q. that the equipment etc. at the gun is complete or otherwise.

10. The following ammunition will be kept at the gun.
    150 rounds   Shrapnel.
    150 rounds   H.E.
    1 round   H.E. 106 Fuze.

11. A copy of "Orders for N.C.O. in charge of BULLY Anti Tank gun is attached.

INSTRUCTION "G" (cont).

12. In each 18-pdr. Battery one gun must be told off to run out, in the event of a tank attack, to position in the open close to its battery.

    Such positions must have a good view to their front and flanks so as to be able to bring direct fire to bear on advancing tanks. Regardless of the position of our own troops these guns must fire at all surviving tanks until the latter are definitely put out of action.

    The remaining guns of batteries will meanwhile continue to engage the hostile infantry either by barrage fire or individual action as the situation may require. O.P.'s will be established and manned near all batteries. These O.P's, should immediately pass the news of the approach of tanks to the selected guns.

13. In dealing with tanks, Shrapnel, which is practically non-effective, and smoke shell, which only serves to increase the tanks power of manoeuvre, will not be used.

14. Experience shows that if tanks are advancing straight towards the guns the aim should be low - a burst just under a tank being nearly as effective as a direct hit. Fire must be maintained on any stationary tank until its extrication is an impossibility.

15. It must be borne in mind that it is not so much the actual tank itself that constitutes the danger but the facilities it affords for the enemy's infantry to break into our defences.

    Hence the necessity that those guns, and those only, which have been specially told off for the purpose should deal with tanks.

    All others must devote the whole of their energies to destroying the enemy's infantry.

INSTRUCTION "G" (cont).

Orders for N.C.O. in charge of

BILLY Anti-Tank Gun.

1. During the day one man will always be in the gun pit.
   At night at least two men will sleep in the gun pit.

2. The complete detachment will stand to :-
   (a) Half an hour before dawn until half an hour after dawn daily.
   (b) When a S.O.S. Signal has been given.
   (c) On the order MAN BATTLE STATIONS.

3. The following will be kept in the gun pit:-
   (a) A fighting map and panorama sketch showing all prominent points within the field of fire of the gun, with ranges marked against each point.
   (b) A copy of the paper showing markings of British Tanks.
   (c) A copy of 34th Div. Arty. "Orders for Anti-Tank Guns".
   (d) A copy of these orders.
   (e) A copy of G.H.Q. Instructions for disablement of guns (OB/251)
   (f) A list of equipment, stores and iron rations to be handed over on relief.
   (g) A paper showing the ranges to the various range boards.
   (h) A copy of MIST LINE ORDERS.

4. The detachment will be drilled with Box Respirators on for 15 minutes daily.

5. Every member of the detachment will be armed with a rifle.

6. The gun and all rifles will be inspected daily.

7. No lights will be allowed in the gun pit at any time.

INSTRUCTION "G" cont.

8. The detachment is responsible for the upkeep of the position.

9. To engage hostile tanks the gun will be run out of the gun pit on to the platform in front.

10. The relieved N.C.O. will take receipts for all equipment, stores and iron rations etc., (see para 5 (f)) and hand it to his Battery Commander not later than 24 hours after completion of relief.

11. One round of H.E. fused with No.106 Fuze will be kept in the gun pit for the purpose of destroying the gun should such a course be necessary.

INSTRUCTION "G" cont.

MIST LINE ORDERS FOR N.C.O. I/C BILLY ANTI-TANK GUN.

1. The gun will be kept laid on the MIST LINE Aiming Posts.

2. On observing the BLACK LINE S.O.S. Signal fired from HARTS CRATER or when he sees that our barrage has been brought back to the BLACK LINE he will open fire on the MIST LINE in accordance with the following table :-

   Range. Open at 1,100 yards and search forward and backward between 1,100 yards and 1,600 yards.
   Angle of Sight.- zero.
   Corrector - 150 and correct so as to get low air bursts.
   Ammunition - Shrapnel until it is all expended, then 50 rounds H.E.
   Rate of fire - 4 rounds per minute for first 10 minutes, then 3 rounds per min.

3. He will not fire at shorter ranges than 1,100 yards unless he sees enemy tanks or infantry under that range, when he will engage them by direct laying.

4. After firing the 100 rounds shrapnel and 50 rounds H.E. as in para 2 above, he will stand to with his remaining 50 rounds H.E. in the hopes of seeing a target through the mist or fog.

5. Should the weather be clear he will on no account fire on this mist line, but will keep all his ammunition for enemy tanks or infantry at short ranges and fire on them by direct laying.

INSTRUCTION "E".

Mutual Support.

The concentrations "BARRAGE COSY" and "BARRAGE HILL 70" will be fired by the Centre Group if called on to support the Right or Left Inf. Bdes. respectively in the event of a raid etc. on their fronts.

For details see Instruction "D"

In this event however they will not be fired until the Battn. Commanders on whose fronts have been consulted.

Liaison Officers are responsible for informing Group H.Q. as quickly as possible of the Battn. Commander's wishes whenever such occasion arises.

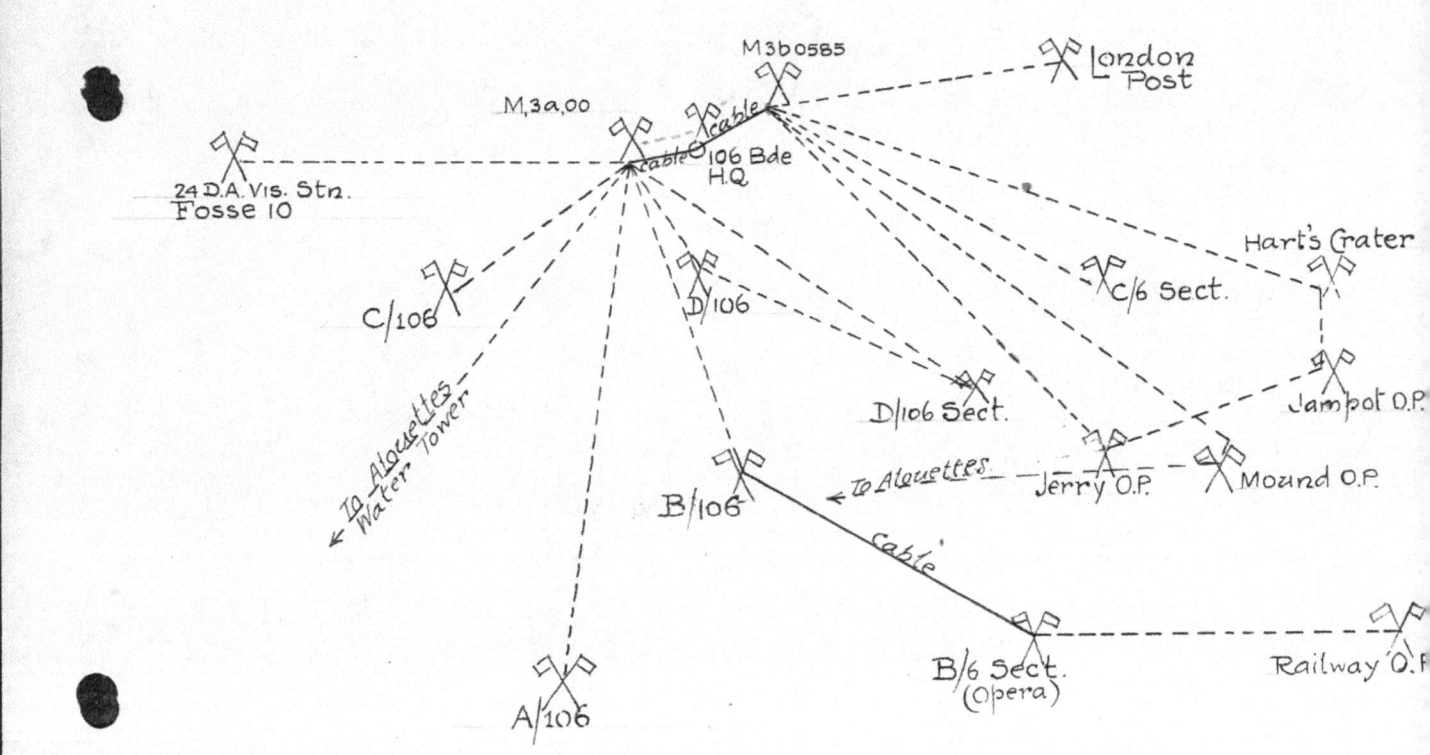

106 Bde. R.F.A.
Visual Communications

INSTRUCTION "K"
HARASSING FIRE

1. Harassing fire is carried out on tracks, tender spots, etc. under orders from Group H.Q. For this purpose only forward guns and detached sections will be used assisted by roving guns and Hows. ~~as detailed by 24th D.A. from the two silent Bdes. (48th Army Bde, RFA, and 52nd Army Bde, RFA.). Orders for targets and number of rounds for roving guns are sent by Group H.Q. to the Brigade concerned~~.

2. The Normal boundaries for harassing fire for the Centre Group are:- H32d34 - H29central - H36d00 - N6c00 - N9656

 ~~Northern Boundary - The E. and W. line through H.32.d.3.4.~~
 ~~Southern Boundary - The E. and W. line through N.8.b.55.60.~~
 ~~Eastern Boundary - The N. and S. line through N.6.c.0.0.~~

3. The normal expenditure of ammunition on harassing fire is 400 rounds 18-pdr. and 200 rounds 6.5" How. from the Group each night.

INSTRUCTION "L"

LOCAL DEFENCE

1. Each Battery position will be protected by wire so as to form "Rallying Points" for local defence.

2. The Lewis guns will be sited by Battery Commanders for defence of the locality.

INSTRUCTION "M".

Arrangements in case of Retirement.

1. The first retiring positions of all batteries have been prepared and the second retiring positions reconnoitred.
These are known as RESERVE POSITIONS and numbers are allotted to them by Corps, each number having a prefix FA for 18-pdr. batteries and FA(H) for 4.5" How. batteries.
2. 100 rounds per gun or How. (boxed) has been dumped in the first retiring position of each battery.
3. 1st. Retiring positions are as follows:-

Battery	Position	Number allotted	Arc of Fire	O.P. (for BROWN Line)	Route from former positions.
H.Q/106	R.12.a.70.53.			M.9.a.35.25.	By road or tracks about Cité du No. 11 and over GRAENAY Bridge N.B. if a ramp can be made on the N. side of Rly. cutting at M.9.c.31 A,B & D/106 will use this route.
A/106	R.12.a.72.05.	FA 209	58-118	G.33.d.7.5.	
B/106	M.7.b.10.51.	FA 210	55-115	G.34.c.5.8.	
C/106	M.7.b.41.86.	FA 211	54-106	M.3.b.05.90.	
D/106	M.8.a.05.30.	FA(H)212			
H.Q/52	R.11.c.20.10.			FOSSE 11 de BETHUNE and M.15.a.50.05.	S & T Tracks
A/52	R.17.a.30.80.	FA 205			
B/52	R.10.d.95.50.	FA 207			
C/52	R.11.c.45.70.	FA 208			
D/52	R.11.c.40.25.	FA(H)206			

INSTRUCTION "M" (contd.)

4. 2nd Retiring positions are as follows:-

Battery	Position	Number Allotted	O.P. (for GREEN Line)	Route from former position
H.Q/106.	R.2.c.1.9.			S Track.
A/106.	R.9.b.70.35.	FA 236.	L.36.c.S/E.	S Track.
B/106.	R.9.b.30.00.	FA 234.	L.35.a.9.3.	do.
C/106.	R.9.b.90.10.	FA 235.	FOSSE 6.	do.
D/106.	R.9.d.45.25.	FA(H)233	M.1.b.1.8.	do.
H.Q/52.	R.7.a.9.4.			
A/52.	R.7.b.4.9.	FA 227.)		T.S. or P Tracks.
B/52.	R.8.a.2.6.	FA 226)	F.5.c.8.8.	do.
C/52.	R.2.c.4.1.	FA 228)	R.15.d.8.6.	do.
D/52.	R.8.a.2.5.	FA(H)125)		

5. Areas for battery positions for defence of the BULLY SWITCH, ARMY H& and G.H.Q. lines have been selected and reconnoitred, but are not allotted to batteries. 2 Maps showing these areas have been forwarded to each battery.

6. All the above positions and areas and the routes to them will be thoroughly reconnitred by all Officers and senior N.C.O's and wherever possible alternative routes will be prepared.

INSTRUCTION "N".
ALTERNATIVE POSITIONS.

1. Each battery will maintain an alternative position for its present and first retiring positions. No ammunition will be kept in these positions but Batteries will keep them in good order and camouflaged.

2. Alternative 2nd. retiring positions have been selected and marked.

3. Alternative positions for the present line are as follows:-

Battery	Position		Battery	Position
HQ/106.	M.9.d.3.8.		*Reinforcing bd.*	
A/106.	M.11.c.3.0.		A/52.	M.14.c.4.5.
B/106.	M.10.a.90.95. & M.11.a.10.65.		B/52.	M.14.c.06.24.
C/106.	M.10.b.25.15.		C/52.	M.15.d.05.20.
D/106.	M.22.b.15.50.& M.10.a.70.25.		D/52.	M.14.d.38.97.

4. Alternative 1st. retiring positions are as follows:-

Battery	Position		Battery	Position
H.Q./106	R.6.c.7.7.		A/52.	
A/106.	R.6.a.95.52.		B/52.	
B/106.	R.6.a.80.68.		C/52.	
C/106.	M.1.b.80.68.		D/52.	
D/106.	R.6.a.70.44.			

5. Alternative 2nd. retiring positions are as follows:-

Battery	Position		Battery	Position
A/106.	L.32.c.8.0.		A/52.	
B/106.	R.2.a.6.6.		B/52.	
C/106.	R.2.a.2.0.		C/52.	
D/106.	R.2.b.1.8.		D/52.	

INSTRUCTION "O"

AMMUNITION.

1. Ammunition will be maintained as follows, the proportion of each nature being adhered to as far as available supplies admit:-

POSITION		A	AX 106 fuze	AX various (20% 106 Fuze if available)	AX other than 106 Fuze	BX	GAS 75% N.C.
Detached Sections.	Present positions A,B,& C/106.	180	–	120	–	–	–
	D/106	–	–	–	–	250	50.
	Alternative positions.						
	A & B/106.	180	XXX	120	–	–	–
	C/106.	180	100	–	20	–	–
	D/106.	–	–	–	–	250	50.
Main Battery Positions	A & B/106.	360	–	240	–	–	–
	C/106.	360	200	–	40	–	–
	D/106.	–	–	–	–	500	100.
1st Retiring Positions	A,B,& C/106.	60	–	40 (any fuze)	–	–	–
	D/106.	–	–	–	–	100	–
In Wagons	A,B,& C/106.	106	35	–	35	–	–
	D/106	–	–	–	–	108	–

2. The ammunition in gun pits will not exceed 250 rds. per gun, the remainder being scattered in small weatherproof dumps of about 200 rds. in or near the battery position.

INSTRUCTION "O" (contd)

3. Batteries will arrange for a turnover of all ammunition on their charge from time to time. This can be done by active guns drawing ammunition from the position of the silent guns, etc., the latter being refilled from the ammunition dump.

4. Ammunition Dump for Centre Group is the GARDEN DUMP at B.29.d.5.6. near NOULETTE, where 200 rounds per 18-pdr. and 4.5" How. are maintain maintained.

INSTRUCTION "P"

RETALIATION SCHEMES

1. Combined Field Artillery, Heavy Artillery and T.M. bombardments have been arranged by the Divl. Artillery. In order that these schemes may be brought into force at short notice code names have been given to them.

2. The Centre Group bombardments will be ordered from Group H.Q. by telephone or wire, giving the code name followed by the time the shoot will commence. Watches will then be synchronised.

3. On receipt of orders Batteries will fire as follows:-

Code Name	Bty	No. of guns	Target	Period of bombdment	Rate of fire
(a) SMASH QUATORZE	D/106	2	T.J.H.27.a.40.24. T.J.H.27.c.62.96.	half hour	Normal
(b) SMASH	B/106	1	H.33.c.58.40. to H.33.d.14.46.		) Rapid) ½ A
MINES	C/106	1	do	5 mins.	) ½ AX
	D/106	2	T.M.H.33.c.26.64. T.M.H.33.c.34.50.		INTENSE

INSTRUCTION "P" (contd.)

RETALIATION SCHEMES

Code Name.	Bty:	No. of guns	Target	Period of bombardment	Rate of Fire.
(c) SMASH St.AUGUSTE	A.:	2	N.3.b.44.10. to N.3.b.66.42	Half hour	) Five 2 min.) bursts of fire) INTENSE rate) at irregular) intervals) ½ A ½ AX
	C.:	1	N.3.b.66.42. to N.3.b.85.65		
	B.:	1	N.3.b.85.65. to N.4.a.00.85		
	D.:	2	T.M.N.3.a.88.76.) T.M.N.3.a.36.80.)		Normal.
(d) SMASH CONDE	A.:	1	N.9.d.10.88. to N.10.c.00.82	5 mins.	INTENSE 18 pdrs. ½ A ½ AX.
	C.:	1	- do -		
	D.:	2	T.M.N.9.c.26.70. T.M.N.9.c.16.62.		

INSTRUCTION "Q"

ZONE CALLS, LL CALLS, & S.O.S. AEROPLANE

LL CALLS
(a) During S.O.S. LL Calls will not be answered.
(b) During counter preparation they will be answered by ~~the forward section of F/196~~ one Section of all batteries that can be brought to bear.
(c) At all other times they will be answered by all forward sections which can be broughtt to bear.

GF Calls

N.B. When sending an LL Call to engage troops on the move, the Observer will send the pin point of the head of the formation, and the direction in which moving. It is then the duty of the battery commander to fix the point on which he will fire, taking into consideration the time which will have elapsed between receipt of call and opening fire.

In the event of no information as to direction and movement being sent, the battery commander will open fire on the point sent by observer.

On receipt of a message from Corps H.Q. this machine will fly to the scene of the bombardment and endeavour to locate any massing of troops and will report all such targets by wireless. If the enemy is seen advancing in strength across "No mans land" the S.O.S Signal will be sent down by wireless, and Red Parachute Bombs will be dropped as nearly as possible over the scene of the attack and also over our field battery positions opposite.

The S.O.S. Aeroplane has the same markings as a contact patrol machine i.e. a black wooden streamer (2 ft. x 1 ft.) attached to the rear edge of each bottom plane. The machine will also have a black band under the right wing.

INSTRUCTION "Q"
ZONE CALLS, LL CALLS, & S.O.S. AEROPLANE

LL CALLS
(a) During S.O.S. LL Calls will not be answered.
(b) During counter preparation they will be answered by ~~the forward section of D/106~~ one Section of all batteries that can be brought to bear.
(c) At all other times they will be answered by all forward sections which can be broughtt to bear.

GF Calls
(a) During S.O.S. or counter preparation, GF Calls will **not** be answered.
(b) At all other times they will be answered by D/106.

Rates of fire for LL and GF Calls at all times will be:-
Intense for 3 minutes.

→ See attached para N.B.

S.O.S. AEROPLANE
An aeroplane is standing by from dawn to dusk daily ready to leave the ground at short notice in the event of hostile bombardment.

On receipt of a message from Corps H.Q. this machine will fly to the scene of the bombardment and endeavour to locate any massing of troops and will report all such targets by wireless. If the enemy is seen advancing in strength across "No mans land" the S.O.S Signal will be sent down by wireless, and Red Parachute Bombs will be dropped as nearly as possible over the scene of the attack and also over our field battery positions opposite.

The S.O.S. Aeroplane has the same markings as a contact patrol machine i.e. a black wooden streamer (2 ft. x 1 ft.) attached to the rear edge of each bottom plane. The machine will also have a black band under the right wing.

INSTRUCTION "B"

COUNTER ATTACK SCHEME.

Reference GRAND TRUNK MAP 1/10,000.

1. In the event of an enemy attack in force being held on the BLACK Line, the 17th I.B. intend to retake the BLUE Line by a Counter Attack.

2. This Counter attack will be carried out by 2 Companies.
    Both Companies will start from ~~the Red Line at Zero, to~~ their assembly positions at ZERO + 30.
    The objective of the LEFT Coy. will be the
    BLUE Line from N.1.b.73.97. to N.1.b.83.30.
    The objective of the RIGHT Coy. will be the
    BLUE Line from N.1.d.93.70. to N.7.b.93.97.
    Subsequently the whole of the BLUE Line will be cleared and NELSON Trench recaptured.

3. This Counter-attack will be known as "COUNTER ATTACK K.B.O."

4. Zero hour for this Counter-attack will be notified by wire as follows :- K.B.O. plus or minus the time in mins. 1.30.pm. on the day in question being taken as the datum time.
    Thus "K.B.O. plus 133" means "Counter attack K.B.O. will take place at 3.43.pm." (i.e. at 1.30.pm. plus 133 minutes).
    "K.B.O. minus 96" means "Counter attack K.B.O. will take place at 11.54.am.
    This notification will be confirmed in clear by runner.

5. Barrage TABLE and TRACING (18-pdrs and 4.5" Hows) attached.

6. The 67th Bde. R.G.A. will bombard the old BLUE Line from N.1.d.8.0. to B.31.d.7.0. with what Hows are available, from Zero to Zero plus 30 mins, then lifting to enemy present front line.
    Counter battery work will be arranged at the same time

7. All available T.Ms will keep up a bombardment on the houses of CITE ST. LAURENT between COSY and COUNTER ALLEYS from Zero plus 30 min onward

INSTRUCTION "R" (cont).
BARRAGE TABLE

(a). **From Zero to Zero plus 30.**

The 3, 18-pdr. batteries covering Group, BLACK S.O.S. & reinforcing battery will search out over ground between BLACK S.O.S. and OUTPOST Line.

(b). **At Zero plus 30** the Barrage will start as under on Line "A":-

Re-inforcing battery 6 guns	N.31.d.37.13.	- N.1.b.46.44.
B/106 2 guns	N.1.b.46.44.	- N.1.b.49.29.
B/106 4 guns	N.1.b.49.29.	- N.1.d.57.65.
C/106 2 guns	N.1.d.57.65.	- N.1.d.61.46.
A/106 6 guns	N.1.d.61.46.	- N.7.b.60.89.

This barrage is arranged in Three parts :-
    Northern part - Re-inforcing Battery and Section B/106 (8 guns)
        Thick opposite LEFT objective.
    Centre part - Two Sections B/106 (4 guns) Thin.
    Southern part - A/106 and Section C/106 (8 guns).
        Thick opposite RIGHT objective.

The above barrage will remain stationary till Zero plus 40 minutes.

(c) **At Zero plus 40.** The barrage will creep forward in 50 yard lifts at the rate of 100 yards in four minutes, according to attached tracing and Line Table, until the following Line is reached :-

Northern part   ) 8 (N.32.c.13.36. - N.32.c.36.00. -
Re-inforcing Battery) guns(N.2.a.35.73. - N.2.a.21.50. -
& Section B/106.   )   (N.2.a.25.85.

Centre part - 2 Section B/106 - 4 guns - N.2.a.35.35. -
                                               N.2.c.29.72.

INSTRUCTION "B" (cont).

(c). (cont).

 Southern part   ) e (N.2.c.29.72.- N.2.c.30.35.-
 A/106 & Sect: C/106)guns(N.2.c.48.02.

(d). All guns will stop creeping forward independently as they reach the above line, where they will remain till Zero plus 78, when the Barrage will be re-arranged, as shown in the Final Protective Barrage for BLUE LINE.

(e) <u>18-pdr. Standing Barrage</u>:-

C/106 - 4 guns - BLUE LINE, N.1.d.93.70.- N.1.b.90.90.
From Zero plus 30 to Zero plus 60 minutes, when it will lift to the Final Protective Barrage for the BLUE LINE. At Zero plus 78, the whole Barrage will be arranged as follows :-

(f). <u>Final BLUE Barrage</u>.:-

   A/106 - 6 guns - N.8.a.73.50. - N.2.c.34.20.
   C/106 - 6 guns - N.2.c.34.50. - N.2.a.85.00.
   B/106 - 6 guns - N.2.a.85.00. - N.2.a.30.90.
 Re-inforcing) - 4 guns - N.2.a.30.90. - N.32.c.15.25.
  Battery) - 2 guns - N.32.c.15.25. - N.32.d.05.50.

(g) <u>RATES OF FIRE</u> :-

0 to 0 plus 30	SLOW)	Rates may have
0 plus 30 to 0 plus 44	NORMAL)	to be altered
0 plus 44 to 0 plus 54	RAPID)	according to
0 plus 54 to 0 plus 70	NORMAL)	ammunition
0 plus 70 to Stop	SLOW)	available.

INSTRUCTION "R" (cont).

(h).   4.5" How. Barrage Table:-

At Zero D/106 will engage the following points:-
(1). 1 How. N.1.b.74.75.   (4). 1 How. N.1.b.82.45.
(2). 1 How. N.2.a.94.80.   (5). 1 How. N.1.d.90.06.
(3). 1 How. N.2.a.82.88.   (6). 1 How. N.2.c.30.25.

(j).   These Hows. will move forward 400 yards (16 minutes) ahead
of the 18-pdr. Creeping Barrage (i.e. (1) (4) and (5) at
Zero plus 35, (2) at Zero plus 45, (3) at Zero plus 30), at
the rate of 100 yards per four minutes, until they reach the
Final How. Barrage Line, with the exception of (6), which will
remain on original target till Zero plus 46, when it will lift
to FINAL BARRAGE LINE.
                (1). Will walk along NELSON Trench.
                (2). Will move due EAST.
                (3). Will walk along NETLEY Trench.
                (4). Will move due EAST.
                (5). Will walk along NESTOR.

(k).   Reinforcing How. battery.
                (a). Two Hows. sweep N.1.a.75.80 - N.2.c.0.0.
                (b). Four Hows. area N.7.b.80.65.- N.8.a.40.00.-
                         N.8.a.60.70.- N.7.b.50.55.
At Zero plus 30 (a). Two Hows. will move to Trench.
N.2.c.60.70.- N.8.a.75.xx 65.
At Zero plus 75, all Six Hows. will lift to FINAL HOW. BARRAGE.

(l).   Final How. Barrage:-
         D/106. - 6 Hows.-N.2.d.00.40.- N.2.b.00.00.
Reinforcing
  How. battery) - 6 Hows.-N.2.b.00.00.- N.2.b.00.80.

I N S T R U C T I O N "R" Cont.

(m) **RATES OF FIRE :-** For 4.5" Hows

```
0 to 0 plus 30              SLOW
0 plus 30 to 0 plus 44      NORMAL
0 plus 44 to 0 plus 54      RAPID
0 plus 54 to Stop           SLOW.
```

18-pdr LINE TABLE.

Line A   from Z plus 30 to Z plus 40.

Line B   from plus 40 to plus 42.

Line C   from plus 42 to plus 44.

Line D   from plus 44 to plus 46.

Line E   from plus 46 to plus 48.

Line F   from plus 48 to plus 50.

Line G   from plus 50 to plus 52.

Line H   from plus 52 to plus 54.

Line J   from plus 54 to plus 56.

Line K   from plus 56 to plus 78.

"COUNTER ATTACK" K.B.O.

INSTRUCTION "S"

"PREPARE FOR ACTION" and "MAN BATTLE STATIONS"

1. The following will be the procedure at "PREPARE FOR ACTION" and "MAN BATTLE STATIONS" respectively:-
    (a) "PREPARE FOR ACTION"
        (1) O.P. Parties in the OUTPOST ZONE will be withdrawn to their Batteries.
        (2) BLACK Line O.P's will be manned.
        (3) Visual Stations will be manned.
        (4) The forward sections of batteries will move to the following alternative positions:-
            A/106   to   Main position.
            B/106   to   do do .
            C/106   to   Main position.
            D/106   to   M.8.a.05.80 (Brown Line position).
        For this purpose ½ the ammunition establishment of these sections is kept at the above positions (see Instruction O).
        (5) Personnel and guns at rest in W.L. will move into action immediately.
    (b) "MAN BATTLE STATIONS"
        All teams in Battery Wagon Lines will be harnessed up.

    (c) In the event of a sudden attack "MAN BATTLE STATIONS" only may be sent in which case the procedure will be as in (a) and (b)

2. TEST ACTION & TEST STATION.
    The action to be taken at "TEST ACTION" or "TEST STATIONS" will be as above except that O.P's in the OUTPOST ZONE will not be withdrawn and guns of forward sections will not be moved.

INSTRUCTION "S" (contd).

2. (cont).

Any guns at rest in W.L. will proceed complete with detachments to C/106 main battery position where they will halt on the road and report to the Group H.Q. Any other personnel at rest will move up into action at once reporting to Group H.Q. when ready for action.

In all cases times will be taken by batteries etc. from "Receipt of Message" to "Ready". In the case of O.P's and Visual Stations time will be taken when communication is opened. The party will then return to their Units at once. Similarly wagon lines will take the times to "Harness Up", when the harness will be taken off again.

Battery disembarked
Havre from England
30.8.15.

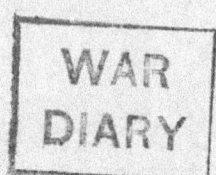

WAR DIARY

"A" Battery,

106th BRIGADE, R.F.A.

(24th Division)

S E P T E M B E R

(29.8.15 to 30.9.15)

1 9 1 5

War Diary. A. Battery 106. Brigade R.F.A.

1915

Aug. 29 | The Battery entrained at Farnborough Station in two trains - Brigade H.Q. sharing 2nd train
Battery Strength 4. Officers
 Captain Hon.ble R.G.O. Bridgeman
 Lieut. W.C. Maskell
 Lieut. D.J. Day
 Lieut. A.G.C. Northcroft.
 130. N.C.O. & Men
 126. Horses
Battery Equipment was still not complete but was sufficient to go into action.
The Battery arrived at Southampton about 3 p.m and embarked on transport "Courtfield" with some men on "Empress Queen"
Boats left at 5 p.m escorted by destroyers.

Aug. 30 | Arrived at Havre late, disembarked and marched to No 5 Rest Camp by 3.30 p.m.
Entrained at 9 p.m and moved off at midnight.

Aug 31	Arrived at Hesdin about 1.30 p.m and disentrained. Marched about 5 miles to billets & bivouac at BEAURAINVILLE, the remainder of the Brigade and other troops being in the same neighbourhood.
Sept.1.	Stormy day - battery settling down after journey. Heavy rain at night.
Sept.2.	Storms at intervals. Rained hard all night.
Sept.3.	Horse lines in a frightful mess - still raining. Changed lines to a new field rather nearer billets. Rained hard all day. Horses nearly stampeded by wasps
Sept.4.	Moved lines to better place - Showery
Sept.5.	Quiet day setting things straight
Sept.6.	Fine. Genl Haking the Corps Commander interviewed senior officers & outlined probable movements.
Sept.7.	Brigade moved off at 7.30.a.m for Divl Field day - returned to billets at 6.p.m.
Sept.8.	Fine day
Sept 9	Do

BEAURAIN-
-VILLE

Sept. 10.	Brigade marched at 9. A.M. via ROYON and FRUGES to billets near LAIRES about 20 miles	LAIRES
Sept. 11.	Moved at 9.15 a.m. by batteries independantly about 10 miles to AIRE.	AIRE
Sept. 12.	Moved at 9. a.m. about 9 miles to billets at HERVESKIRKE	HERVESKIRKE
Sept. 13.	B.C. went forward at 8 AM to reconnoitre position near RICHEBOURG St-VAAST. Battery followed later to billets at LESTREM. Battery took up position by 8.30 p.m. already partially prepared.	RICHEBOURG ST VAAST
Sept. 14.	Worked at position all day. In afternoon fired 35 registering rounds on 2nd line German trenches. O.P. in RUE DE BOIS. Day & telephonists sleep at Inf.y Batt.n H.Q.	
Sept. 15.	Fired 40 rounds in the morning registering various points.	
Sept. 16.	Fired 43 rounds, registering front German trenches.	
Sept. 17.	Fired 12 rds early and a few more later. Withdrew the battery at 7 p.m. to wagon line near LESTREM and at 10 p.m. got orders to march.	

Sept. 18	At 10.30.p.m. marched via LOCON and GORRE BRIDGE to a position at VERMELLES previously prepared. At GORRE a guide met us, and at BEUVRY another officer took 1st line wagons to near VERQUIGENUL. Got into position by 5 a.m. and had a short rest. Busy squaring things up for the remainder of the day. A lot of work still to be done to the position. In the afternoon O.C. reconnoitred German position from trenches, the lie of the land being pointed out by O.C. "T" R.H.A. The battery is now attached to 14th Bde R.H.A. - (Col. Sudor - and is working under orders of C.R.A. 7th Divn - Brig.Genl Rotton -	VERMELLES.
Sept 19th	Fired some 35 rounds to register a zero line and test ranges. Observation from a much battered mine shaft. Continued the same in afternoon, but had to return before completion to the battery in order to register certain targets with aeroplane & wireless observation. Work continued on battery position, but still a lot to do.	

Sept 20	Continued registration by aeroplane and also from O.P. firing about 100 rounds in all. Enemy fired a good many heavy H.E. into VERMELLES – but only a few splinters near the battery.	
Sept 21	Constructed a new O.P. in the trenches last night – carried out further registration in the morning. When light was sufficiently good, a bombardment commenced of the whole German position – especially for wire cutting purposes. At 6 p.m. A. Batt^y took on the task of firing all night to neutralize the wire already cut. Firing continued through the night. About 8.45 p.m. very heavy firing to the South towards ARRAS but it only lasted about half an hour.	1st Day of Bombardment
Sept 22	Fired 327 rounds during the night up to 7.55 a.m. At that hour a feint attack took place and rate of fire was increased. 50 rounds including 50% H.E. fired in 13 mins. Firing then stopped. Germans fired some 30. H.E. 5.9" at the battery in the morning no damage done. Firing continued in the afternoon with H.E. to knock out enemy's machine guns &c.	2nd Day of Bombardment

Firing continued by Left Section throughout the night to neutralize the wire already cut – 264 rounds

Sept. 23. Night firing stopped at 6.a.m. Battery had a short rest till wire cutting began at 11 a.m. At the last moment the battery was relieved of this task.
The battery rested without firing during the day.
Other Artillery busy – especially the French to the South during the afternoon. Night firing as usual.

3rd Day of Bombardment

Sept. 24 Fired 288 rounds during the night up to 6.a.m. Did not fire during the day – rain last night made all telephone lines into a bad way – got them right by evening. Neutralization of wire at night as usual

4th Day of Bombardment.

Sept. 25. Fired 288 rounds during the night. At 5.45 a.m. the attack began. Tasks had been allotted by a detailed programme – at 6.30 a.m. the Infantry assaulted and were successful though the extent of the success cannot be reckoned at present. Fired about another 600 rounds during the day, forming barrages

Sept 25 (cont⁴) of fire in front of the Infantry. Lt. Day - who was Forward Observing Officer was dangerously wounded in the head early in the morning. No shell anywhere near the battery. German Artillery not at all in evidence.

In the evening the Battery received orders to prepare to move forward and rejoin the 24th Divⁿ. But later this was stopped as the 7th Divⁿ's attack was held up and our support was still required. Battery continued firing all night - a portion of the time at a rapid rate. Rained most of the night - some light German shell round about.

Sept 26. Fine morning - battery still firing barrages towards Sᵗ ELIE.
Lieut Spice joined from Amᵘⁿ Colⁿ to take Lt Day's place.
Battery continued to fire at intervals throughout the day, firing some 700 rounds in all. Attacked counter attacks towards Sᵗ ELIE and to the North, succeeding each other rapidly.
The 1ˢᵗ Army took 2300 odd prisoners yesterday, the French some 8000.

Sept 27	Except for a counter attack a little further North, the night was fairly quiet. Fired some 50 rounds in the early morning. A & B batteries still working with 4th R.H.A. Bde, 7th Divn. Attacks and counter attacks at intervals throughout the day. Fired about 200 rounds in all.
Sept 28	Fired 2 bursts of fire into St ELIE during the night. The morning fairly quiet. In the afternoon the battery withdrew from its position with a view to rejoining 24th Divl Artillery. Bivouaced in the rain near NOYELLES-LES-VERMELLES.
Sept 29	In the morning O.C. & staff went to reconnoitre position for the battery in advance of LE RUTOIRE to support the Guards Divn, but orders were cancelled before the battery was brought up. Heavy rain
Sept 30	Very cold but fine, battery still bivouacing in the same place awaiting orders to move

NOYELLES LES VERMELLES

| Sept 3th (Cont:) | Rained again in the afternoon — Orders received late at night to be ready to march early in the morning.
Still no news of Lieut Day. |

Henry. G.O. Bridgeman
Capt R.F.a.
Commdg "A" Batty
186. Bde R.F.a.

121/7431

24th Division

"A" Battery 106th Bde: RFA.
Vol I

Oct 15.

Herewith War Diary for October
of "A" Battery 106 Brigade R.F.a.
Kindly acknowledge receipt.

H. Bridgeman
Capt R.F.a.
Comm'g A/106.R.F.a.

1/11/15.

Oct 1	The Battery marched at 5.30 a.m via BETHUNE and LILLERS to ISBERGUES and billeted. Very cold march of about 20 miles.	ISBERGUES
Oct 2	March resumed at 9 a.m. to LYNDE about 10 miles, billeted.	LYNDE
Oct 3	Marched about 20 miles to billets and bivouac in an area near PROVEN. The 24th Division now forms part of 6th Corps and remains at present in Reserve, refitting. Billets bad.	PROVEN
Oct 4	Rain - busy cleaning up.	
Oct 5	Rain - drawing stores &c.	
Oct 6	Fine day. Battery inspected in Drill Order in the afternoon by new G.O.C. Divn - Genl Capper.	
Oct 7	Battery inspected on a route march in Drill Order by the Army Commander - Genl Sir H. Plumer. One Officer 2Lt Spicer and a party of NCO's & telephonists went forward for attachment to Artilly whose place in the line we expect shortly to take over. Fine day.	
Oct 8	Fine day. 3 Drivers joined - Battery now complete except for 1 Gunner	

Oct 9	At 9 a.m orders received to march at 12.15p.m to the neighbourhood of RENINGHELST.— about 9 miles Reached billets about 5 p.m. The farm chosen for the battery's billets was one in which both Capt Bridgeman and Lt Maskell had spent 6 weeks in Jany and Feby last when with 52nd Battn. No orders as yet for going into action. News received with great regret of the death at BOULOGNE from wounds of Lt. D.I. Day.	RENINGHELST
Oct 10	Busy cleaning up billets & arranging for permanent standings for horses &c in view of the probability of our spending the winter here. 6 Pairs of Wheelers sent on fatigues to POPERINGHE.	
Oct 11.	Considerable quantity of Ordnance Stores drawn.	
Oct 12	Lt Northcroft transfered as Orderly Officer to O.C Bde as Signalling Officer. Lt. A.S. Dallas joined in his place. Baths at RENINGHELST. Lt Spicer's party returned & others went in their place. O.C reconnoitred position	

Oct. 13.	Battery got baths in RENINGHELST. Work continued on lines, & standings
Oct. 14.	Fine day. Considerable firing on our front yesterday evening. In the afternoon B.C. reconnoitred position & O.P. of A/51 R.F.A with a view to forthcoming reliefs
Oct. 15	Very misty all day.
Oct. 16.	Still misty. Batt? is to relieve A/51 on the nights of 17-18 and 18-19
Oct. 17	One Section into action at 6.30.p.m in relief of one section A/51. Position is due South of DICKEBUSCH
Oct. 18	O.C. went to trenches and finally registered Right Section on their zone. Left Section came into position at 7pm & A/51 handed over command and withdrew
Oct. 19	Some trouble with telephone wires. Batt? fired about 70 rounds in retaliation and registering.
Oct. 20	Fired about 20 rounds registering - trench wires left to us in a very bad condition. Observation from trenches
Oct. 21	Still putting wires in order. Rain at night.
Oct. 22	Fired about 40 rounds, observation from trenches. Possible new O.P. found.

Oct. 23. Quiet day – improving position and telephone lines – a mine fired under German sap in front of T1 Trench in the evening produced no reply.

Oct. 24 Very misty – nothing doing. Rain at night.

Oct. 25. Heavy rain – all dugouts leaking. S.O.S. received from Infy about 9.20 p.m. the Germans having exploded a mine. Battery fired about 100 rds & stood by twice during the night, but nothing more resulted. Communications interrupted.

Oct. 26 Started to register with aeroplane but wireless broke down. Fine sunny day.

Oct. 27 Stormy, trenches in a bad state & wires consequently troublesome.

Oct. 28. Rain all day – all dugouts very wet. Fired 20 rds in retaliation about 3 p.m.

Oct. 29 Quiet night inspite of rumours of a german mine going up in honour of Kaiser's birthday. Some retaliation during day. B.C. to Wagon line.

Oct 30	B.C. to battery - & then round with new C.R.A. - Brig Genl Philpotts - looking for a new position. No definite decision arrived at. Lt Dalles up from Wagon Line in relief of Lt Spicer
Oct 31	Last night North Staffords took possession of the 3 craters in front of T.1 trench & successfully held them against several bomb attacks. B.C. further reconnoitred proposed new position.

Henry G.O. Bridgeman
Capt R.F.A.

Commanding A/106 R.F.A.

34th Brown

A/to 6 Battery R74.
Vol: 2

1748/131

Nov 15.

Army Form C. 2118

WAR DIARY
or
INTELLIGENCE SUMMARY.
(Erase heading not required.)

A. Batty 106 Bde R.F.A.

Instructions regarding War Diaries and Intelligence Summaries are contained in F.S. Regs., Part II. and the Staff Manual respectively. Title pages will be prepared in manuscript.

Place	Date	Hour	Summary of Events and Information	Remarks and references to Appendices
DICKEBUSCH	Nov 1.		Rain most of the day. Genl. Capper GOC. 24th Divn. visited position. A new position is to be started on at once for 3 Guns - the 4th Gun being kept in reserve with a roving Commission	
	-2.		Rain all day - Communications destroyed - nearly all trenches having collapsed and broken & buried the lines.	
	-3.		Communications more or less destroyed but difficult to maintain. Fired a few rounds in the afternoon. Started work on new position - a possible new O.P. found for gun to be carried	
	-4.		Work continued on new position. Fired about 70 rounds on points behind front trenches	
	-5.		Misty. Fired about 100 rounds on enemy's roads & communications. Work on new position progressing - Fired about 50 rounds	
	-6.		Work on new position & OP continued.	
	-7.		Strong S.W. wind. Fired about 100 rounds.	
	-8.		Heavy rain & S.W. wind last night. Clear day with good light. German guns active	
	-9.		Heavy rain - water rising in all dug outs, B.C. accompanied Rec Cmdr to Infantry OP.	
	-10.		Still raining & flowing a sea. Position flooded. Permission obtained to move at dawn tomorrow to new position, though it is still incomplete.	
	-11.		A bad night - all dug outs flooded & falling in - Liff Station moved to new position at dawn & 3rd Gun in the evening, the 4th going into reserve. Rain & gale all day - no visibility therefore possible - & the position being incomplete, everything very uncomfortable	
	-12.			
	-13.			

WAR DIARY or INTELLIGENCE SUMMARY

Army Form C. 2118

Place	Date	Hour	Summary of Events and Information	Remarks and references to Appendices
DICKEBUSCH	Nov 14.		Fine day – Frost – fired about 90 rounds registering. German aeroplanes active. 8" howitzers heavily shelled the area immediately behind the position. Enemy the morning and evening. One Driver & horse with wagon slightly wounded.	
	-15.		Opened fire at 6.30 am at request of Infy on Germans working outside their trenches & dispersed them. At 3 p.m. a combined bombardment of enemy's communications took place. Work on position continued. Registered a new zone – namely the German Salient at ST ELOI including "The MOUND" – a good deal of trouble in laying fresh wire – trenches very shallow.	
	-17		Very cold hailstorms at intervals – good light at times – fired about 100 rounds.	
	-18		Frost last night. Heavy rain in afternoon – Fired 80 rounds.	
	-19		Forkazan – fired about 100 rounds – doing a good deal of damage to enemy trenches and works.	
	-20.		Fine day – Bombarded Enemy's Communications at 5 am & 8.30 am – a deserter having reported that troops would be moving at these hours. 24th Divn to be relieved shortly by 3rd Divn in consequence O.C. 6 Bg R.H.A came and reconnoitred wagon line.	
	-21.		Fine day but rather misty – some firing.	
	-22.		Hard Frost – thick fog all day.	

Army Form C. 211

WAR DIARY
or
INTELLIGENCE SUMMARY.
(Erase heading not required.)

Instructions regarding War Diaries and Intelligence Summaries are contained in F.S. Regs., Part II. and the Staff Manual respectively. Title pages will be prepared in manuscript.

Place	Date	Hour	Summary of Events and Information	Remarks and references to Appendices
DICKEBUSCH	Nov 23		Preparing for relief. One gun section evening to VERBRANDENMOLEN as all guns are to be handed over in position to relieving battery.	
	24		Left section relieved at dusk - & marched at 9 p.m. to new billets.	
ST SILVESTRE CAPPELL	25		Right section relieved & position handed over to O.C. 6 By R.F.A. Remainder of Battery marched at 4 p.m. - reaching billets at ST. SILVESTRE CAPPELL at 10 p.m. Hailstorms.	
	26		Halted - A Staff muddle in connection with ammunition. Had to send the Battery lorry to turn out & refill with ammunition at night.	
BROXEELE	27		Marched 13 miles to BROXEELE - very cold march. Inspected en route by Maj. Gen.? Strathan. Had frost.	
	28		Marched at 9 a.m. for TATTINGHEM - but owing to Staff having made a muddle of billetting areas - the whole brigade had to go on a further 3 miles after last movement to HEURINGHEM.	
HEURINGHEM	29		Rain - and no supplies. Marched back to TATTINGHEM.	
TATTINGHEM	30		Rain & cold wind. Battery engaged in trying to straighten itself out & refit.	

H. Bridgman Capt R.F.A.
Comng A/108 R.F.A.

106th Bde: R.7a.
Yols: 4.

24

Army Form C. 2118.

Vol 5

WAR DIARY
INTELLIGENCE SUMMARY.
(Erase heading not required.)

Instructions regarding War Diaries and Intelligence Summaries are contained in F. S. Regs., Part II. and the Staff Manual respectively. Title pages will be prepared in manuscript.

Place	Date	Hour	Summary of Events and Information	Remarks and references to Appendices
TATINGHEM	1/12/15		Inspection of billets and horse lines by Maj. Gen. J.E. Capper, C.B. comdg 24 d Divn.	
"	2/12/15		Inspection of billets and horse lines by Colonel Edgerton, G.S.O. 2nd Army.	

#353 Wt. W2544/1454 700,000 5/15 D. D. & L.   A.D.S.S./Forms/C. 2118.

Army Form C. 2118.

WAR DIARY
or
INTELLIGENCE SUMMARY.

(Erase heading not required.)

Vol IV

Instructions regarding War Diaries and Intelligence Summaries are contained in F. S. Regs., Part II. and the Staff Manual respectively. Title pages will be prepared in manuscript.

Place	Date	Hour	Summary of Events and Information	Remarks and references to Appendices
TATINGHEM	3.12.15		In billets. Weather wet.	
"	4.12.15		Draft of 1 acting Bombardier, 1 saddler, 1 shoeing smith, 5 gunners and 4 drivers joined Brigade. Weather wet.	
"	5.12.15		In billets. Weather showery.	
"	6.12.15		In billets. Showery.	
"	7.12.15		In billets. Showery.	
"	8.12.15		In billets. Fair.	
"	9.12.15		In billets. Fair.	
"	10.12.15		In billets. Very wet.	
"	11.12.15		Inspection by C.C.R.A. 24th Division. Weather	
"	12.12.15		In billets.	
"	13.12.15		In billets.	
"	14.12.15		In billets.	
"	15.12.15		In billets.	
"	16.12.15		In billets.	
"	17.12.15		In billets.	
"	18.12.15		Inspection by G.O.C. 2nd Army.	
"	19.12.15		In billets.	
"	20.12.15		Draft of 1 fitter, 12 gunners + 8 drivers joined the Brigade.	
"	21.12.15		In billets.	
"	22.12.15		Inspection of 'A' 'B' + 'D' Batteries by Colonel Commanding.	
"	23.12.15		Inspection of 'C' Battery and Amm Col. by Colonel Commanding.	
"	24.12.15		Inspection of 'B' Battery by Colonel Commanding.	
"	25.12.15		Xmas day. Weather showery.	

Army Form C. 2118.

VOL V

WAR DIARY
or
INTELLIGENCE SUMMARY.
(Erase heading not required.)

Place	Date	Hour	Summary of Events and Information	Remarks and references to Appendices
TATINGHEM	26/12/15		In billets. Weather fair.	
"	27/12/15		In billets. Weather showery	
"	28/12/15		In billets. Weather wet.	
"	29/12/15		In billets. Weather. Very windy. Gale in afternoon.	
"	30/12/15		In billets. Weather fair.	
"	31/12/15		In billets. Preparing for move. Collecting stores etc.	
VOORDPEENE				

24. 106ten 7a. Bde:
Vol: 6

a/106 Avery
Vol: 4

24

Herewith War Diary A Batty 106 Bde R.F.A. at present acting independantly of the remainder of the Brigade.

In the field
6/3/16

H. Bridgeman
Maj R.F.A.
Comdg A/106 R.F.A.

Army Form C. 2118.

WAR DIARY
or
INTELLIGENCE SUMMARY.
(Erase heading not required.)

Instructions regarding War Diaries and Intelligence Summaries are contained in F. S. Regs., Part II. and the Staff Manual respectively. Title pages will be prepared in manuscript.

Place	Date 1916	Hour	Summary of Events and Information	Remarks and references to Appendices
TATINGHEM NOORDEPENE	Jan.1		The Brigade left TATINGHEM and marched to NOORDEPENE - wet cold march. March continued - Another cold wet march. Orders received for carrying out reliefs.	
STEENVOORDE	Jan 2			
YPRES	Jan 3		Advance section marched to Wagon line of A/79 R.F.A. 17th Div; detachments taken up by bus at 4.30 to YPRES and thence marched to gun position near the École de BIENFAISANCE just E of YPRES. Zone taken HOOGE&MENINROAD	
	Jan 4		Remaining section arrived, & position finally taken over from A/79.	
	Jan 5		Fired 90 rounds checking the register. Fine day.	
	Jan 6		A good deal of trouble with telephone lines which were taken over in a bad state. a fair light - some firing.	
	Jan 7		Communications with Infantry still indifferent. A good light and so considerable firing - Strong S.W. wind	
	Jan 8		24th Div: Infantry began reliefs last night. Fired about 700 rounds. Wind dropped & gone to N.W. fine light and a good deal of shooting. Enemy's guns active against YPRES in afternoon. One Gunner slightly wounded.	
	Jan 9			
	Jan 10		Heavy firing early this morning apparently W. of Still be-lasted about 1 hour, rather misty - wind back in S.W.	
	Jan 11		A good deal of shooting G.O.C. & C.R.A. Div visited the position. New O.P.selected	
	Jan 12		B.C. went round trenches- work on O.P. begun at night. a good deal of work also going on a gun position	

2353 Wt. W2541/1454 700,000 5/15 D. D. & L.   A.D.S.S./Forms/C. 2118.

WAR DIARY
or
INTELLIGENCE SUMMARY.
(Erase heading not required.)

Army Form C. 2118.

Place	Date	Hour	Summary of Events and Information	Remarks and references to Appendices
YPRES	Jan 13		Work continued on O.P at night - a new wire laid to it.	
	Jan 14		Lt. Haskell to Wagon Line - Lt. Spicer to guns - work on O.P continued. Telephone lines now in better order. New O.P in use. Fired about 90 rounds during day, doing a good deal of damage to German trenches. Some A.P. & HE fire found about Suspension.	
	Jan 15		New wire completed to C.3 trench. German guns active & wire cut more than once. Fired about 80 rounds knocking out a snipers post and silencing a minenwerfer which was registering C.3	
	Jan 16		9.1. Spicer ofish'ing in the trenches	
	Jan 17		A good deal of firing in Hill 60 sector. Wind S. Some rain in the evening.	
	Jan 18		Brisk - No firing - work at the gun position continued.	
	Jan 19		Fine day. aeroplanes active and a good deal of shelling & trouble with wires. About 120 - H.E. 5-9" shows - close to battery but no damage done - Hostile artillery unusually active in afternoon.	
	Jan 20		Fine day. Quieter on the whole. Wires cut once or twice.	
	Jan 21		Dull quiet day - fired some rounds registering a good deal of work done at gun position. Lt Spicer did some registering from C.H. - quiet day. but Now. Battery to our front got heavily shelled in the afternoon	

Army Form C. 2118.

WAR DIARY
or
INTELLIGENCE SUMMARY.
(Erase heading not required.)

Instructions regarding War Diaries and Intelligence Summaries are contained in F. S. Regs., Part II. and the Staff Manual respectively. Title pages will be prepared in manuscript.

Place	Date	Hour	Summary of Events and Information	Remarks and references to Appendices
YPRES	Jan 23		Frosty morning - must kill 11 am. then good light. Works now in good order. Our 9" How. shelled Enemy trenches at HOOGE - battery stood by to open fire. Germans doing a lot of work on their trenches - fired at some of these places doing considerable damage.	
	Jan 24		About noon Germans shelled our front & support trenches at HOOGE heavily - we retaliated. Enemy artillery rather active all day. 2/Lt Franklin attacked whilst 2/Lt Dallas is on leave.	
	Jan 25		Frosty & fine - aeroplanes active - did some registering & retaliation. Work at O.P. at night.	
	Jan 26		Dull day - a lot of fresh work visible in German trenches & work going on - stopped this & did a good deal of damage with 60 HE.	
	Jan 27		Good light. Howitzers did some bombing of above C3 last night. Fire about 80 rounds doing a good deal of damage to fresh work in German trenches. Working party to complete O.P. at night.	
	Jan 28		Dull & misty - very little artillery activity - work continued at O.P.	
			Bull. Enemy shelled our front trenches at HOOGE about 3.15 p.m. Retaliation effective.	
	Jan 29		Tick most of day. No firing.	
	Jan 30		Misty & kind. Fired 40 rounds in afternoon. No 2 gun out of action with a broken spring case.	
	Jan 31			

XXIV

106 RFA
Vol 87

Army Form C. 2118.

VOL VII

WAR DIARY
or
INTELLIGENCE SUMMARY.
(Erase heading not required.)

Instructions regarding War Diaries and Intelligence Summaries are contained in F.S. Regs., Part II. and the Staff Manual respectively. Title pages will be prepared in manuscript.

Place	Date	Hour	Summary of Events and Information	Remarks and references to Appendices
16 Rue du Casset POPERINGHE	1.2.16		Nothing to chronicle. Weather fair.	
	2.2.16		Colonel Commanding visits Lt group. Weather fine.	
	3.2.16		Nothing to chronicle. Weather fine.	
	4.2.16		Storm during night. 3rd/4th which did some damage to B.A.C. lines shelters. Weather dull	
	5.2.16		Nothing to chronicle. Weather fine. Lieut Dallas wounded by splinter of 5.9" H.E. at YPRES.	
	6.2.16		Nothing to chronicle. Weather dull. Captain Ho. Hos. 116 O. Brodman promoted Major	
	7.2.16		Nothing to chronicle. Weather dull.	
	8.2.16		Nothing to chronicle. Weather fair.	
	9.2.16		Colonel H.C. Burrows proceeds to England on leave.	
	10.2.16		Nothing to chronicle. Weather fine.	
	11.2.16		Nothing to chronicle. Weather fine.	
	12.2.16		Nothing to chronicle. Weather war. On account of activity at YPRES order given to 'Stand to'	
	13.2.16		POPERINGHE Station shelled three times during day and trains dropped from aeroplanes on Tain.	
	14.2.16		Nothing to chronicle. Weather wet	
	15.2.16		Nothing to chronicle. Weather fine.	
	16.2.16		Nothing to chronicle. Weather fine. Capt Cruber & Lieut Jackson attached to 'B' & 'C' Btys for 14 days	
	17.2.16		German aeroplane bombed POPERINGHE at about 1.30 am. 3.30 am to 7.30 am	
	18.2.16		Nothing to chronicle. Colonel C.O.P. returns from leave. Weather wet.	
	19.2.16		Nothing to chronicle. Weather fair.	
	20.2.16		Nothing to chronicle. Weather fair. Night 20th/21st German aeroplane dropped bombs on Pt-eninghe at 11.30 pm	
	21.2.16		At 3.0 am and 7.0 am. Weather cold	

Army Form C. 2118.

VOL VII

WAR DIARY
or
INTELLIGENCE SUMMARY
(Erase heading not required.)

Instructions regarding War Diaries and Intelligence Summaries are contained in F. S. Regs., Part II and the Staff Manual respectively. Title pages will be prepared in manuscript.

Place	Date	Hour	Summary of Events and Information	Remarks and references to Appendices
6 Rue de Cassel POPERINGHE	22.2.16		Night 21st/22nd German shelled POPERINGHE at about 5.0 a.m. Some areas in morning.	
	23.2.16		Enemy dropped bombs on POPERINGHE during night. Weather fair.	
	24.2.16		Weather cold and snow storms at intervals. D Battery detailed for special work	
	25.2.16		Weather cold all this Snow in afternoon	
	26.2.16		Snow in morning turning to rain in evening	
	27.2.16		Nothing to chronicle	
	28.2.16		" "	
	29.2.16		" "	

Alfred Clark Lieut
Adjutant for Major in command
108 Hy Bde RGA
7.3.16

To/
Officer i/c
  A.G's Office at the Base.

Herewith A.F. C2113, War Diary for the Unit under my command for March 1st to 12th 1916

23.3.16

J. Bridgeman
Major.
Commdg A/106th F.A. Bde.

WAR DIARY or INTELLIGENCE SUMMARY

Army Form C. 2118.

Place	Date	Hour	Summary of Events and Information	Remarks and references to Appendices
YPRES	March 1		Clear day - did some firing in the morning checking registers to selected points. At 5 p.m. Battery took part in a bombardment carried out by the whole Division and by the Divisions on our right & left. Firing was very intense to the South in the neighbourhood of the BLUFF. The hostile artillery only replied in that direction. An unusually quiet night.	
	March 2		At 4.32 a.m. last nights bombardment repeated (with variations, and kept up on our front till dawn. Bombardment very intense to the South where an attack was launched to recapture the BLUFF, which from present accounts was entirely successful, some 300 prisoners being taken. Fire continued in that neighbourhood throughout the day. HOOGE trenches shelled in the afternoon - our retaliation effective. The position of B/108 on our immediate right heavily shelled about 10 p.m. with 15cm Howitzers.	
	March 3 Friday		Quiet day - rain	
	March 4		Snow last night and still falling in the morning - cleared in afternoon - attacks Single Shot of B/107 registered to enfilade enemy trenches at HOOGE. Snow melting - a sprinkling of shell round our billet in the ECOLE at intervals throughout the day. Sgt Ling slightly wounded in the foot with shrapnel.	
	March 6		More snow last night and thaw) later. Quiet day.	
	March 7		Snow all day - quiet	
	March 8		Fine & clear, about 4 inches of snow on the ground. Engaged & dispersed working party in the early morning	

Army Form C. 2118.

WAR DIARY
or
INTELLIGENCE SUMMARY.
(Erase heading not required.)

Place	Date	Hour	Summary of Events and Information	Remarks and references to Appendices
YPRES	March 9		A lot of snow still on the ground, with occasional further falls	
	March 10		Still snowing at times. About 20 4.2" H.E. fired at ECOLE about midday - no casualties. The Battery is being relieved by B/106. on nights of 11/12th & 12/13th but leaves one detachment in charge of single gun at POTIJZE	
	March 11		Enemy artillery active against HOOGE - we retaliated at intervals. A/106 took over detached gun & 1 sec" B/106 relieved 1 sec" A/106	
	March 12		Misty - Remaining section relieved by B/106. 2Lt Westberg attached for duty A/106 now rejoined 106th Brigade & ceases to be employed independently	

N.B. [signature] Major.
Commanding "A" Bty. 106th [Brigade R.F.A.]

106th Bde: R.F.A.
Vols 2 & 3

121/7931

Sep '15
to
May '19

24th

Army Form C. 2118.

VOL. III. A

Vol II / 2

WAR DIARY
or
INTELLIGENCE SUMMARY

(Erase heading not required.)

Instructions regarding War Diaries and Intelligence Summaries are contained in F. S. Regs., Part II. and the Staff Manual respectively. Title pages will be prepared in manuscript.

Place	Date	Hour	Summary of Events and Information	Remarks and references to Appendices
NOVELLES LEZ VERMELLES	29.9.15		Draft consisting of 1 corporal, 1 shoeing Smith, 2 gunners & 8 drivers received from Base.	
"	30.9.15	8.30 pm	C & D Batteries withdrew from their positions to their wagon lines. See Vol. 2. Sect E.	
ISBERGUES	1.10.15		Brigade bivouacked at wagon lines.	
E			Brigade marched at 5.30.a.m. via BETHUNE – CHOQUES – LILLERS to billets at ISBERGUES	
LYNDE	2.10.15		Brigade marched via SERCUS to billets at LYNDE	
N of WATOU	3.10.15		Brigade marched via WALLON CAPELLE – CASSEL – STEENVOORDE to billets 1½ miles N. of WATOU. Captain H.S. Browne joined and took over command of D Battery. In Billets. 1 NCO. 1 Saddler, 5 drivers sent from No 2 General Base Depot.	
"	4.10.15		"	
"	5.10.15		"	
"	6.10.15		In Billets. Inspected by Major Gen. J.E. Capper CB. Comm dg 24th Division. Captain J.F. Mascall joined and took over command of B Battery.	
"	7.10.15		Inspected during a route march by Lieut. Gen. H.C.O. Plumer K.C.B. Comm dg 2nd Army. Colonel Comm dg and parties from H.Q. Staff. Each Battery & B.A.C. proceeded to be attached to Brigades of 9th Divisional Artillery in neighbourhood of DICKEBUSCH.	
"	8.10.15		In Billets.	
"	9.10.15		Brigade marched at 12.30.p.m. via POPERINGHE to new billeting area 1 mile E of RENINGHELST.	

Army Form C. 2118.

WAR DIARY
or
INTELLIGENCE SUMMARY.

(Erase heading not required.)

Vol. III. B.

Instructions regarding War Diaries and Intelligence Summaries are contained in F. S. Regs., Part II. and the Staff Manual respectively. Title pages will be prepared in manuscript.

Place	Date	Hour	Summary of Events and Information	Remarks and references to Appendices
1MILE E/ RENINGHELST	10.10.15		In Billets.	
"	11.10.15		In Billets	
"	12.10.15		do do Captain L.E. Mascall, Commdg "B" Battery promoted Major	
"	13.10.15		do do	
"	14.10.15		do do	
"	15.10.15		do do	
"	16.10.15		do do	
"	17.10.15		1 Section from each Battery relieved 1 Section of corresponding Batteries of 51st Brigade. Remaining Sections relieved remaining 51st Brigade Sections and Headquarters. Colonel Commanding took over command of the Right Artillery Group, the Composition & positions of the Group being as follows:– 24th Division. The Composition & positions of the Group being as follows:– Head Quarters. I.29.c.2.6. Map Reference VOORMEZEELE 2nd Army Sheet 6. A/106.B*a* N.4.a.2.6. Right Sec. B/106 N.4.a.1.10 Left Sec. B/106 H.36.b.5.7. C/106. H.28.d.3.0. D/106. I.9.6.3.2. B/108. H.35.c.1.6. D/109 (Howitzer) H.36.a.8.7. 2/7 Belgian Battery H.36.a.8.7. 2/7 Belgian Battery	
"	18.10.15		4.30.a.2.7. 1 Section 5th Mountain Battery I.31.6.1.4. and the 27th + 32nd Trench Mortar Batteries. Reliefs completed at 8.30 pm	

Army Form C. 2118.

WAR DIARY
or
INTELLIGENCE SUMMARY.
(Erase heading not required.)

Vol. III. C

Place	Date	Hour	Summary of Events and Information	Remarks and references to Appendices
H.29.c.2.6	19.10.15		Battery registering. Day very quiet. Weather fine & sunny after heavy morning	
"	20.10.15		Very quiet. Ammunition Expenditure limited to 200 rds per Battery per week for 18 prs & 40 rds per week for Howitzer Battery. Fine & sunny day.	
"	21.10.15		Very quiet day. Foggy morning. Capt Gray 2i/c B Battm proceeded to Base	
"	22.10.15		1 shoeing smith. 2 gunners & drivers joined Brigade from Base	
"	23.10.15		Quiet day. Enemy shelled DICKEBUSH — YPRES Road after 7 pm with Heavy Howitzers.	
"	24.10.15		Very quiet - a foggy day.	
"	25.10.15		A wet day. Enemy artillery fairly active. A mine fired opposite Trench T1 at 9 pm brought a S.O.S. call from the West Kents but no infantry action ensued. Our Batteries	
"	26.10.15		A very bright clear day. Many Aeroplanes hostile & otherwise out. Batteries registered points with Aeroplane observation.	
"	27.10.15		A dull day & very quiet till evening when Enemy shelled roads east of ORE Hoë Q.2 for a considerable time.	
"	28.10.15		Usual shelling from both sides. A wet day.	
"	29.10.15		Nothing of importance occurred. Weather dull.	
"	30.10.15		Quiet day. Fine & cloudy.	
"	31.10.15		Artillery of both sides fairly active all day. Weather dull.	

Army Form C. 2118.

Vol IV/3

VOL. IV.

WAR DIARY
or
INTELLIGENCE SUMMARY.

(Erase heading not required.)

Place	Date	Hour	Summary of Events and Information	Remarks and references to Appendices
Ayette	31/10/15		Artillery of both sides fairly active all day. Weather dull. see Vol. III. closed.	
"	1.11.15.		Some Artillery activity in the morning, remainder of day quiet. Weather wet.	
"	2.11.15		Infantry demanded a certain amount of Retaliation during the middle of the day, otherwise quiet. 2 Gunners joined Brigade from N°2 General Base Depot. Weather very wet. Lieut. H.P. Clarke 'D' Battery joined H.Q. to take over duties of Adjutant from Captain K.J. Scott-Smith who is to be withdrawn. 2/Lt S.P. Lievaart from B.A.C. to 'D' Battery.	
"	3.11.15		Enemy shelled road in vicinity of Brigade Headquarters during afternoon. Weather showery.	
"	4.11.15		Very quiet day. C/106 registered 0.8.a.7.4. with aeroplane. Weather fine.	
"	5.11.15		Considerable aircraft activity during evening, otherwise very quiet on this front. Weather showery.	
"	6.11.15		Bombardment of enemy position by Heavy Guns from 6-8 a.m. Lieut. W.P. Clarke appointed acting Adjutant vice Captain K.J. Scott-Smith posted to 2nd Divisional Ammunition Column.	
"	7.11.15		Weather fine but windy. D/106 & B/106 each fired 50 rounds into HOUPLINES village at about 2 p.m. retaliating on account of Belgian Battery being shelled. 3rd Belgian Battery came under orders of OC Right Artillery group at 10 a.m.	
"	8.11.15		Very quiet day. Weather brisk, some showers.	
"	9.11.15		Very wet. A B & D Batteries fired on road C.15.a.3.2. from 5 p.m - 6 p.m. 20 to 10 rounds per gun. 2/Lt Hony Sergt C.H. Massey 26711 posted to A Battery as BQMS from D/107 F.A. Bde.	
"	10.11.15		2/Lieut. W.H.P. Clarke is appointed adjutant vice 2/Capt. K.J. Scott-Smith from 4.11.15.	
"	11.11.15		Very wet. Some Artillery activity from 2.0 p.m. - 3.0 p.m.	
"	12.11.15			

Army Form C. 2118.

WAR DIARY
or
INTELLIGENCE SUMMARY

Vol. IV. B.

(Erase heading not required.)

Instructions regarding War Diaries and Intelligence Summaries are contained in F. S. Regs., Part II. and the Staff Manual respectively. Title pages will be prepared in manuscript.

Place	Date	Hour	Summary of Events and Information	Remarks and references to Appendices
HDQRS 2.6	13/11/15		Quiet day. Weather very windy.	
"	14/11/15		Enemy shelled heavily cross roads at H.29.C.3.9 at 12.30 pm & 2.0 pm and from 5.15 pm – 6 pm. The enemy did not retaliate.	
"	15/11/15		Artillery of 5th Corps joined in Combined Retaliation from 5.0 pm – 8.0 pm.	
"	16/11/15		B Battery moved into rest at 1 pm. "Artillery Groups reallotted Right group now consists of A/101 & 2/1st D/101 & a section of B/101 which has not yet taken up its position. Zone of Right group is from Trench P.16 R, both inclusive. Weather showery.	
"	17/11/15		Considerable activity on the part of our Artillery.	
"	18/11/15		2/Lt. A.H Cooper joined Brigade posted to Ammunition Column.	
"	19/11/15		Activity shewn by our Artillery.	
"	20/11/15		Quiet day. Frosty.	
"	21/11/15		Foggy weather. Very quiet.	
"	22/11/15		Weather foggy. Very quiet.	
"	23/11/15		Weather fine. Quiet day.	
"	24/11/15		Batteries parties went back to ST SYLVESTRE CAPPEL to take over billets occupied by 40th F.A Brigade.	
"	25/11/15		Head Quarters. B Battery and one Section of remaining Batteries marched via POPERINGHE – ABEELE – STEENWOORDE to ST SYLVESTRE CAPPEL. Sections were relieved by sections of the 40th F.A Brigade guns were exchanged the 40th Brigade leaving theirs at ST SYLVESTRE to be taken over on arrival.	
ST SYLVESTRE CAPPEL	26/11/15		Remaining sections of Batteries and marched by same route as first sections	

WAR DIARY
or
INTELLIGENCE SUMMARY.

Army Form C. 2118.

Vol. IV. C

Place	Date	Hour	Summary of Events and Information	Remarks and references to Appendices
ST SYLVESTRE CAPPEL	26/11/15		to billets at ST SYLVESTRE CAPPEL. Ammunition Column also marched in this day. All movements were carried out under cover of darkness. A little snow. At 8 pm the Brigade was ordered to fill up with ammunition from 5th Batt. 3rd Division. This was done by motor lorries taking ammunition to Batteries.	
BROXEELE	27/11/15		Brigade marched via FLAESTRAETE - OXELAERE - BAVINCHOVE - WEMAERS CAPPEL - BAMEMBERG - POINT DU TOUR to BROXEELE. Starting at 9 a.m. and arriving at 2.15 pm. The Brigade was inspected by the G.O.C 2nd Army when passing CASSEL. Forty three.	
HEDRINGHEM	28/11/15		The Brigade was ordered to march to TATINGHEM via HEDRINGHEM - CREME STRAETE - WATTEN. Where East of WATTEN, LEBAS - BERQUES - TILQUES. The billeting party however found that TATINGHEM was occupied by 4th ARMY SIGNALS, and the Brigade was ordered to rest for the night at HEDRINGHEM. Weather frosty.	
TATINGHEM	29/11/15		Brigade marched at 11.30 am to TATINGHEM via BILQUES - HELFAUT - WIZERNES. No supplies arrived either on 28th until on the morning of 29th until so orders were issued to requisition what was necessary.	
TATINGHEM	1/12/15		In billets. Weather wet.	
"			Inspection of billets and horse lines by Maj. Gen. J. E. Capper @ B. Bridge 24th Division	
"	2/12/15		Inspection of billets and horse lines by Colonel Staynton G.S.C 1 2nd Army. 21st Hows and 2/4 Hows join Brigade and attached to the Brigade and attached to B. Battery and Ammunition Column respectively. Weather wet.	

Army Form C. 2118.

WAR DIARY
or
INTELLIGENCE SUMMARY
(Erase heading not required.)

Vol VI

Place	Date	Hour	Summary of Events and Information	Remarks and references to Appendices
VOORDPEENE	1.1.16		Brigade marched to NOORDPEENE via ST OMER and CLARMARAIS starting at 10.0 a.m.	
STEENVOORDE	2.1.16		Brigade marched to STEENVOORDE via ZUTYPERVE - OXELAERE - QUAESTRAETE starting at 10.0 a.m.	
"	3.1.16		1st Section of A & C Batteries moved to wagon lines of corresponding batteries of 79th Bgd R.F.A. starting at 8.0 a.m. & 9.0 a.m. respectively. Personnel of these Sections relieved personnel of Sections of 79th Brigade during night. 2/Lt R Boully slightly wounded	
16 Rue de Cassel POPERINGHE	4.1.16		Head Quarters moved to 16 Rue de Cassel POPERINGHE and took over from Hd Qrs 79th Brigade R.F.A. Ammunition Column marched to wagon lines & took over from 79th B.A.C. 2nd Section of A & C Batteries moved to wagon lines in course of the morning. Personnel of these sections relieved personnel of 79th Bde in course of afternoon. In all cases the guns were exchanged. The guns of 79th Bde being left in action.	
"	5.1.16		Inspection of new wagon lines by Colonel Commanding. A Battery passes into Right Group commanded by Colonel Cardew who will be relieved by Lt Col Valtholl 109th Bde R.F.A. C Battery passes into Left Group under Lt Colonel Coates 10th Bde R.F.A.	
	6.1.16		Draining wagon lines and cleaning harness. Major C C Robertson leaves for England.	
	7.1.16		Weather fair	
	8.1.16		Nothing to chronicle. Weather showery.	
	9.1.16		Nothing to chronicle. Weather fair	
	10.1.16		Nothing to chronicle. Dull in morning Rain about 5 pm	
	11.1.16		Inspection of wagon lines by G.O.C. R.A. Weather fair	
	12.1.16		Recieved A.B. 57 & C. 2118 Corporal from Base	

WAR DIARY or INTELLIGENCE SUMMARY

Army Form C. 2118.

VOL VI

Place	Date	Hour	Summary of Events and Information	Remarks and references to Appendices
Rue di Caral PERING HE	13.1.16		Inspection of wagons by Colonel Commanding. 17 Remounts posted to Brigade. Weather fair in morning, colder after noon. Sleet showers.	
	14.1.16		Nothing to chronicle. Weather colder but fine.	
	15.1.16		Nothing to chronicle. 2/Lt Fairhurst & 2/Lt Ball joined the Brigade attached to 'B' & 'D' Batteries respectively.	
	16.1.16		Nothing to chronicle. Weather fair	
	17.1.16		Walton C Battery withdrawn from position to wagon lines	
	18.1.16		Nothing to chronicle. Weather wet	
	19.1.16		- do - - do - weather fine.	
	20.1.16		2nd Lieut Franklin joined the Brigade – attached to Am. Col. weather fair – late wet	
	21.1.16		Capt. Nable joined the Brigade & posted to 'C' Battery – OC C/106. weather dull. Colonel Cameron Ansling went up to the firing line.	
	22.1.16		Weather dull, late fine. Enemy aeroplane dropped 10 bombs in vicinity of 106" & Brigade Ammunition Column. One civilian wounded. At 11 p.m. six bombs dropped – Principle on camp & close to 106 & Bde Hd Qrs. during two Infantrymen	
	23.1.16		Weather fine – afternoon showery. Nothing to chronicle	
	24/1/16		Nothing to chronicle – weather fine.	
	25.1.16		- do -	
	26/1/16		- do -	
	27/1/16		Twelve gunners – nine drivers – 7 LD horses posted to Brigade. weather dull Return to Chronicle – weather dull	
	28/1/16		- do -	

Army Form C. 2118.

WAR DIARY
or
INTELLIGENCE SUMMARY.
(Erase heading not required.)

Vol VI

Place	Date	Hour	Summary of Events and Information	Remarks and references to Appendices
29.1.16	29.1.16		Nothing to chronicle. Weather dull.	
16 Rue de Cassel	30.1.16		Nothing to chronicle. Weather dull.	
Poperinghe	31.1.16		Nothing to chronicle. Weather fair.	

a/106 Battery
vol: 5

24

Army Form C. 2118.

A/106 Battery

4/3

WAR DIARY
or
INTELLIGENCE SUMMARY.
(Erase heading not required.)

Instructions regarding War Diaries and Intelligence Summaries are contained in F. S. Regs., Part II. and the Staff Manual respectively. Title pages will be prepared in manuscript.

Place	Date	Hour	Summary of Events and Information	Remarks and references to Appendices
YPRES	Feb 1		O.C. to POPERINGHE for a lecture. Heavy howitzers carried out a bombardment on our front in which the Battery cooperated. Enemy replied vigorously on our trenches. 18 P.rs successfully installed. New gun brought into action in the evening.	
	Feb 2		Infantry called for retaliation in the morning - which Battery provoked the German artillery to reply to a lively exchange for a time. 17th Inf. Bd. Bde. new in our sector. Fine day - strong S. wind - a good deal of firing in the morning particularly by our 4" & 6" Hows.	
	Feb 3		Good night. Strong S. wind still. Artillery of both sides active towards Hill 60 but fairly quiet on our front. Fine day - extraordinarily clear. Aeroplanes active. Fired about 120 rounds dispersing a working party & doing a lot of damage to trenches. Cold & dull S.W. wind. Artillery very active in afternoon. Our trench trench bombarded. Bdr. Dallas to hospital with damaged shoulders owing to fall from his horse when riding up to guns after return from Faye. Gr. Hood badly wounded and I. Roise by a shell burst close to Cook's cart last night on its return from Gun position to Wagon line. Aeroplanes active - bombs dropped close to Wagon line. Enemy artillery busy all day - wires much cut near O.P. Fired a good deal at intervals in reply	
	Feb 2			

Army Form C. 2118.

WAR DIARY
or
INTELLIGENCE SUMMARY.
(Erase heading not required.)

Place	Date	Hour	Summary of Events and Information	Remarks and references to Appendices
YPRES	Feb 8		A very marked increase of activity on part of hostile artillery today. The front trenches were shelled almost continuously, and there were few areas that escaped entirely. Our retaliation did not succeed in stopping it.	
	Feb 9		The neighbourhood of the Battery shelled a good deal in the early part of the night. Aeroplanes actors apparently registering for artillery. Enemy guns appeared to be registering everywhere. Wires often cut but repaired.	
	Feb 10		Hostile artillery active against our back area in afternoon & on roads and communications at night. Cpl. Vickers wounded by S.9 when returning with empty ration cart to wagon line.	
	Feb 11		Dull day - Hostile artillery still active - we repaired Telephone Lines now again in order.	
	Feb 12		North & NE wind. Heavy artillery & Infy: fire to the North in afternoon. Battery stood to for a time & received the warning "Gas Alert". All normal again at 7 p.m.	
	Feb 13		Enemy artillery active all day - Front line trenches at HOOGE so knocked about that infantry had to evacuate them till dusk. We retaliated for a time & Heavy Howitzers taken on. Wires much cut. Light shell round Battery. Major to Wagon Line with a view to going on leave. Lt Haskell at guns & in Command.	

Army Form C. 2118.

WAR DIARY
or
INTELLIGENCE SUMMARY.
(Erase heading not required.)

Instructions regarding War Diaries and Intelligence Summaries are contained in F.S. Regs., Part II. and the Staff Manual respectively. Title pages will be prepared in manuscript.

Place	Date	Hour	Summary of Events and Information	Remarks and references to Appendices
	Feb. 14		Our heavy artillery fired on enemy trenches in the morning. At 3 p.m. Enemy commenced a very heavy bombardment of front trenches all along the line. Battery stood to. S.O.S. signal received about 3.30 p.m. Battery opened a prompt & rapid fire — rate of fire reduced after about ½ an hour until situation was reported satisfactory. Battery standing to all night. Infantry report that artillery fire was very prompt & effective.	
	Feb. 15		A lot of work needed on telephone wires. Some retaliation during the morning. Aeroplanes very active in afternoon. Heavy fire to the South at 5 p.m. preparatory to an attempt to regain a French post (restored).	
	Feb. 16		"S.O.S." signal from Infantry at 2.30 a.m. proved a false alarm. Mr Spicer secured a direct hit on a Tree used as an observation post by enemy — another heavy bombardment to the South at 3 p.m.	
	Feb. 17		A quiet & misty day — aeroplanes active.	
	Feb. 18		Quiet day. If Franklyn to Wagon Line.	
	Feb. 19		Aeroplanes active. German working party dispersed in GLENCORSE WOOD. Some H.E. found Battery during the day. C.R.A. visited Battery & expressed his own & GOC's satisfaction at present good work of Battery.	

Army Form C. 2118.

WAR DIARY
or
INTELLIGENCE SUMMARY.
(Erase heading not required.)

Instructions regarding War Diaries and Intelligence Summaries are contained in F. S. Regs., Part II. and the Staff Manual respectively. Title pages will be prepared in manuscript.

Place	Date	Hour	Summary of Events and Information	Remarks and references to Appendices
YPRES	Feb 20		Aeroplanes again active - did some firing at working parties & hostile communication trenches	
	Feb 21		Misty morning but clear later - Battery engaged in cutting enemy's wire which was satisfactorily done. Battery was heavily shelled with 4·2" & 5·9" between 3 & 7 p.m. A few gas shell amongst them.	
	Feb 22		A thick morning followed by fall of snow. Battery position again shelled - a direct hit on No. 3 gun pit did considerable damage to equipment but no casualties. Gas shell round billet.	
	Feb 23		Quiet misty day, a few shell round about the billet.	
	Feb 24		Cold - hard frost - Major Bridgeman returned from leave.	
	Feb 25		Frost & misty. N.E. wind - German working party dispersed. Some retaliation in the afternoon. Snow at night at knobbolt to wagon line	
	Feb 26		Snow & thick - considerable shelling in the evening to South. Aeroplane dropped bombs close to billet - no damage. I Brit. to Flying Corps. Group retaliation at 9 p.m.	
	Feb 27		Thaw - fired 125 rounds Group Retaliation at 8 p.m.	
	Feb 28		S. wind misty. Lt Franklyn to a Trench Mortar Course	
	Feb 29		Clear - aeroplanes active - strong E wind in afternoon.	

J. Bd? Swan Major R.A
Comdr A Mob R.F.A

C/O
A.G.s Office, Base

Herewith volume
VIII of War Diary.

Butler
Major
6.4.16   Comdg 106th FAE

Army Form C. 2118.

WAR DIARY
or
INTELLIGENCE SUMMARY.
(Erase heading not required.)

Vol VII

Place	Date	Hour	Summary of Events and Information	Remarks and references to Appendices
16 Rue du Cacul POPERINGHE	1/3/16		2/Lt G.F. Bell detached Orderly Officer.	
	2/3/16			
	3/3/16		2/Lt A.G. Burrases proceeds to England Sick, Storres.	
	4/3/16			
	5/3/16		Major T.E. Heescale comes to Hd Qrs to command Bde.	
	6/3/16			
	7/3/16			
	8/3/16			
	9/3/16		One section of C Battery goes to I.20.c.3.6 (sheet 28) under Capt. Burns in Right Group.	
	10/3/16		Remaining section of C Battery wt position.	
	11/3/16		One section B Battery relieves one section A Battery in ECOLE DE BIENFAISANCE. Position I.15.6.3.10 (Sheet 28)	
	12/3/16		Remaining section A Battery relieved by section B Battery.	
	13/3/16		Major D.W. Spiller pricd & took over command of Brigade.	
	14/3/16		Nothing to chronicle.	
	15/3/16		O.C. 101st Bde R.F.A. takes over command of Left Group. 24th Divie Arty, composed of 6 F.A. Batteries to one 4.5" Hows Reg and a call on 6 in Siege Howitzers.	
	16/3/16		Five Casualties in C Battery. One man killed.	
	17/3/16		In evening the 5 in Hows fired 112 rounds at the BIRDCAGE	

Army Form C. 2118.

WAR DIARY
or
INTELLIGENCE SUMMARY.
(Erase heading not required.)

VOL VIII

Place	Date	Hour	Summary of Events and Information	Remarks and references to Appendices
RAMPARTS YPRES	17.3.16		at point where a field gun was supposed to have been put in front trenches. Section of LAHORE D.A. relieve section of 24th D.A. unfit	
	18.3.16		17th/18th Section relieved March to EECKE 18th/19th 11ph March completed and Sto proceed to EECKE	
EECKE	19.3.16		On march	
	20.3.16		On march	
	21.3.16		On march	
	22.3.16		On march	
	23.3.16		On march	
	24.3.16		On march	
	25.3.16		On march	
	26.3.16		Major Spiller goes up to front of 1st Canadian F.A. Brigade	
	27.3.16		On march	
	28.3.16		On march	
	29.3.16		On march	
	30.3.16		On march	
	31.3.16		First section from EECKE at 9.a.m. March to 10 a.p.m. line 1st Bde: Canadian Field Artillery. Relief of section completed under cover of darkness.	

XXIV

106 RFA
Vol 8

O.i/c,
    A.G's Office
        Base.

        Herewith Vol.9.(April) of
War Diary.

                        Major.R.F.A.
2.5.16.   Comdg.106th.F.A.Bde.

Army Form C. 2118.

WAR DIARY
or
INTELLIGENCE SUMMARY.
(Erase heading not required.)

VOL IX

Instructions regarding War Diaries and Intelligence Summaries are contained in F.S. Regs., Part II. and the Staff Manual respectively. Title pages will be prepared in manuscript.

Place	Date	Hour	Summary of Events and Information	Remarks and references to Appendices
T20.c.29 (Sheet 28)	1.4.16		Last sections march to water lines and relief is completed by 9.30pm. Head Quarters relieving when all battery relief complete.	
	2.4.16		Registration by Batteries.	
	3.4.16		Registration by Batteries.	
	4.4.16		Registration by Batteries.	
	5.4.16		Shoot by Heavy Howitzers 6.45 witness on LA PETITE DOUVE FARM. Retaliation given for shelling of Frost Trenches.	
	6.4.16		C Battery shelled with lap cruzado. 4 casualties, none killed.	
	7.4.16		Two retaliations given in reply to enemy shell fire.	
	8.4.16		Quiet day.	
	9.4.16		Artillery actively on both sides.	
	10.4.16		Night 10/11. Turned at night on 100F. SW of MESSINES. Flashes were hidden by VERY lights fired on 11.40p63.	
	11.4.16		Quiet day, wet.	
	12.4.16		Quiet day, wet.	
	13.4.16		Nothing to record.	
	14.4.16		Enemys artillery active. Retaliations given.	
	15.4.16		Nothing to record.	
	16.4.16		Fine day. Aeroplane activity.	
	17.4.16		Registration of MESSINES - GAPAARD road.	
	18.4.16		Nothing to record.	

Army Form C. 2118.

WAR DIARY
or
INTELLIGENCE SUMMARY.
(Erase heading not required.)

VOL IX

Place	Date	Hour	Summary of Events and Information	Remarks and references to Appendices
Trench C & D	19.4.16	8.0 pm	Continued transport shoot at MESSINES and GAPAARD road. 106ᴿ, 107ᴿ & 109ᴿ Bass RFA. 60 p.m. & 12 in. Heavies Co operated.	
	20.4.16		Quiet day.	
	21.4.16		Wet. Quiet day.	
	22.4.16		Normal	
	23.4.16		Normal	
	24.4.16		Normal	
	25.4.16		Col Digh spoken to England on leave. Maj Hamilton O Bridgeman & HQrs	
	26.4.16		Artillery activity	
	27.4.16		Quiet day.	
	28.4.16		A Battery registered with aeroplane observation.	
	29.4.16		B Battery registered with aeroplane observation. Later 29/4 about 1 am	
	30		Gas Alarm sounded on Right. O certain number of rounds were fired. Nothing happened. A 106ᵗʰ Bn took	
	31.4.16		C Battery registered with aeroplane observations etc. Apl 30/1ˢᵗ Gas Alarm sounded on Left trenches & Division. No Gas	
			in 106ᵗʰ Bn front	

106th Bde R.F.A.

RF/A-106
Vol 9
XIV

Army Form C. 2118.

WAR DIARY
or
INTELLIGENCE SUMMARY.
(Erase heading not required.)

Instructions regarding War Diaries and Intelligence Summaries are contained in F.S. Regs., Part II. and the Staff Manual respectively. Title pages will be prepared in manuscript.

Place	Date	Hour	Summary of Events and Information	Remarks and references to Appendices
PLOEGSTEERT	May 1 1916		Fine, warm mostly. Wind E.N.E. Bar. 29.32. Quiet day. Little artillery activity.	
"	" 2		Fine but cloudy later, cooler. Rain later. Bar. 29.19. Generally quiet. Minor artillery bombardment on right sector arranged for midnight. Gas alert cancelled	
"	" 3		Cloudy, dull. Bar. 29.14. C.O. visited Batteries and advance gun of A/109 with G.O.C. R.A. Little artillery activity. Gas alert at 10.30 p.m.	
"	" 4		Warm. Cloudy. Bar. 28.96. C.O. visited Wagon Lines. Quiet on front.	
"	" 5		Dull, close & hot. Bar. 28.67. G.O.C. & B.M. visited A & B. Batteries gun positions and O.P's with C.O. Quiet day. Some activity S. of Armentières. Gas alarm heard about 8.30 p.m. Breeze S.E.	
"	" 6		Showery with fine intervals. Bar. 28.85. Lt Col Burne proceeded on leave. Major Cowan D/109 assumed temporary command of the Brigade.	

169th Bde R.F.A

Army Form C. 2118.

WAR DIARY
or
INTELLIGENCE SUMMARY.
(Erase heading not required.)

Instructions regarding War Diaries and Intelligence Summaries are contained in F.S. Regs., Part II. and the Staff Manual respectively. Title pages will be prepared in manuscript.

Place	Date	Hour	Summary of Events and Information	Remarks and references to Appendices
PLOEGSTEERT	1916 May 7		Dull, colder, showery. Bar 29.90. Arranged shoot for 2.30pm N.E. edge of L'Enfer Wood. Too gusty for much artillery shooting. Evist. day Major Bowen visited Batteries and C/169 O.P.	
"	" 8		Gusty, cold & cloudy. Bar 29.1. Little activity. Trial of signal lights at 9-15 pm.	
"	" 9		Cold, rain & windy. Bar 29.2. Adjutant & Lt Mitton visited Batteries to see "Listening Apparatus" demonstration.	
"	" 10		Calmer & mild. Bar 29.4. Some artillery activity on whole front from noon till 4 pm. Capt Schaur posted to Trench Mortars	
"	" 11		Mild. Cloudy. Bar 29.43. Quiet day. Arrangements for re-organisation of Bdes begun.	

106" Brigade R.F.A
(late 109th Army Bde R.F.A)

Army Form C. 2118.

WAR DIARY
or
INTELLIGENCE SUMMARY.
(Erase heading not required.)

Instructions regarding War Diaries and Intelligence Summaries are contained in F. S. Regs., Part II. and the Staff Manual respectively. Title pages will be prepared in manuscript.

Place	Date	Hour	Summary of Events and Information	Remarks and references to Appendices
PLOEGSTEERT	1916 May 12		Mild. Cloudy. warmer. Bar 29.34 Enemy shelled farm at T.29.d.6.5. heavily	
	13		Rained during night, & day was wet. Bdes re-organised Headquarter Staff took over 106th Bde R.F.A at noon consisting of C.10 & C.106th Bde & A/109th Bde (South) to be known as B/106th Bde. B.O.B/109th Bde completed units of 109th Bde & No.1 Section D.a.C also bought for 106th, 109th & 108th Bdes	
	14		Dull & showery. Bar 29.32 Adjt. visited B/106 Waggon Line	
	15		Rain during night. overcast & gusty. Bar 29.05 Quiet generally	
	16		Bright. Warmer. Bar 29.5 Col Burne returned from leave at 2.30 am. Quiet generally.	

106" Brigade T.F.A

Army Form C. 2118.

WAR DIARY
or
INTELLIGENCE SUMMARY.
(Erase heading not required.)

Instructions regarding War Diaries and Intelligence Summaries are contained in F. S. Regs., Part II. and the Staff Manual respectively. Title pages will be prepared in manuscript.

Place	Date	Hour	Summary of Events and Information	Remarks and references to Appendices
	1916			
PLOEGSTEERT	May 17		Bright, warm. Bar 29.65. 2/Corp Bde had B.Fitch whilst killed at Gun position at 6 am. One horse belonging to Bdqrs run over by Motor Bus & had to be destroyed at 3 am. Quiet generally on front. Interpreter reported hended. (Sauvegarde)	
"	18		Bright, warm Bar 29.45. Gas alarm at 12-15 am must have been false. Took over command of 106R Group tactically at 2pm. Hostile aeroplane brought down in enemy lines. Capt Welch machine leave	
"	19		Bright, hot. Bar 29.62. C.O. visited trenches with Col Spiller. Held conference of O.C.s at 2pm. Quiet on front generally.	
"	20		Bright, hot. Bar 29.74. Quiet generally. 2/Lt Miles from D.A.C. attached A/106	

106th Brigade R.F.A.

Army Form C. 2118.

WAR DIARY
or
INTELLIGENCE SUMMARY.
(Erase heading not required.)

Place	Date	Hour	Summary of Events and Information	Remarks and references to Appendices
PLOEGSTEERT	1916 May 21		Bright hot. Bar 29.65. Enemy artillery very active shelling "Ferme de vacinity" of Headquarters D.I./H. Maj Cowah reported 1 man (took out) killed. Quiet at noon. Hostile artillery shelled B/106 x A/109 in afternoon. All quiet at 3 pm No further casualties reported. 2/Lt Strake arrived on signalling instructions by 19th I.B.	
"	22		Hot. Bar 29.51. C.O. visited trenches at 5am. G.O.C. "D" accompanied by G.O.C. R.A. visited gun positions in forenoon. 2/Lt Davel to T.M. Cowah.	
"	23		Cloudy cooler. C.O. to Ballent for conference G.O.C. R.A. Conference of B.C. of group at 6.30pm Airplane activity above average. Bar 29.52. 2/Lt Hudnich to Hospital.	
"	24		Cooler & overcast. Bar 29.28. 2/Lt Strake (12th Lancers) left Headquarters. C.O. visited trenches at 5am. Arranged 5 min bombardment of Messines	

106th Brigade R.F.A.

Army Form C. 2118.

WAR DIARY
or
INTELLIGENCE SUMMARY.

(Erase heading not required.)

Instructions regarding War Diaries and Intelligence Summaries are contained in F. S. Regs., Part II. and the Staff Manual respectively. Title pages will be prepared in manuscript.

Place	Date	Hour	Summary of Events and Information	Remarks and references to Appendices
	1916			
PLOEGSTEERT	May 24		at 8.45pm for transport.	
"	" 25		Showery, cooler. Bar 29.16 C.O. visited trenches. All quiet.	
"	" 26		Cloudy, cool. Bar 29.32. Slow retaliation by 6de for enemy shelling of Bh. G.O.C. R.A. visited Headquarters.	
"	" 27		Cloudy, cool. Bar 29.24. Quiet on front generally.	
"	" 28		Cloudy, some sunshine. Bar 29.31. G.O.C. R.A. visited Headquarters at 2pm. Naval party visited guns from 2pm to 6pm.	
"	" 29		Bright, warm. Bar 29.42. Quiet generally. Rain at night.	
"	" 30		Dull at first. Sunshine later. Bar 29.48. Artillery activity on both sides from noon to 3pm. Special retaliation 2-50pm. Several attached officers arrived	

106" Brigade R.F.A.

Army Form C. 2118.

WAR DIARY
or
INTELLIGENCE SUMMARY.
(Erase heading not required.)

Instructions regarding War Diaries and Intelligence Summaries are contained in F. S. Regs., Part II. and the Staff Manual respectively. Title pages will be prepared in manuscript.

Place	Date	Hour	Summary of Events and Information	Remarks and references to Appendices
	1916			
PLOEGSTEERT	May 31		Sunshine warm Bar 29.58 Major Bridgeman returned from leave. Quiet generally. Lt Lockhart on Signalling Instruction to Bailleul.	

A.W.Dougan.
Lieut T.F.A.
for O.C. 106" Brigade T.F.A.

APPENDIX 1.

NEW ORGANIZATION of 24th Divisional Artillery.

May 13th 1916.

106th F.A.B.   T/Lt.Col.E.R.BURNE, D.S.O.

   A/106 Battery.   Maj.Hon.H.G.O.BRIDGEMAN.
   B/106   "   Lt. C.S.GOODWIN.
   C/106   "   Capt.W.M.M.O'D.WELSH.
   D/106(How) "   Capt.H.GARDNER.   (Formerly A/109 Battery.)

107th F.A.B.   Lt.Col.D.R.COATES.

   A/107 Battery.   Capt.R.L.GALLOWAY.
   B/107   "   Capt.W.S.N.CURLE.
   C/107   "   Capt.H.A.S.WURTELE.
   D/107(How) "   Maj.J.de B.COWAN.   (Formerly D/109 Battery.)

108th F.A.B.   T/Lt.Col.E.C.W.D.WALTHALL. D.S.O.

   A/108 Battery.   Capt.R.N.V.MONTGOMERY.
   B/108   "   Capt.G.A.CAMMELL. D.S.O.
   C/108   "   Maj. Hon.R.G.A.HAMILTON.
   D/108(How)   Capt.O.HART.   (Formerly B/109 Battery.)

109th F.A.B.   T/Lt.Col.D.W.L.SPILLER.

   A/109 Battery.   Capt.H.S.BROWNE.   (Formerly D/106 Battery.)
   B/109 Battery.   Capt.W.L.LUCAS.   ("   D/107   "   )
   C/109 Battery.   Capt.P.Y.BIRCH.   ("   D/108   "   )

24th D.A.C.   Lt.Col.G.J.F.TALBOT.

"A" ECHELON.

   No.1 Section.   Capt.W.BROADBRIDGE.
    " 2   "   Capt.J.R.GRIEVE.
    " 3   "   Capt.E.D.L.SAUNDERS.

"B" ECHELON.

   No.4 Section.   Maj.B.B.GILPIN.

APPENDIX 11.

Temporary Tactical Grouping of 24th Divisional Artillery.

May 13th 1916.

106th F.A.B.GROUP.   T/Lt.Col.D.W.L.SPILLER
                         & H.Q. 109th F.A.B.
                         (Until return of Lt.Col.E.R.BURNE, D.S.O.)

                         A/106 Battery.
                         B/106   "
                         C/106   "
                         A/109   "
                        *D/107(How) "

107th F.A.B.GROUP.   Lt.Col.D.R.COATES.
                         & H.Q. 107th F.A.B.

                         A/107 Battery.
                         B/107
                         C/107   "
                         B/109   "
                         *D/106(How) "

108th F.A.B.GROUP.   T/Lt.Col.E.C.W.D.WALTHALL, D.S.O.
                         & H.Q. 108th F.A.B.

                         A/108 Battery.
                         B/108   "
                         C/108   "
                         C/109   "
                         D/108(How) "

H.Q. 106th F.A.B. In Rest.

* This grouping of Howitzer batteries is adopted
  to avoid changing their present zones, which would
  entail fresh registration.

106th Brigade. R.F.A.

Army Form C. 2118.

WAR DIARY
or
INTELLIGENCE SUMMARY.
(Erase heading not required.)

Place	Date	Hour	Summary of Events and Information	Remarks and references to Appendices
	1916.			June
PLOEGSTEERT	June 1 Thurs.		Cloudy, warm. Artillery active on night. Observation Balloon broke loose in our lines and drifted over enemy lines at 7.30 p.m. Observers descended in our lines in parachutes. Bar. 29.46.	
"	2 Fri		Fine, some clouds. Bar. 29.40. Heavy Artillery active towards YPRES. Quiet generally. Aeroplanes active. G.O.C., R.A. visited O.P.s with R.E. Officer. C.O. had conference with Battery Commanders.	
"	3 Sat		Fair, cloudy. Bar. 29.36. Trench Mortars active, otherwise quiet. Enemy attack on 3rd Div. CANADIAN Front, heavy bombardment on left.	
"	4 Sun.		Dull, windy, colder. Bar. 29.22. Organised bombardment of enemy trenches by Div: at 12.30 a.m. slight retaliation only. Quiet generally during day. G.O.C., R.A. visited gun positions	
"	5 Mon.		Dull. Bar. 28.58. Enemy attitude quiet during day. G.O.C., R.A. visited gun positions in afternoon	

Army Form C. 2118.

WAR DIARY
or
INTELLIGENCE SUMMARY.
(Erase heading not required.)

Instructions regarding War Diaries and Intelligence Summaries are contained in F.S. Regs., Part II. and the Staff Manual respectively. Title pages will be prepared in manuscript.

Place	Date	Hour	Summary of Events and Information	Remarks and references to Appendices
	1916			
LOEGSTEERT	June 6 Tues		Met. Bar 29.2. C.O. visited trenches with Major BRIDGEMAN at 5.0. a.m	
"	7 Wed		Met. Bar 29.13. Fair cloudy. At 3.0 a.m 6 wires in French leading into Headquarters found cut, cuts were clean as if done with pliers. Full enquiries elicited no information to lead to detection. Conference of B.C's held at Headquarters. Visual signalling between H.Q. & B/107 carried out. Working party of some Group Batteries supplied to D.A. for O.P. fatigues on Hill 63.	
"	8 Thurs		Met. Bar 29.19. Wet. G.O.C. R.A. accompanied by C.O. made round of inspection to B/106 Wagon line	
"	9 Fri		Met. Bar 29.32. Showery. Experimental Shoot for purpose of wire cutting carried out by B/106 and observed by O.C. Group. Visual signalling between Batteries and Group H.Q in the evening. O.C attended Conference at D.A, N.Q.	

WAR DIARY or INTELLIGENCE SUMMARY.

Army Form C. 2118.

Place	Date	Hour	Summary of Events and Information	Remarks and references to Appendices
	1916			
PLOEGSTEERT	June 10 Sat		Fine. Showery at night. Bar. 29.56. Enemy Artillery not so aggressive in this sector today. A/109 cut wire for instructional purposes at Ygo 2.2/2. Enemy retaliated chiefly with 10 c.m. Hows. Battery on our Battery position but was countered by D/107 How. Battery.	
"	" 11 Sun		Fine. Bar. 29.52. Enemy attitude quiet during day. Proposed visit of Sir HUBERT GOUGH and Major General FRANKS to visit O.P's of this Group cancelled. Wire cutting for instructional purposes practised.	
"	" 12 Mon		Raining & Cloudy all day. Bar. 29.31. G.O.C., R.A. visited H.Q. 106" Bde. Heavy Artillery bombardment in the neighbourhood of YPRES.	
"	" 13 Tues		Raining hard all day. Bar. 29.05. Very hard for observation. O.C. held a conference of B.C's in connection with proposed operations	
"	" 14 Wed		Raining off & on. Bar. 29.43. C.O. visited Batteries & O.P.S. C/106 engaged in wire cutting. At 11 o'clock fire one hour in accordance with instructions from R.A.	

WAR DIARY
or
INTELLIGENCE SUMMARY.
(Erase heading not required.)

Army Form C. 2118.

Place	Date	Hour	Summary of Events and Information	Remarks and references to Appendices
	1916	Day		
PLOEGSTEERT	June 15 Thurs		Raining Bar 29.51. Very poor for observation. G.O.C.R.A. held a meeting of Group Commanders in BAILLEUL at 9.0 a.m. O.C. attended. Later O.C. visited Batteries & O.P's	
"	" 16 Fri		Cloudy, warmer. Bar. 29.61. C.R.E's conference on gun pit construction at A/106. Bombardment on night about ARMENTIERES.	
"	" 17 Sat		Fine night. Cloudy during day. Bar. 29.47. Enemy gas emitted along Div'n Front at 12.30 a.m and lasted until 2.30 a.m when bombardment ensued. Enemy did not leave his trenches. Enemy shelled B/106 A/109 admirality from 2.30 a.m to noon. Casualties 1 man wounded, 1 man gassed (slightly)	
"	" 18 Sun		Cloudy, cold. Bar. 29.32. Quiet during morning. Enemy shelled trenches 130-132 about 4.30 p.m. Retaliated. Gas alarm on night of Div'n Front. Proved to be false alarm.	

Army Form C. 2118.

WAR DIARY
or
INTELLIGENCE SUMMARY.
(Erase heading not required.)

Instructions regarding War Diaries and Intelligence Summaries are contained in F.S. Regs., Part II. and the Staff Manual respectively. Title pages will be prepared in manuscript.

Place	Date	Hour	Summary of Events and Information	Remarks and references to Appendices
	1916			
PLOEGSTEERT	June 19 Mon		Cloudy. Cold. Bar. 29.23. Quiet generally. Some shelling of 130 & 131. Retaliated	
"	20 Tues		Cloudy. Bar. 29.57. C.O. visited A/109 Wagon Line to see Bridging Demonstration by R.E. Quiet on front.	
"	21 Wed		Cloudy, warmer. Bar. 29.60. G.O.C., R.A. ANZAC. CORPS. visited O.P's and Gun Positions. C.O. attended conference at BAILLEUL. Quiet generally.	
"	22 Thurs		Cloudy, close. Bar. 29.30. Enemy shelled COURT DREVE FARM in vicinity of Brigade H.Q with 5.9 Hows about 2 hours (10. a.m – 12. a.m.). Gas alarm heard on right and "Div" on our right commenced heavy Bombardment about midnight all due to false alarm and S.O.S. rocket. Commenced work on "Fallen Tree"	
"	23 Fri		Cloudy, close. Some showers. Bar. 29.24 Relief of 17th I.B. by 2nd Australian Inf y Brigade commenced. Quiet generally. C.O. went to BAILLEUL for conference	

Army Form C. 2118.

WAR DIARY
or
INTELLIGENCE SUMMARY.
(Erase heading not required.)

Instructions regarding War Diaries and Intelligence Summaries are contained in F. S. Regs., Part II. and the Staff Manual respectively. Title pages will be prepared in manuscript.

Place	Date	Hour DAY	Summary of Events and Information	Remarks and references to Appendices
PLOEGSTEERT	1916 Tues 25	Sat.	Cloudy rain. Bar. 29.40. Infantry in trenches relieved by ANZACS. Enemy Artillery active at night about 7 p.m. Group wire cutting demonstration by 18 pdr. Batteries.	
"	25	Sun	Cloudy with fine intervals. Bar. 29.29. Aeroplanes active. Quiet along front – heavy artillery fire near ARMENTIERE.	
"	26	Mon	Showery, wet at night. Bar. 29.19. Our aeroplanes attacked German observation balloons at 8.30 p.m. and brought 3 down in flames. Quiet day on front. C.O. visited trenches at 6.0 a.m.	
"	27	Tues	Wet. Bar. 29.01. Continued wire cutting. Col. TURNER Second Army G.S. visited gun positions. Quiet generally.	
"	28	Wed	Wet. Bar. 29.12. Wire cutting continued. Some slight retaliation on part of enemy over trenches 132 & 135. Quiet otherwise. Raid by 8" Buffs (Continued) on	

T 2134. Wt. W708—776. 500000. 4/15. Sir J. C. & S.

Army Form C. 2118.

WAR DIARY
or
INTELLIGENCE SUMMARY.
(Erase heading not required.)

Instructions regarding War Diaries and Intelligence Summaries are contained in F. S. Regs., Part II. and the Staff Manual respectively. Title pages will be prepared in manuscript.

Place	Date	Hour	Summary of Events and Information	Remarks and references to Appendices
	1916		Cont'd	
LOEGSTEERT	Tues 28		on ASH ROAD BARRIER at 11.31 p.m. Right party entered trench and killed 3 Boschs, and brought back some rifles and other material. Left party were not able to find gap in wire and therefore did not enter trench. Bombardment very successful. Enemy sap encountered rather spoilt surprise. Our casualties slight. Retaliation very feeble.	
"	29 Thurs		Cloudy with few fair intervals. Bar 29.28. Enemy attitude quiet. Slight shelling of gun positions on left of sector with 77 m.m gun at 9.30 p.m Heavy bombardment heard on right of S of ARMENTIERE.	
"	30 Fri		Cloudy, fine in evening. Bar. 29.37. Enemy shelled B/106 and A/109 and road near Bde H.Q about 9 p.m. Div- on our right raided enemy trenches at 9.20 p.m.	

H.W. Douglas Lieut R.F.A.
for O.C. 106" (?) Brigade R.F.A.

106 / July
Army Form C. 2118.
106 RFA
Vol II

WAR DIARY
or
INTELLIGENCE SUMMARY.
(Erase heading not required.)

Place	Date	Hour	Summary of Events and Information	Remarks and references to Appendices
PLOEGSTEERT	July 1st		Fine morning, dull later. Two discharged from trenches 128 & 130, wind about 5-10 m.p.h. accompanied by bombardment 2-26 am. All quiet at 1-30. Tribulation alight, mostly T.M's. Enemy shelled Courte Dreve Farm Group retaliated on Bethlehem & Seignent Farms. Heavy firing about Armentieres during night. "Willow Tree" observatory erected.	
"	2		Fine, some clouds. All quiet generally. Some shelling behind our lines on farms.	
"	3		Fine intervals. Enemy registered & shelled farms in Petit Pont, with very little damage.	
"	4		Dull at night first: wet night. Relief of Group by 101st & 2nd Divt Artillery (A & NZ A C) by sections. One section completed relief by midnight. Batteries relieved took over Wagon lines in Kemmel Area.	
"	5		Fair cloudy. One section of each Battery relieved proceeded to new wagons lines near Locre at 10 am. Second half of relief cancelled for 24th hours. HQ staff to new Wagon line near Kemmel Ave. to relieve 251st Bde (Scrivilliers) SCM Diff	

106" T.A.B

Army Form C. 2118.

WAR DIARY
or
INTELLIGENCE SUMMARY.
(Erase heading not required.)

Instructions regarding War Diaries and Intelligence Summaries are contained in F.S. Regs., Part II. and the Staff Manual respectively. Title pages will be prepared in manuscript.

Place	Date	Hour	Summary of Events and Information	Remarks and references to Appendices
KEMMEL	July 6.		Fine mostly. C.O. arrived at Kemmel. Able to look over zone. Quiet on front. Relief of 1st Section completed.	
"	7.		Fine with few intervals. 2nd section relief of Batteries of 25 1st Bde Group cancelled. Section relieved returned to original positions. Orders received to return to PLOEGSTEERT Area on 8th to relieve 21st Australian Bde S.A.	
"	8		Warm, cloudy in evening. Batteries passed through Bailleul at noon and returned to Wagon Lines in Hoegsteert Area. Complete relief at 11·30pm Command handed over. Quiet all day. Argoes went out.	
PLOEGSTEERT	9.		Cloudy order C.O. to G.O.C.R.A. conference. A.Q. billet shelled with whizzbangs no casualties. Raid by Bde on our right at 11·30pm. Enemy aeroplanes very active with bombs. A.Q. wagon line had to move.	
"	10		Cloudy, fair at intervals. Quiet generally. Orders received to re-group at 4 pm on 12/7/16.	
"	11		Dull. Enemy aeroplanes active at 7·30am. Registered farm house Bde H.Q. at 9am. Wireless station demolished and operator wounded. Bde H.Q. moved to T5pa 5.6 at 10·30pm. Enemy aeroacks of a/106 & C/106.	

106" F.A.B

Army Form C. 2118.

WAR DIARY
or
INTELLIGENCE SUMMARY.

(Erase heading not required.)

Instructions regarding War Diaries and Intelligence Summaries are contained in F. S. Regs., Part II. and the Staff Manual respectively. Title pages will be prepared in manuscript.

Place	Date	Hour	Summary of Events and Information	Remarks and references to Appendices
ROMARIN	July 12		Dull, occasional drizzle. Moved from temporary Transport camp to T.21.d.3.1. New group camp under control at HQrs A.B. & D/106 & A.B. & B/107 H.A.B. (Capt Earle)	
"	13		Dull, rain during afternoon & night. C.O. visited batteries. Enemy shelled some Battery positions. Quiet otherwise. C.O. visited C.R.A.	
"	14		Dull, warmer in afternoon, cold at night. 16/106 came out of action and moved to Romarin for Gun pit construction. Lieut McCulloch took over Gun pit making from O.E. B/106 2/Lt Wilmot posted to B/106 2/Lt while to Ajax	
"	15		Warmer, cloudy at times. C.O. visited trenches A.O.T. shelled enemy Battery at O.28 C.2.5. D/106 co-operated. Wire cutting was carried out by 18 pdr Batteries.	
"	16		Misty, some rain in morning. Wire cutting by 18 pdr Batteries continued. C.O. & C.R.A. visited H.Q. at 12.50 p.m. C.O. inspected new gun positions.	
"	17		Cloudy, drizzling. Wire cutting continued. Bombardment of enemy trenches on left sector carried out at 11 p.m. by 108 H.A.O.B. & rec.d by 1/1st S.B. Bombardment arranged by Div. pastnard. Group fired on presences where a good deal of	

106th T.A.B.

Army Form C. 2118.

WAR DIARY
or
INTELLIGENCE SUMMARY.
(Erase heading not required.)

Instructions regarding War Diaries and Intelligence Summaries are contained in F. S. Regs., Part II. and the Staff Manual respectively. Title pages will be prepared in manuscript.

Place	Date	Hour	Summary of Events and Information	Remarks and references to Appendices
ROM A RIN.	July			
	18.		Transport was heard. Cloudy, cooler. C.O. visited trenches and new Gun Positions. Corps commander & C.R.G.S. visited O.P's on Hill 63. Quiet day.	
"	19		Cold night, warmer in day, cloudy. Wife sitting returned. Infantry On Reliefs at 2am. Letter 12 & J.B. received by 20th Div. Infantry.	
"	20		Misty, warm. Orders issued for D.A. to be ready to move out at short notice. Quiet day. Orderly Officer 153rd Bde R.F.A. arrived	
"	21.		Warm, misty & close. Orders issued to relieve on night 22/23 & to Brigade Group, and move to rest area at Ecke. Envoy shelled during morning & afternoon. No damage.	
"	22		Misty & close. E.O. & Adjt 153rd Bde R.F.A. arrived after breakfast. C.O. took Col. 153rd Bde round Battery positions. Hill 63 etc. Adjt. explained administration & tactical positions to Adjt 153 Bde, & captured Telephone system to Orderly Officer 153 Bde who took over same. H.Q. 106th Bde advance party under O.C. march out at 4-30 pm reached Ecke at 8-30 pm. Col. & Adjt remaining behind	

T2134. Wt. W708—776. 500,000. 4/15. Sir J. C. & S.

106th F.A.B.

Army Form C. 2118.

WAR DIARY
or
INTELLIGENCE SUMMARY.
(Erase heading not required.)

Instructions regarding War Diaries and Intelligence Summaries are contained in F.S. Regs., Part II. and the Staff Manual respectively. Title pages will be prepared in manuscript.

Place	Date	Hour	Summary of Events and Information	Remarks and references to Appendices
	July			
POMMIN	23		to hand over. C.O. hands over to Col 152 Bde & arrives at Ecke on the morning of 23rd.	
ECKE	24		Misty & slight rain during night. C.O. & Adjt visit wagon lines & A.A.D.A.	
"	25		Fine. C.O. & Adjt visit wagon lines & H.Q. D.A.	
"	25.		Fine C.O. & Adjt depart at 10 am for Bailleul to see East of Batteries. 106 Bde entrain full H.Q. Staff march out at 1-45 pm for Bailleul The whole of H.Q. Staff entrain at Bailleul and depart at 7-30 pm for Hangest & Somme	
LONGUEAU	26		Cloudy. arrived at Longueau at 4 am & marched out to Hangest-&-Somme. Arrived at 11 am. C.O. & Adjt visit wagon lines. Veterinary Officer visits 2/106 wagon line & inspects the horses.	
HANGEST -S- SOMME	27		Fine & warm. C.O. visits wagon Lines & reconnoitre country for training purposes.	
"	28		Fine & warm. Scheme for training purposes detailed by O.C. Wheeler. Battery Staffs with signallers & junior officers passed on scheme with O.C. Brigade at 9-15 am. Batteries practice Driving Drill & coming into action with Guns & Living Battery wagons. Capt takes Brigade	

T2134. Wt. W708—776. 500000. 4/15. Sir J. C. & S.

106 "T.A.B.

Army Form C. 2118.

WAR DIARY
or
INTELLIGENCE SUMMARY.
(Erase heading not required.)

Place	Date	Hour	Summary of Events and Information	Remarks and references to Appendices
HANGEST -S- SOMME	July		Staff on signalling & wire laying course, & "communication on the move", at 2-30 pm programme of work carried out in morning and afternoon by Batteries. test joined drafts practice laying of fuze setting & a map reading course for young officers was practised together with Director Pole & Bty Staff, communication on the move	
"	29.		Fine, warm. Training programme continued. C.O. proceeds on aeroplane with skeleton Battery staffs signalling &c. Programme of work carried out morning and afternoon by Batteries. Adjutant takes H.Q. Staff on the telegraph and visual signalling in the afternoon	
"	30		Fine warm. Church Parade 9.30 am at D/107 wagon line Conference Brigade & Bty commanders, D.A. H.Q. at 11-30 am Col inspects all wagon lines.	
"	31.		106th Bde R.F.A. left Hangest-S-Somme at 10-30 am and arrive at Vecquemont at 6.15 pm.	

Wm Douglas
Lieut R.F.A.
for O.C. 106" Brigade R.F.A.

T2134. Wt. W708—776. 500000. 4/15. Sir J. C. & S.

24th Divisional Artillery.

106th BRIGADE

ROYAL FIELD ARTILLERY

AUGUST 1916

106th Brigade R.F.A.

Army Form C.2118.
WA06.92
106 R.F.A

WAR DIARY
or
INTELLIGENCE SUMMARY.
(Erase heading not required.)

Instructions regarding War Diaries and Intelligence Summaries are contained in F. S. Regs., Part II. and the Staff Manual respectively. Title pages will be prepared in manuscript.

Place	Date	Hour	Summary of Events and Information	Remarks and references to Appendices
	1916			
NICQUEMONT	Aug 1st		Fine & very warm. C.O. visited wagon lines of all Batteries. Brigade and Battery staffs signalling practice	
"	" 2nd		Fine. Signalling practice continued. C.O. visited wagon lines	
"	" 3rd		Fine & warm. Preparations made for move to new area	
"	" 4th		Fine night. Brigade marched off at 1.30 a.m. for BOIS-DE-TAILLES at 1.30 a.m. and arrived at Corps reserve area at 6.0. a.m	
BOIS-DE-TAILLES	" 5th		C.O. and Battery Commanders visited R.A. Dvl HQ at the CITADEL and proceeded to reconnoitre positions in the vicinity of LA BRIQUETERIE and TRONES WOOD, later visited heavies and obtained good views of DELVILLE WOOD, GINCHY & GUILLEMONT. Shelling heavy in the area at times mostly 4.2" & 5.9"	

Army Form C. 2118.

WAR DIARY
or
INTELLIGENCE SUMMARY.
(Erase heading not required.)

Instructions regarding War Diaries and Intelligence Summaries are contained in F. S. Regs., Part II. and the Staff Manual respectively. Title pages will be prepared in manuscript.

Place	Date	Hour	Summary of Events and Information	Remarks and references to Appendices
	1916			
BOIS DE TAILLES	Aug 6		Parties at 106 Bde "dug in" on proposed new forward gun positions near LA BRIQUETERIE & TRONES WOOD. Shelling heavy at times with 8inch, several falling near parties causing 3 casualties	
"	"	7"	Parties continue "digging in", shelling very heavy. C.O. has conference with B.C's and later in the day accompanied by the Adjt inspected work at new gun positions	
"	"	8"	C.O. accompanied by C.O. 108" Bde visited forward gun positions and on return arranged with C.O. 2d D.A.C. for loan of G.S. Wagons for transport of necessary material for building O.T's in forward trenches	
"	"	9"	C.O. had conference with B.C's and afterwards visited R.A.H.Q. at CITADEL. Orderly Officer with Battery & D.A.C. Wagons took material from forward dumps to various Battery positions	

WAR DIARY
or
INTELLIGENCE SUMMARY.

(Erase heading not required.)

Army Form C. 2118.

Place	Date	Hour	Summary of Events and Information	Remarks and references to Appendices
	1916			
BOIS-DE-TAILLES	Aug 10		C.O and Adjutant visit forward position. Wires are laid out from Bde. H.Q to Battery positions and Infantry H.Q at LA BRIQUETERIES	
"	"	11"	Batteries left in sections at 4 + 4.30 A.M for new positions. Colonel and Adjutant left for new Bde H.Q at 10.0 a.m calling at R.A.H.Q en route. At noon O.C left Sagon line with staff for new H.Q	
"	"	12	Batteries engaged in improving gun positions and registering. C.O. has conference with B.C's and later visited Infantry H.Q, arranging for laying of frozen Offices and for signal and telephone station at LA BRIQUETERIE. Wagon lines moved to MEAULTE	
MEAULTE	"	13	Great difficulty experienced in making of communications owing to heavy shelling	

Army Form C. 2118.

WAR DIARY
or
INTELLIGENCE SUMMARY.
(Erase heading not required.)

Instructions regarding War Diaries and Intelligence Summaries are contained in F. S. Regs., Part II. and the Staff Manual respectively. Title pages will be prepared in manuscript.

Place	Date	Hour	Summary of Events and Information	Remarks and references to Appendices
MARTINSART	1916 Aug 14		Batteries engaged in wire cutting and fuzing to enfilade with movement. Communications broken owing to heavy shelling. Heavy bombardment in vicinity of POZIERES from 10.15 pm	
"	15		Brigade was heavily shelled. Lt. Dallas A/106 slightly wounded.	
"	16		Communications cut early in day, runners arranged for. Bombardment begun at 5.10 pm with view to capture of trenches.	
"	17		Feint bombardment at 4.7 pm or for 5 minutes at intense rate. At 1.0 p.m another bombardment commenced and lasted till 11.0 p.m then slow rate till 5.0 a.m	
"	18		9.17 a.m Feint bombardment. At 2.45 p.m heavy bombardment on our front, also on Right & Left. Infantry assaulted at 2.45 p.m	

Army Form C. 2118.

WAR DIARY
or
INTELLIGENCE SUMMARY.
(Erase heading not required.)

Instructions regarding War Diaries and Intelligence Summaries are contained in F. S. Regs., Part II. and the Staff Manual respectively. Title pages will be prepared in manuscript.

Place	Date	Hour	Summary of Events and Information	Remarks and references to Appendices
MARICOURT	Aug 19		Bombardment & further infantry action arranged for 5.0 A.M. cancelled	
"	21	4.30 p.m	Bombardment opened to cover Infantry attack. Enemy aeroplanes active during firing	
"	24		Bombardment of GUILLEMONT at 5.45 p.m & continued until 8.0 p.m. Lieut W.A. Spicer to hospital badly wounded. S.O.S. called at 9.0 p.m	
"	25	5.0 p.m	Batteries ordered to "stand by" in anticipation of enemy attack which did not materialise. 8.45 p.m. S.O.S received followed by "Gas Alert".	
"	27		2/Lt Maskell temporarily attached to A/106 and took over command 2/Lt Blackburn joined and posted to A/106.	
"	28		No 2 Gun A/106 sent to Workshops, replaced by one from 35 D.A.	

T2134. Wt. W708—776. 500000. 4/15. Sir J. C. & S.

WAR DIARY or INTELLIGENCE SUMMARY

Army Form C. 2118.

Place	Date	Hour	Summary of Events and Information	Remarks and references to Appendices
MARICOURT	1916 Aug 28	6.0 p.m	On leave. Heavy shelling in vicinity. Dug out of C/106 blown in by 8in A.P. shell. Lieuts. Walsh, Winter & Totheby wounded & sent away.	
	29		Bombardment of GUILLEMONT began at 8.0 a.m with view to attack but cancelled after a little shooting. Violent storm at 5.0 p.m. S.O.S received at 6.10 p.m, firing stopped at 6.40 p.m. Eff. rifles of B/106 attached to C/106. 2/Lt. Bingham Newland joined from D.A.C and attached to C/106.	
	30		General offensive cancelled owing to bad weather. Considerable bombardment on our left about 4.0 p.m. S.O.S received at 9.30 p.m, firing stopped after 15 minutes.	
	31		Heavy shelling with gas shells, and 17cm shells. Batteries opened fire on approaches to GINCHY as attack was anticipated. S.O.S at 10.0 p.m but very little firing.	

Wm Douglas Lieut. R.F.A
for O.C 106 B.Q.B.

Royal Artillery

24th Division.

106th BRIGADE R. F. A.

SEPTEMBER 1916

Head Qrs (Q)
24th Division

Herewith War Diaries for the month of September 1916 for the following units:—

106th Bde R.F.A.
107th " "
108th " "
24th D A C
X)
Y) Batty T. Mortars
Z)

Kindly acknowledge receipt hereon

R.H. Fox
Captn
for 24th D A
for CRA 24 D A

9/10/16

106TH Brigade R.F.A.

Vol 3

Army Form C. 2118.

WAR DIARY
or
INTELLIGENCE SUMMARY.

(Erase heading not required.)

Instructions regarding War Diaries and Intelligence Summaries are contained in F. S. Regs., Part II. and the Staff Manual respectively. Title pages will be prepared in manuscript.

Place	Date 1916 Sept	Hour	Summary of Events and Information	Remarks and references to Appendices
BRIQUETRIE	1		Raining. Gas shells sent over by enemy during the night. Batteries engaged area shooting. G.O.C. visited Batteries & H.Q.	
"	2		Heavy bombardment started at 8 am. Batteries engaged, firing all day with occasional heavy bursts during the afternoon. Brigade Staff repairing forward wires.	
"	3		Bombardment began at 8 am & proceeded according to programme. Right section Kane of A/106 ordered up from wagon line to "stand by" at Carnoy ready to advance if required. Teams sent back at 6 pm. C.O. & O.O. attend at BRIQUETERIE all day and remain during the night. Position of GUILLEMONT & GINCHY taken.	
"	4		Bombardment continued. C.O. & O.O. at Briqueterie all day. Guillemont & up to Leuze wood taken, but Division on our left turned out of Ginchy.	

2353 Wt W2544/1454 700,000 5/15 L. D. & L. A.D.S.S./Forms/C. 2118.

Army Form C. 2118.

WAR DIARY
or
INTELLIGENCE SUMMARY.
(Erase heading not required.)

Instructions regarding War Diaries and Intelligence Summaries are contained in F. S. Regs., Part II. and the Staff Manual respectively. Title pages will be prepared in manuscript.

Place	Date	Hour	Summary of Events and Information	Remarks and references to Appendices
BRIQUETRIE	1916 Sept 4 (cont^d)		C.O. & B.C's Guard's Divisional Artillery (who are to relieve us) report and are shown positions at 6-30 pm. Bombardment renewed in support of further infantry attack.	
"	5		Rain at intervals. One section of each battery relieved by Guard's Divisional Artillery. Position for Brigade in front of Guillemont reconnoitred. O.O. accompanied by 2 B.C's of the Guard's Division and inspect proposed positions and report Agft feasible. Batteries reply to S.O.S. call, for about an hour. Lt Westerberg A/106 killed by a shell on returning from O.P. after handing over to Guard's Officer.	
"	6		Remaining section of Batteries relieved, & B.C's left position C.O. and H.Q. Staff arrive at Wagon line at Bois-de-Tailles at 6 pm.	

WAR DIARY
or
INTELLIGENCE SUMMARY.
(Erase heading not required.)

Army Form C. 2118.

Place	Date	Hour	Summary of Events and Information	Remarks and references to Appendices
BOIS - DE - TAILLES	1916 Sept 7.		Brigade at rest at Bois-de-Tailles. G.O.C. Dir. visits Brigade. C.O. visits all Wagon lines & was received of each of G.O.C. R.A. & Brigade Major.	
"	8.		Brigade at rest Bois-de-Tailles. C.O. visits all wagon lines.	
"	9.		Bde at Rest at Bois-de-Tailles. Lt Lloyd leaves for London & Capt Cathcart reports and takes over duties as M.O. C.O. and Adjutant attend funeral of General PHILLIBOTTS & B.M. at the Citadel.	
"	10		Orders received to go into action at B.1.c.26. C.O. holds conference with B.C's & subsequently left to reconnoitre new positions and has conference with the Brigade Major.	

Army Form C. 2118.

WAR DIARY
or
INTELLIGENCE SUMMARY.
(Erase heading not required.)

Instructions regarding War Diaries and Intelligence Summaries are contained in F. S. Regs., Part II. and the Staff Manual respectively. Title pages will be prepared in manuscript.

Place	Date	Hour	Summary of Events and Information	Remarks and references to Appendices
BOIS-DE-TAILLES	1916. Sept. 11		C.O. Adjt, & B.C's leave Bois-de-Tailles for new Battery positions at 11am with parties for digging in etc. Brigade leaves Bois de-Tailles for new wagon Lines at Méricourt at 10am.	
"	12		Batteries leave wagon Lines at 2am for new gun positions and arrive at positions without casualties although position shrapnelled upon arrival. Trench Mortar party & Brigade parties engaged digging in all day. O.O. spent all day visiting various dumps for the purpose of drawing material for Batteries. C.O. returns from new gun positions very little to be got. C.O. returns from new gun positions to attend Generals conference at 10½h Bde wagon line at 5·30 pm. H.Q. staff move into advanced position in the evening leaving Méricourt Post at 4pm. Ammunition brought up during night.	

WAR DIARY or INTELLIGENCE SUMMARY.

Army Form C. 2118.

Place	Date	Hour	Summary of Events and Information	Remarks and references to Appendices
MALTZ & MORN RAVINE	1916 Sept 13		C.O. visits all batteries and has conference with Battery Comdrs. Forward communications laid and Batteries registered.	
"	14		C.O. visit Batteries and has conference with F.O.O. Lt Halel slightly wounded while on duty. Plan (general) of operations received later in day & explained to B.C's by C.O. Batteries registered C.O. visit 10th Bde to attend G.O.C. R.A's conference which was postponed (per telephone) after to find left. Teams & Limbers of B. & C. batteries in preparation for advance brought up to valley in rear of gun positions night 14/15K.	
"	15		Forward communications repaired & extended for operations tomorrow. Bombardment (in accordance with programme) commenced at 6-30 am. F.O.O's out at daylight & Liaison Officer sent to Infantry previous evening. Attack towards MORVAL & LES BOEUFS made progress on left but held up in centre.	

WAR DIARY
or
INTELLIGENCE SUMMARY.
(Erase heading not required.)

Army Form C. 2118.

Place	Date	Hour	Summary of Events and Information	Remarks and references to Appendices
MALTZ	1916 Sept			
CORN RAVINE	15 (contd)		FLERS was taken and a considerable number of prisoners.	
"	16		Supported attack on LES BOEUFS at 9-25 am. At about 10 am part of German entrenched line taken and prisoners. Attack on left held up for a bit. C.O. reconnoitred advanced new positions for guns near LEUZE WOOD with view to moving up tonight. Orders received from G.O.C. that Brigade should not move tonight.	
"	17		Batteries engaged registering with Aeroplane on trench T.14.d.8½.4. to T.14.c.8.2.5. and the Quadrilateral with a view to registration for barrage. C.O. holds conference with B.C's. Batteries engaged wire cutting. Heavy rain all day.	
"	18		Supported attack on Quadrilateral & obtained all objectives in spite of heavy rain. 300 prisoners and some machine guns	

Army Form C. 2118.

WAR DIARY
or
INTELLIGENCE SUMMARY.

(Erase heading not required.)

Instructions regarding War Diaries and Intelligence Summaries are contained in F. S. Regs., Part II. and the Staff Manual respectively. Title pages will be prepared in manuscript.

Place	Date	Hour	Summary of Events and Information	Remarks and references to Appendices
MALTZ HORN RAVINE	1916. Sept. 18 (cont'd)		captured. attack commenced at 5-50 am. Reconnoitred advanced new gun positions in front of Guillemont. 1 section from each Battery dug itself in	
"	19.		in morning. Raised heavily in morning Batteries registered Ammunition brought up to guns. H.Q. & Batteries continued digging in. In consequence of rain operations postponed 24 hours. C.O. visited D.Q. & 15. I.B. Batteries engaged in night firing in accordance with instructions.	
"	20.		Raining heavily. operations postponed 24 hours. Batteries continue digging in as far as weather permits and engaged in wire cutting operations.	
"	21.		Raining intermittently the whole day. operations postponed on account of weather conditions. H.Q. & Batteries engaged	

Army Form C. 2118.

WAR DIARY
or
INTELLIGENCE SUMMARY.

(Erase heading not required.)

Instructions regarding War Diaries and Intelligence Summaries are contained in F. S. Regs., Part II. and the Staff Manual respectively. Title pages will be prepared in manuscript.

Place	Date	Hour	Summary of Events and Information	Remarks and references to Appendices
MALTZ HORN TRVINE	1916 Sept 21 (contd)		on forward positions. Ammunition brought up to the Guns. Forward communications to OP laid & established.	
LEUZE WOOD	22		Weather fine. Working party from D.F.C. assisted in completing H.Q. and Battery positions. Operations still further postponed. H.Q. move forward to advanced positions. Arrangements made for forward communications, & liason for Right Group in the event of the capture of LES BOEUFS.	
"	23		Weather fine. H.Q. and Batteries engaged completing forward positions.	
"	24		Bombardment commenced in accordance with programme and continued until 6-30 pm.	
"	25		Weather fine. Bombardment resumed at 6-30 am & continued	

WAR DIARY or INTELLIGENCE SUMMARY

Army Form C. 2118.

Place	Date	Hour	Summary of Events and Information	Remarks and references to Appendices
LEUZE WOODS (cont'd)	1916 Sept 25		till zero 12-35 p.m. Supported an attack on LES BOEUFS & MORVAL. All objectives gained & large number of prisoners surrendered. Counter attack reported but did not materialize.	
"	26		Weather fine. C.O. & Officers of 32nd F.A.B. H.Q. & Div: report at H.Q. & are shewn battery positions & front covered etc. Our batteries engaged registering.	
"	27		Fine in morning. Wet at night. one section of 32nd Bde relieved one section of Right Group. New batteries registered. Aeroplanes bombed our wagon lines in the evening, killing 6 horses outright & wounding 20 others so badly that the V.O. ordered them to be shot. These belonged to A/1C6.	
"	28		Remaining sections of 32nd Bde relieved remaining section R't Group. C.O. R't Group hands over to C.O. 32nd Bde. Brigade	

Army Form C. 2118.

WAR DIARY
or
INTELLIGENCE SUMMARY.
(Erase heading not required.)

Instructions regarding War Diaries and Intelligence Summaries are contained in F. S. Regs., Part II. and the Staff Manual respectively. Title pages will be prepared in manuscript.

Place	Date	Hour	Summary of Events and Information	Remarks and references to Appendices
	1916 Sept			
LEUZE WOOD	28 (cont'd)		marched to Bois-de-Tailles.	
BOIS DE TAILLES	29.		Raining. Brigade marched out of Bois-de-Tailles at 7.0 am. arrived at PIERREGOT at 2 pm.	
PIERREGOT	30.		Fine. Bde marched out of PIERREGOT at 2.30 pm arrived at AUTHIEULLE 6.30 pm. Standard time put back one hour from this date (i.e from 3 pm to 2 pm)	

Wm Dewyas. Lieut. R.F.A.
for O.C. 106 Brigade R.F.A.

Army Form C. 2118.

WAR DIARY
or
INTELLIGENCE SUMMARY
(Erase heading not required.)

106th Bde R.F.A.

Place	Date 1916	Hour	Summary of Events and Information	Remarks and references to Appendices
AUTHIEULE	Oct 1		Brigade marched out Authieule at 7-30 am. and arrived at Vacquerie-le-Bourcq at 2.30 pm.	
VACQUERIE LE BOURCQ	" 2		Left Vacquerie-le-Bourcq at 8-15 am. for Gricourt & Bours	
BOURS	" 3		Left Bours at 5-30 am and arrived at Verdrel at 5-30 pm. One section of each Battery relieved corresponding unit of 51st Brigade in action.	
VERDREL	" 4		Left Verdrel at 9.30 am. Remaining sections completed relief.	
"	" 5		Wagon lines moved up to Fauchin-le-Gal.	
BERTHONVAL	" 6		Two 18 pdrs (A/106 & B/106) taken out and sent gk DA.	
"	" 7		Hostile Trench Mortars Batty. 4.5" How. retaliated.	
"	" 8		Nothing to report.	
"	" 9		Enemy raided ERSATZ CRATER about dawn, but easily repulsed by our Infantry. No Artillery assistance called for. Casualties slight.	
"	" 10		Hostile aeroplane brought down.	
"	" 11		Hostile T.M's busy on CHORD. Artillery retaliated.	
"	" 12		Nothing to report	

Army Form C. 2118.

WAR DIARY
or
INTELLIGENCE SUMMARY

(Erase heading not required.)

Instructions regarding War Diaries and Intelligence Summaries are contained in F. S. Regs., Part II. and the Staff Manual respectively. Title Pages will be prepared in manuscript.

Place	Date 1916	Hour	Summary of Events and Information	Remarks and references to Appendices
BERTHONVAL	Oct 13		Nothing to report.	
"	" 14		Arranged registration for 6" Siege Battery.	
"	" 15		Hostile T.M's busy.	
"	" 16		6" Siege Battery fired at 10am and 3pm on front line. Aeroplanes very active.	
"	" 17		Aeroplanes active. Raid by 14 of our machines. Infantry Raid by Right Battn not successful due to listening post being manned.	
"	" 18		Nothing to report.	
"	" 19		Slight hostile Trench Mortar activity.	
"	" 20		Registration by aeroplane.	
"	" 21		Nothing to report.	
"	" 22		Aeroplanes active.	
"	" 23		Nothing to report.	
"	" 24		Nothing to report.	
"	" 25		Nothing to report.	

2449 Wt. W14957/M90 750,000 1/16 J.B.C. & A. Forms/C.2118/12.

Army Form C. 2118.

WAR DIARY
or
INTELLIGENCE SUMMARY

(Erase heading not required.)

Instructions regarding War Diaries and Intelligence Summaries are contained in F. S. Regs., Part II. and the Staff Manual respectively. Title Pages will be prepared in manuscript.

Place	Date 1916	Hour	Summary of Events and Information	Remarks and references to Appendices
BERTHONVAL	Oct 26		Nothing to report.	
"	" 27		C.O and one Officer for Battery to see new area at Mazingarbe	
"	" 28		#/Trench Mortar shoot at noon.	
"	" 29		Nothing to report	
"	" 30		Nothing to report.	
"	" 31		Nothing to report.	

H.W.Douglas. Lieut
for O.C. 106th Bde. R.F.A

WAR DIARY or **INTELLIGENCE SUMMARY**

106th Bde RFA   Army Form C. 2118.

November 1916

Vol 15

Place	Date	Hour	Summary of Events and Information	Remarks and references to Appendices
	1.11.16			
	2.11.16			
	3.11.16			
	4.11.16			
	5.11.16		Batteries carried out usual day and night bombardment.	
	6.11.16			
	7.11.16			
	8.11.16			
	9.11.16			
	10.11.16		Gen. Mercer, G.O.C, R.A., 1st Army visited Group Head Qrs & Battery positions.	
	11.11.16		"A" & "B" Battery wagon lines moved to CAMBLAIN L'ABBE.	
	12.11.16			
	13.11.16			
	14.11.16		Batteries carried out usual day and night bombardment.	
	15.11.16			
	16.11.16			

Army Form C. 2118.

WAR DIARY
or
INTELLIGENCE SUMMARY.
(Erase heading not required.)

November 1916

Place	Date	Hour	Summary of Events and Information	Remarks and references to Appendices
	17.11.16			
	18.11.16			
	19.11.16			
	20.11.16			
	21.11.16		Batteries carried out usual day & night bombardment.	
	22.11.16			
	23.11.16			
	24.11.16			
	25.11.16			
	26.11.16			
	27.11.16		Batteries supported a raid on enemy trenches on VIMY RIDGES following the successful blowing up of a mine in enemy lines which caused considerable casualties; raid carried out by 2nd Canadian Brigade. Enemy trenches entered and two identifications secured. We suffered some casualties also from hostile artillery, and the explosion of a trench mortar dump in our lines.	

Army Form C. 2118.

WAR DIARY
or
INTELLIGENCE SUMMARY

(Erase heading not required.)

November 1916

Place	Date	Hour	Summary of Events and Information	Remarks and references to Appendices
	28.11.16		Enemy made several unsuccessful counter attacks on mine crater which we occupied the near lip.	
	29.11.16		} Usual day & night firing by Batteries.	
	30.11.16			

B.C. Burne 1/Col
(comdg) 106 Bde RFA
30/11/16-

106 Bde R.F.A.
December 1916

WAR DIARY or INTELLIGENCE SUMMARY.
(Erase heading not required.)

Army Form C. 2118.

Place	Date	Hour	Summary of Events and Information	Remarks and references to Appendices
	1916 Dec. 1		Nothing to chronicle.	
	2		On night of 2nd, 4 guns of 18 pdr Batteries and a section of How: Battery were relieved by corresponding guns of 5th Bde Lahore Div: Arty. These sections proceeded to billets in the Commune of NIEUX-LES-MINES.	
	3		On night of 3rd remaining sections were relieved by corresponding sections of Lahore Div: Arty. Head Qrs. Staff handed over by 3.0.p.m. to Col. Strover commanding 5th Bde. These sections moved into billets in NIEUX-LES-MINES. The guns relieved on the 2nd and the afternoon of the 3rd relieved corresponding guns of Left Group 40th Div: Arty in Loos area.	
	4		Remaining sections relieved corresponding guns of 40th Div: Arty. H.Q were taken over by the O.C. by 6.p.m. The Group were responsible for firing from 12 noon. The Left Group consists of A/106, B/106, N/106 and a section of C/106 (attached) Remaining 4 guns of C/06 attached to Right Group.	
	5–23		Weather generally dull & rainy. Enemy Trench mortars, light, medium & heavy very active during the period. Most of the heavy trench mortar	

WAR DIARY or INTELLIGENCE SUMMARY

Army Form C. 2118.

December 1916

Place	Date	Hour	Summary of Events and Information	Remarks and references to Appendices
	5-23		emplacements have been marked down and engaged by our 18 pdrs & 4.5" Hows with assistance occasionally from H.A. 60 pdrs & 6" Hows for retaliation purposes.	
	24		At 5.0 a.m enemy Heavy T.M. became very active and a bombardment opened out with 77 m.m guns. 10.5 a.m to 10.15 am Hows, a barrage being put up on our supports in H.19 a 9.c. Our artillery replied on enemy. T.M. communications & support trenches, and a slow barrage was put up on their front line in H.19.C. The bombardment quieted down at 10.30 a.m but the Heavy T.M's were active throughout the day.	
	24-26		Our Batteries were active throughout the Xmas period, special Secret two minute bombardments being carried out on enemy trenches etc. Enemy field guns & Heavy T.M's were also active.	
	29-31		General Trench mortar activity by enemy.	

A.W.Beham Lieut for Lt. Col.
Comdg. 106th Bde. R.F.A.

G.S.M.

WAR DIARY
INTELLIGENCE SUMMARY
(Erase heading not required.)

106 F.A Brigade

Army Form C. 2118.

January 1917

Place	Date	Hour	Summary of Events and Information	Remarks and references to Appendices
1.1.	1/1/17		at 11.20. A.M. a bombardment of enemy H.T.M's in H.13.C & H.19.D was carried out by our 9.2" in conjunction with 6" others & Group 4.5" others firing on front line and supports in H.13.C. General effect good. Two dumps were blown up and several H.T.M's must have been put out of action. One H.T.M. re opened fire in the afternoon for a few rounds only.	
	2/1/17 to 5/1/17		Weather dull. Enemy quiet except for occasional heavy trench mortar activity.	
	9/1/17		A raid was carried out at H.19.a.6c.9c. The raiding party entered enemy trenches at H.19.a.6c.9c. brought back one prisoner and sustained no casualties. A preliminary bombardment of C.T.'s and supports was carried out by H.T.M's in H.13.a. & H.19.d. Enemy artillery retaliation was small & slow in coming into action. B/106 moved forward to a new position near Rue y at H.24.a.45.65.	
	10/1/17		Weather dull.	
	11/1/17 to 31/1/17		Night firing by batteries on enemy roads in co operation with H.A.	

Army Form C. 2118.

WAR DIARY
or
~~INTELLIGENCE SUMMARY~~

(Erase heading not required.)

January 1917

Instructions regarding War Diaries and Intelligence Summaries are contained in F. S. Regs., Part II. and the Staff Manual respectively. Title pages will be prepared in manuscript.

Place	Date	Hour	Summary of Events and Information	Remarks and references to Appendices
	17/1/		After dark our shelling by Group Batteries and H.A. enemy tembered VERMELLES from about 8.30 P.M. to 12 midnight and then barraged our trenches in region of CRATERS. Our 18 pdrs opened a slow barrage over CRATERS and left sub-section. Firing died down about midnight.	
	18/1/	23/1/	Weather dull, changing to snowy then frosty weather. Nothing to chronicle.	
	24/1/		At 11.0. P.M. enemy attempted to raid the CRATERS. They were beaten off by our sentries leaving 1 dead & 2 wounded behind them, our casualties were nil. At 4.0. P.M. Lt. Col. E.H. Perre. D.S.O. commanding left Group was wounded whilst in front line trenches of left sub-section.	
	25/1/		At 12 noon a raid was carried out by 9th East Surreys. They entered enemy trenches at H.19. a. 60. 35. They took 3 prisoners killed a large number of the enemy in dug outs. The party had 11 men wounded.	
	26/1/		At 6.45 a.m. B/106 & B/106 a. shewed with enemy Group when carrying a raid by Centre Group, in which 18 prisoners were taken	

WAR DIARY
~~INTELLIGENCE SUMMARY~~
(Erase heading not required.)

Army Form C. 2118.

January 1917.

Place	Date	Hour	Summary of Events and Information	Remarks and references to Appendices
	27/1		All quiet. Nothing to chronicle	
	28/1, 29/1, 30/1		do.	
	31/1		Lieut Col. G.H. Batson took over command of Left Group.	

J. L. M.

A.F. Bokam Lieut
for O.C. 106th Brigade R.F.A.

WAR DIARY or INTELLIGENCE SUMMARY

Army Form C. 2118.

106th Bde RFA
FEBRUARY 1915

Vol 18

Place	Date	Hour	Summary of Events and Information	Remarks and references to Appendices
PHILOSOPHE.	1.2.14 to 10.2.14		All quiet. Have post. Nothing to shortcut. recvd	
	11.2.14		Enemy attempted a raid about 5.20 A.M. against our trenches at Boyan 64 after a H.T.M. bombardment of about half an hour, to which fresh artillery replied. The raid was repulsed by Lewis gun fire, one Officer and 3 men being captured and several dead being left on our wire. Artillery stood to, but was not required.	
			Cl. recd by the N. Staffords was attempted against enemy trenches at 4.15 A.M. at H.19.A.65.60. The enemy were ready and their barrage opened 2 minutes after our own.	
	12.2.14		On the night 12th/13th, 2 sections A/106, B/106 and 1 section D/106 were relieved by corresponding guns from 123rd Bde. R.F.A., 37th Division, and proceeded to the rest area at EQUEDECQUES, near LILLERS.	
	13.2.14		On the night 13th/14th, the remaining guns of the Brigade and Bough. H.Q. were relieved by corresponding units 123rd Bde. R.F.A. and proceeded to rest area at EQUEDECQUES.	
EQUEDECQUES	14.2.14 to 18.2.14		On rest billets.	
	19.2.14		Major J. Myler D/106 returned from Course of Instruction (W.2.14) (16.2.14) Major J. W. Eye McCash C.A. B/106 to England on Course of Instruction. 2/Lt. S.P. Kewart C/106 appointed Adjutant, vice 2/Lt. C.L. Botham posted to D/106. 2/Lt. W.B. Buchanan C/106, appointed Orderly Officer. England	

Army Form C. 2118.

WAR DIARY
or
INTELLIGENCE SUMMARY.
(Erase heading not required.)

1 FEBRUARY 1917.

Instructions regarding War Diaries and Intelligence Summaries are contained in F. S. Regs., Part II. and the Staff Manual respectively. Title pages will be prepared in manuscript.

Place	Date	Hour	Summary of Events and Information	Remarks and references to Appendices
ECQUEDECQUES	20.2.17		No rest killed.	
	21.2.17		" " " Major H. HOBDAY O.C. B/106 returned from Course of Instruction in ENGLAND.	
	22.2.17		" " "	
	23.2.17		" " "	
	24.2.17		" " "	
	25.2.17		" " "	
	26.2.17		" " "	
	27.2.17		" " B/106. (Stokes) calibrated their guns at new Practice Range. FONTAINES-LES-HERMANS	
	28.2.17		" " B/106 (18 pdrs.) " " " " "	
			2nd Lieut. A.B. Whitworth attached C/106 proceeded to MECHIN	
			T.M. Course at 1st Army T.M. School.	
			1.3.17	

S.P. Manly
2nd Lieut.
for O.C, 106th Infantry T.M.B.

Army Form C. 2118.

10 Bde RFA

WAR DIARY
or
INTELLIGENCE SUMMARY.

March 1917

Vol 19

Place	Date	Hour	Summary of Events and Information	Remarks and references to Appendices
	1/3/17		A/106 calibrated their guns at Bactric Range. Guns & detachments of B/106 & D/106 proceeded to ANNEZIN to relieve guns & detachments of C/107 & D/107 at their wagon lines, & enable latter to calibrate their guns on 2nd inst, at FONTAINE-LES-HERMANS.	
	2/3/17		Nothing to chronicle. recnd	
	3/3/17		"	
	4/3/17		"	
	5/3/17		Brigade marches from ECQUEDECQUE to NOEUX-LES-MINES to wagon lines there.	
	6/3/17		Brigade relieves 2nd Brigade C.F.A. in the line as Left Group of 24th Divl. Artillery. None from DOUBLE CRASSIER to South end of Cité CALONNE. (See 24th D.A. Operation Order No 37)	
	7/3/17		(CALONNE Sector) Relief complete, as form q.am. q'nist.	
	8/3/17		Nothing to chronicle. recnd	
	9/3/17		"	
	10/3/17		"	
	11/3/17		"	
	12/3/17		Group Commanders conference. recnd	
	13/3/17		Nothing to chronicle.	
	14/3/17		4 Guns A/106 detailed for duty with 6th Divisional Artillery (Division on our Left)	

Army Form C. 2118.

WAR DIARY
or
INTELLIGENCE SUMMARY.
(Erase heading not required.)

Instructions regarding War Diaries and Intelligence Summaries are contained in F. S. Regs., Part II. and the Staff Manual respectively. Title pages will be prepared in manuscript.

Place	Date	Hour	Summary of Events and Information	Remarks and references to Appendices
	15/3/17		Nothing to chronicle.	
	16/3/17		4 Guns A/106 return to Left Group front from 1st Division area.	
	17/3/17		Nothing to chronicle recvd.	owing to Enemy mistaking our Test-Rocket for his own S.O.S.
	18/3/17		Slight disturbance on Left Group & Centre Group front lasting half an hour. 8 – 8.30 pm	
	19/3/17		Hostile T.M. Posns bombarded by Heavies at 2 P.M. in retaliation for hostility on opposite.	
	20/3/17		Nothing to chronicle recvd.	
	21/3/17		" " "	
	22/3/17		6 Guns A/106 & 2 Guns B/106 leave Left Group area for special work on 6th Div. front, 2 guns from Centre Group occupy A/106 position Y.24. T.M.B. fires 50 Lethal Gas Bombs into houses & dug outs in M.20.b (Sheet 36.c. S.W.1) Enemy sends up rockets, but no reply by his artillery or T.Ms.	
	23/3/17		Aun planes very active flying low over Battery positions all afternoon.	
	24/3/17		" " " one flying very low over Les-BREBIS at 11. a.m. Summer time adopted, 11 p.m. becomes 12 midnight.	
	25/3/17		6 Guns A/106 & 2 guns B/106 return from 6th Division area. 2 guns return to Centre Group. Some enemy shelling near Wagon Lines NOEUX-LES-MINES.	

Army Form C. 2118.

WAR DIARY
or
INTELLIGENCE SUMMARY.
(Erase heading not required.)

Place	Date	Hour	Summary of Events and Information	Remarks and references to Appendices
	25/3/17		Disturbance at 5.35 P.M. started by a Bombing Patrol from Left Battery, Cinks Brigade. Huns opens up on our front line towards Left Battn front of Left Brigade. Left Group fired on enemy front line at a slow rate till 9.20 P.M. when all was quiet.	
	26/3/17		C.O. discovers (C.P. for A/106 in Oxford Street (CALONNE) M.I.K.C.91.4.7	
	27/3/17		Left Group extends its front N of DOUBLE CRASSIER to Welch Trench as from 6 a.m. C/106 move 1 18-Pdr to MAROC M.2.b.77.95 to enfilade the 2 CRASSIERS.	
	28/3/17		2 guns A/106 & Centre Group in "Bombardment No 6" in support of raid by 6th Buffs. R/106 (6 4.5" Hows) registered by F.O.O. of Right Group on Ratum Point with a view to forthcoming operations. B/106 moves to new position in order to cover zone further North.	
	29/3/17		Hd Qrs, 24th Battery, & 38 A.F.A. B (Centre Group) withdraw from the line. Left Group takes over defence of the line as far S. as BULLY ALLEY and assumes control of remaining Centre Group Batteries.	
	30/3/17		Nothing to chronicle noted.	
	31/3/17		Small shoot with Heavies on suspected gas cylinders in M.10.c. at 9 a.m. BULLY GRENAY shelled during night by 10 c.m & 15 c.m Howitzers in retaliation for evening's firing	S Pimand 2/Lieut for O.C. 106e Bde. R.F.A.

106th BRIGADE R. F. A.

24th DIVISION

APRIL 1917

Army Form C. 2118.

106th Brigade R.F.A.
April 1917.

Vol 20

WAR DIARY
or
INTELLIGENCE SUMMARY.
(Erase heading not required.)

Place	Date	Hour	Summary of Events and Information	Remarks and references to Appendices
Field	1/4/17		Snow. BULLY GRENAY shelled with 10.cm.	
	2/4/17		Group front extended Southwards to BRISSON BOYAU, as from midnight 1/2nd April. 4 18-pdrs of C/107 attached to Left Group to cover its extra front. Z-6 day for VIMY Operation. B/38 and B/106 shoot on front of Division on our right.	
	3/4/17		B/38 and B/106 shoot on GIVENCHY.	
	4/4/17		MAROC reported shelled by enemy Infantry gun (7.65 cm). Battalion with special "Sturmtruppe" suspected opposite our (72nd Inf. Bde) front.	
	5/4/17		Raid by 8th Buffs at 2.30.a.m on Right Group front. B/38 and C/107 fire from 2.50.am to 3.15.am covering his raid. Three casualties in B/106 from aeroplane bombs.	
	6/4/17		BULLY GRENAY shelled, 4.10cm fell in garden of Hd Qrs Billet. 2 Casualties in A/106.	
	7/4/17		Z day for VIMY Operations postponed 24 hours. Group shoot on GIVENCHY postponed till 8th	

Army Form C. 2118.

106th Brigade R.F.A.
April 1917.

WAR DIARY
or
INTELLIGENCE SUMMARY.
(Erase heading not required.)

Place	Date	Hour	Summary of Events and Information	Remarks and references to Appendices
Field	8/4/17		R/38 and D/106 shoot on GIVENCHY.	
	9/4/17		Zero day for VIMY operation. B/106 & R/38 were to fire Gas Shell under orders of 31 H.A.G, & 15 H.A.G, respectively, & 6 guns C/107 & 2 guns B/106 to fire Smoke Shell, but this was rendered impossible by a very high wind.	
	10/4/17		Snow.	
	11/4/17		Snow & Sleet.	
	12/4/17		Lt. MACKAY, Bde Signals Officer, killed at No 7 Test Box, MAROC. Fired at 10 PM in support of a raid by 6th Division, to destroy tunnels in DOUBLE CRASSIER.	
	13/4/17		Enemy commences retirement towards LENS. 6 guns D/38 and 2 guns B/106 move to forward positions in CALONNE. Front line advanced about 800 x.	
	14/4/17		Bde H.Q moves to POMPEY O.P. (in S. MAROC) Wagon Lines move up to BULLY and LES BREBIS. A/106, B/106, C/106 move to forward positions (see Appendix 1)	

Army Form C. 2118.

106th Brigade, R.F.A.
April 1917.

WAR DIARY
or
INTELLIGENCE SUMMARY.
(Erase heading not required.)

Place	Date	Hour	Summary of Events and Information	Remarks and references to Appendices
	15/4/17		Advance held up till evening by M.G. at Hesse 12. 4 Howitzers D/106 to 2nd advanced position.	
	16/4/17		4 guns B/106, 2 guns A/106, 2 guns C/106 move to 2nd advanced position. 2/Lt J. HEMSTED D/106 reported missing, last seen making reconnaissance for forward O.P. Raining, no further move forward. Enemy consolidating the COWDEN - CRIMSON - CRAZY line.	
	17/4/17		Snow & rain. All Batteries firing on 6th Division front at steady rate, for attack on Hill 70.	
	18/4/17		Slow rate of fire maintained on trenches N of DOUBLE CRASSIER (N.1.c. and N.1.d. Map LENS 36.c. SW 10,000). 2 guns C/106 knocked out by shell fire, guns in open, camouflaged.	
	19/4/17		Fire continued on 6th Division front. Colonel Tonge (230 Bde R.F.A.) killed at D/106 O.P. whilst taking over gone for pending relief. Lieut R. McCULLOCH, D/106 also killed. Lieut WEBB, O.C. 230th Bde R.F.A, wounded. 138 I.B. (46th Divn) relieve 72nd I.B. (24th Div)	

Army Form C. 2118.

(4)

WAR DIARY
or
INTELLIGENCE SUMMARY.
(Erase heading not required.)

106ᵗʰ Brigade. R.F.A.
April 1917.

Instructions regarding War Diaries and Intelligence Summaries are contained in F. S. Regs., Part II. and the Staff Manual respectively. Title pages will be prepared in manuscript.

Place	Date	Hour	Summary of Events and Information	Remarks and references to Appendices
	20/4/17		Funeral of Lieut. R. McCULLOCH at MAROC. A/106 Battery joins Left Group.	
	21/4/17		Firing in support of :— (a) Attack on Hill 70 Objectives by 6ᵗʰ Div at 4.a.m. (b) 138. I.B. attack on enemy Strong Points at N.I.C.40.32. and N.I.C.60.37. and objectives in NARWAL ALLEY and COOPER TRENCH, at 5 p.m. S.MAROC shelled with Lethal Gas Shell from 11 p.m till 3.p.m (22ⁿᵈ), Casualties slight, about 10,000 rounds fired over. Bdr GILLETT 106ᵗʰ Bde H.Q. killed (Gassed).	
	22/4/17		Firing at 8 a.m in support of 138. I.B. operation to take NARWAL TRENCH, from junction with COOPER TRENCH (N.7.q.5.7.) to Railway about N.I.d.2.5. Bde. H.Q. moves forward to junction of EDGEWARE ROAD Trench with BOYAU 1.	
	23/4/17		46ᵗʰ Division advances its line to the line SOUCHEZ RIVER (about M.30.d.4.3) – FOSSE 3 de LIEVIN – HILL 65 – ADVANCED TRENCH. A/114 & B/106 fire in support of this operation from 4.45. a.m. to 4.50.a.m.	

Army Form C. 2118.

106th Brigade R.F.A.
April 1917.

(5)

WAR DIARY
or
INTELLIGENCE SUMMARY.
(Erase heading not required.)

Place	Date	Hour	Summary of Events and Information	Remarks and references to Appendices
	24/4/17		Relief of 1 Section of 106th Brigade. Batteries by 1 section Batteries 230th Bde. Relieved sections march to billets in VERQUIN. 2PM.	
	25/4/17		Remaining sections relieved, March to VERQUIN 2PM. Hd.Qrs., C/106, B/106 in VERQUIN. C/106 & D/106 in VAUDRICOURT	
	26/4/17		Brigade marches to billets in WITTERNESSE, via BETHUNE – LILLERS – ST. HILAIRE – ROMBLY.	
	27/4/17		Brigade marches to billets in MATRINGHEM (Hd.Qrs., C/106, & D/106) and VINCLY (A/106, B/106) via BLESSY – ENQUIN-LES-MINES – BOMY.	
	28/4/17		In rest Billets. Visit of A.D.V.S.	
	29/4/17		" " " Visit of I.O.M.	
	30/4/17		" " "	

SPLman
2/Lieut. R.F.A.
for O.C. 106th Brigade R.F.A.

24 DIV

WAR DIARY APRIL 1917.   Ref. LENS 1   36.c.S.W.
                                               10,000

APPENDIX I.

Advanced Positions of Batteries, LEFT GROUP 24th. D.A. April 1917

Battery.	1st. Advanced Position.	2nd. Advanced Position
A/106.	M.14.b.4.4.	M.16.a.5.6.
B/106.	M.14.b.8.3.	M.16.a.6.2.
C/106.	M.9.b.2.8.	M.10.b.8.5.
D/106.	M.14.b.4.0.	M.10.d.5.1.
D/38.	M.14.c.5.5.	M.17.c.0.5.
A/14.	M.3.d.7.1.	

Final alternative Position of A/106 and B/106,

M.16.c. 38-32., behind cottages.

Army Form C. 2118.

WAR DIARY
or
INTELLIGENCE SUMMARY
(Erase heading not required.)

106 Bde R.F.A.
Oct 21

Instructions regarding War Diaries and Intelligence Summaries are contained in F. S. Regs., Part II. and the Staff Manual respectively. Title Pages will be prepared in manuscript.

Place	Date	Hour	Summary of Events and Information	Remarks and references to Appendices
WATRINGHEM	MAY 1st		In Rest Billets.	
"	" 2nd		2/Lt TRIMBLE joins from 2nd D.A.C.	
"	" 3		In Rest Billets.	
"	" 4		"	
"	" 5		"	
"	" 6		"	
"	" 7		Lt. Col. G.R. BALSTON proceeds on leave to ENGLAND. Major T. RYDER assumes command of Brigade.	
"	" 8		In Rest Billets.	
"	" 9		Brigade marches at 7.30 a.m. to LILLE in WITTERNESSE via BEAUMETZ-LES-AIRE-CUHEM-ESTREE-BLANCHE-LIETTRES. Inspection by G.O.C. 24th Division at CUHEM.	
"	" 10		Brigade marches at 5.45 a.m. to HAZEBROUCK via AIRE - BOESEGHEM - STEENBECQUE. Billets in farms S. of HAZEBROUCK.	
"	" 11		Brigade marches at 7.30 a.m. to CASSEL via HAZEBROUCK - ST. SYLVESTRE - CAPPEL - TERDEGHEM. Billets at LE BUNDER.	
"	" 12		In Billets at LE BUNDER.	
"	" 13		Capt. H.M. DOUGLAS proceeds on leave to ENGLAND.	
"	" 14		In Billets at LE BUNDER. Brigade working party of 6 Officers and 150 Other Ranks to HALIFAX CAMP, OUDERDOM, for work on Gun Positions.	
"	" 15		Sect. of A/106 into action for wire cutting under 23rd Divisional Artillery. Personnel of A/106 Station returns, leaving guns on loan to 23rd D.A.	

WAR DIARY or INTELLIGENCE SUMMARY

Army Form C. 2118.

Place	Date	Hour	Summary of Events and Information	Remarks and references to Appendices
	May 16		Second Sect. A/106 into action in YPRES under 1st Brigade R.C.A. Maj. the Hon. R.G.A. HAMILTON posted to command A/106.	
	" 17		LE BUNUER in billets.	
	" 18			
	" 19		Lieut. W.C. FAIRER and 2/Lieut J.B. TUFFLEY proceed on leave to ENGLAND	
	" 20		LE BUNUER in billets	
	" 21		Capt. A.S. DALLAS proceeds on leave to ENGLAND. 2/Lt. G.S. RICKERS and 6 O.R's proceed to Corps Army Rest Camp.	
	" 22		Lt. RUNDER. 2/Lt. R.C. BINGHAM-NEWLAND proceeds on leave to ENGLAND. Brigade marches at 8.0 p.m. to Wagon Lines near OUDERDOM via WINNIZEELE – WATOU – ST JANS-DER-BRIEZEN.	
	" 23			
	" 24		Capt. H. MORTIMER R.A.M.C. joins as M.O. vice Lt. F.G. PEDLEY to 4th Field Ambulance. Lt. Col. G.P. RALSTON returns from leave. Capt. J.S. NEAKES proceeds on leave to ENGLAND.	
	" 25		Brigade Commander and Battery Commanders reconnoitre positions round KLAUWERPORT FARM and FRENCH FARM	
	" 26		2/Lt. A.F. BOTHAM proceeds on leave to ENGLAND.	
	" 27		OUDERDOM – VLAMERTINGHE road. Lulin with Germans during the night. 1 Sect. 15th Battery into action in positions reconnoitred on 25th (D group positions) Second Sect. of Batteries into Action Brigade Hd. Qrs. opens at ZILLEBEKE BUND under 2 & 3 Divisional Artillery.	
	" 28			
	" 29		Brigade commences wire cutting on Mt. SORREL zone.	
	" 30		ZILLEBEKE BUND heavily shelled with 15 c.m. from 6 p.m. to 5.0 p.m. Lt. Col. RALSTON slightly wounded. Major R.G.A. HAMILTON assumes command of Brigade. (D Group) Brigade H.Q. moves to RAILWAY DUGOUTS	

Army Form C. 2118.

WAR DIARY
or
INTELLIGENCE SUMMARY

(Erase heading not required.)

Instructions regarding War Diaries and Intelligence Summaries are contained in F. S. Regs., Part II. and the Staff Manual respectively. Title Pages will be prepared in manuscript.

Place	Date	Hour	Summary of Events and Information	Remarks and references to Appendices
	May 21		All guns less 1 Section of A/106 were in Action. Wire cutting on Group Front.	

S P Leonard
Lt & Adjt
106 in Bde, R.F.A.

106th Brigade R.F.A. WAR DIARY June 1917.
Army Form C. 2118.
INTELLIGENCE SUMMARY.

Place	Date	Hour	Summary of Events and Information	Remarks and references to Appendices
In the field	June 1917.			
	Fri. June 1st		Batteries wire cutting on Mt. SORREL Zone.	
	Sat " 2nd		Ditto. Batteries also fire in support of small raid on SPOIL BANK sector.	
	Sun " 3rd	3.15 pm	Practice Barrage at 3.15 pm. Batteries wire cutting.	
	Mon " 4th		Brigade Commanders Conference at BUSSEBOOM.	
	"	2.30 am	RAILWAY DUGOUTS shelled with gas shell.	
			B/106 shelled 9 casualties. Total Brigade casualties for first week. 34.	
	Tues " 5th	3 pm	Practice Barrage 3 pm for 10 minutes. A/106 shelled.	
	Wed " 6th		Brigade Headquarters moves to vicinity of BLAUWE POORT FARM.	
		10 pm	Gas shell barrage across BLAUWE POORT VALLEY. 10 pm to midnight.	
	Thurs " 7th		Zero day for MESSINES battle. All Batteries firing from 3.10 am to 8.10 pm. "Black line" gained and held. Small counter said by enemy at 10.30 pm, but no enemy attack developed.	
	Fri " 8th		Very quiet. Small S.O.S shoot at 5 pm, but no enemy attack develops.	
	Sat " 9th		Promiscuous enemy fire on BLAUWE POORT VALLEY and SANDBAG TRACK at dawn and dusk.	
	Sun " 10th	11.30 pm	Disturbance S. of Brigade Zone. No attack.	
	Mon " 11th	10.10 pm	Firing on S.O.S. No attack.	

W Smith Lt. Adjt.
for Colonel R.A.
Commanding 106 Bde. R.F.A.

106th Brigade R.F.A. June 1917.

Army Form C. 2118.

WAR DIARY
or
INTELLIGENCE SUMMARY.
(Erase heading not required.)

Place	Date	Hour	Summary of Events and Information	Remarks and references to Appendices
	Tues 12th		Usual barrage on BLAUWE POORT VALLEY. Batteries fire on SHREWSBURY FOREST at night.	
	Wed. 13th		BLAUWE POORT VALLEY shelled. 4.am - 5.am. A/106 shelled.	
	Thurs 14th		Brigade Wagon Lines move up from OUDERDOM to DICKEBUSCH. BLAUWE POORT VALLEY shelled all day. Batteries fire on minor operation at 7.30 pm. Line of trenches taken from SPOIL BANK to LOCK 6 BIS.	
	Fri. 15th		Brigade Commander reconnoitres new positions in triangle LOCKS - ST.ELOI - THE BLUFF. Lt. Col. G.R. BALSTON returns to Command the Brigade.	
	Sat. 16th		Brigade H.Q. established in new area S of CANAL. Sections of Batteries established in new positions. Lt. Col. G.R. BALSTON Commands "A" Group (4 Batteries 106th Bde, 4 Batteries 64th Army F.A.(Bde) as from 4 pm.	
	Sun. 17th		Enemy shelling area CHESTER FARM - BEDFORD HOUSE all day. Lt. Col. G.R. BALSTON returns to hospital. Major the Hon. R.G.A. HAMILTON takes over temporary Command of the Group.	
	Mon 18th		Consolidation of new gun positions and registration of new S.O.S. lines.	

Wilmot Att??
Lt Colonel R.A.
Commanding 106th Bde R.F.A.

106th Brigade R.F.A. WAR DIARY June 1917.

Army Form C. 2118.

INTELLIGENCE SUMMARY.
(Erase heading not required.)

Place	Date	Hour	Summary of Events and Information	Remarks and references to Appendices
	Tues 19th		Further registration of S.O.S. lines	
	Wed 20th		Nil	
	Thurs 21st		"	
	Fri 22nd		Colonel H.E. STREET C.M.G. assumes Command of the Brigade & of "A" Group, on posting. Brigade H.Q. moves to SPOIL BANK TUNNEL T.33.d.1.7. SPOIL BANK heavily shelled.	
	Sat 23rd		Nil	
	Sun 24th		"	
	Mon 25th		"	
	Tues 26th		The Brigade remained in positions near SPOIL BANK	
	Wed 27			
	Thurs 28			
	Fri 29th			
	Sat 30th			

R Wilmot 2/Lt RFA
for Colonel R.A.
Commanding 106th Bde R.F.A.

106th BDE. R.F.A.

WAR DIARY
JULY 1917.

Army Form C. 2118.

Place	Date	Hour	Summary of Events and Information	Remarks and references to Appendices
In the Field	JULY			
	1		Intermittent shelling of our battery positions.	
	2		Lt. Col. B. THORNHILL comdg. 102nd Bde. R.F.A. 23rd D.A. inspects gun positions preparatory to taking over. C & B batteries shelled during the day, 2 guns C/106 & 1 gun B/106 put out of action.	
	3		All batteries register new zone in II Corps area.	
			One Section per battery 106th Bde. relieved by 102nd Bde.	
	4		"A" Group transferred to II Corps from 9 a.m., and takes over new zone covering 70th I.B. 23rd Div.	
			Relieving Sections of 102nd Bde. registers during afternoon.	
			Remaining Sections of 102nd Bde. relieve those of 106th Bde. Relief complete 11.15 p.m.	
			106th Bde H.Q. moves to Wagon Lines H 31 c 5.1. (sheet 28) near RENINGHELST	
	5		Bde. marches at 10 a.m. to BORRE via RENINGHELST - BERTHEN - PRADELLES. Billets in BORRE.	
	6		Bde. marches at 10 a.m. to RACQUINGHEM via HAZEBROUCK - WALLON CAPPEL - LYNDE. Billets in RACQUINGHEM	
	7		At rest - billets in RACQUINGHEM	
	8		"	
	9		"	
	10		"	
	11		"	

H. Strutt Colonel RA
Commanding 106th Bde. R.F.A.

106th BDE. RFA.   JULY 1917   Army Form C. 2118.

WAR DIARY
or
INTELLIGENCE SUMMARY.
(Erase heading not required.)

Instructions regarding War Diaries and Intelligence Summaries are contained in F. S. Regs., Part II. and the Staff Manual respectively. Title pages will be prepared in manuscript.

Place	Date	Hour	Summary of Events and Information	Remarks and references to Appendices
In the Field.	JULY			
	12		At rest billets in RACQUINGHEM	
	13		Bde. marches at 8 am. to billets in BORRE via EBBLINGHEM + HAZEBROUCK.	
	14		Bde. marches at 5 am to Wagon Lines at RENINGHELST via STRAZEELE – BAILLEUL – LOCRE Arr. 10 am	
	15		Bde. Comdr. reconnoitres positions for Bde. H.Q. and Batteries.	
	16.		Further reconnaissance by battery commanders.	
	17		Two sections per battery move up into action in the following positions:– A/106 I.28 a 15.45	
			B/106 I.28 a 60.20, C/106 I.28 a 60.70 D/106 I.28 d 02.08.	
	18.		Remaining sections and Bde. H.Q. move up into action. All batteries register.	
	19.		Bde. takes over zone from 103rd Bde. at 10 am. All batteries bombard ILLUSIVE AVENUE J.25 a & c	
	20		All batteries night firing on back areas 9 pm – 4 am. Night firing trenches + back areas J.25 + J.30	
	21		All batteries :– Day bombardment ILLUSIVE DRIVE " " Trenches in J.25 a & c " " " " " J.25, 26 + 20	
	22		" " " " " SEFFERY AVENUE J.19 c " " " " " " " " "	
			298th ARMY F.A.B. joins 106th Bde. to form "D" group under command of Col. H.E. STREET, C.M.G.	
			A + C/298 move to new positions as follows:– A/298 I.29 a 08.45 C/298 I.28 d 25.40	
	23		All batteries 106th Bde.:– Day bombardment – rectangle in J.25d. Night firing – trenches + back areas J.25, 26 +20	

[signature]
Lt Colonel RA.
Commanding 106th Bde. R.F.A.

106th Bde. RFA.　　　WAR DIARY　　　JULY 1917　　　Army Form C. 2118.
or
INTELLIGENCE SUMMARY.

Place	Date	Hour	Summary of Events and Information	Remarks and references to Appendices
In the Field	JULY			
	23 cont.d		Batteries of 298th Bde. register. B/298 move to new position T 28 d 30.50	
	24		All batteries 106th Bde. Day bombardment - rectangle in J 25 c & d. Night firing - trenches & back areas J 25, 26 & 20	
	25.		Batteries of 298th Bde. register.	
			1st day of intensive counter battery work.	
			All batteries 106th Bde. Day bombardment - area in J 21 d. Night firing - trenches & back areas J 25, 26, 20 & 19	
	26.		" " " " - new trench in J 25 b & c. " " " "	
			Practice barrage in conjunction with raid by 30th Division. Zero hour 5 pm. All batteries of group fire first 25 minutes of the Barrage Tables.	
	27.		All batteries 106th Bde. - Day bombardment - JEFFERY AVENUE & curr.ts area. Night firing on back areas J 25, 26 & 20	
			Practice barrage on II Corps front. Zero hour 5.15 am. All batteries of group fire	
			Barrage Tables from + 1 hr. 15 mins. to + 1 hr. 45 mins. Firing ceased 5.45 am.	
			Results observed: satisfactory.	
	28.		Second day of intensive counter battery work. All batteries 106th Bde. bombard	
			hostile battery No. J W 82 from 6 am to 1.30 pm. Night firing on back areas in J 25, 26 & 20	
			D/106 fires special gas task on hostile battery from 9 pm + Yanks move up into position	

hu Stuart
Colonel R.A.
Commanding 106th Bde. R.F.A.

106th BDE R.F.A. WAR DIARY

JULY 1917

INTELLIGENCE SUMMARY

Army Form C. 2118.

Place	Date	Hour	Summary of Events and Information	Remarks and references to Appendices
In the field	JULY 29		"X" day. Batteries of 106th Bde bombard JEFFERY AVENUE and JAVA DRIVE during day + back areas in J.25.19 & 20. during night.	
	30th		"Y" day. Third day of intensive counter battery work. Batteries of 106th Bde. bombard area in square J 33 during day. B/106 + D/106 night firing on trenches etc. in back areas	
	31st		"Z" day. Zero hour 3·50 a.m. Attack on whole Fifth Army front. All batteries of group firing from 3·50 a.m. throughout the day. Attack on 24th Division front held up in neighbourhood of JEER TRENCH and LOWER STAR POST. Line finally held J 20 c 40.55 – J 26 a 15.50 – J 25 a 84 28 – J 25 d 00 60 – J 31 a 85.60. – J 31 a 72.30. – J 31 d 05.99. D Battery 52nd ARMY F.A.B. joins group at 10·10 a.m. in position at I 28 c 65. 45.	

F Street

Colonel R.A.
Commanding 106th Bde. R.F.A.

106th Brigade R.H.A WAR DIARY or INTELLIGENCE SUMMARY

Army Form C. 2118.

August 1917.

Vol 24

Place	Date	Hour	Summary of Events and Information	Remarks and references to Appendices
In the field	1st Wed.		All batteries of Group firing occasional rounds on S.O.S points throughout the day. 6 p.m. - Our front trenches bombarded. Batteries fire slow barrage on S.O.S. until situation clear. Counter attack expected. All batteries ring firing on back areas on T.26. & T.20.	
	2nd	3.30 am	Batteries firing at slow rate on S.O.S. at request of infantry until 5.30 am. Bombardment by all batteries searching tracks etc, East of S.O.S. lines in T.26.C.	
	3rd		" " " " " " as on 2nd inst.	
	4th		" " " " " 3rd "	
	5th		" " " " " in T.26. and T.27.	
	6th		Our trenches heavily shelled 9.15 p.m. All batteries firing on S.O.S. until 10.15 p.m. all quiet 10.30 pm.	
	7th		Bombardment by all batteries as for 5th inst.	
	8th		" " " " " 6th "	
			" " " " " 7th "	
			At 9.9 P.M. S.O.S. reported on left. All quiet 10.30 pm.	

Mannington Lt. Col. R.H.A
Comdg 106th Bde. R.H.A.

106th Brigade R.F.A. WAR DIARY   August 1917.   Army Form C. 2118.

INTELLIGENCE SUMMARY.

(Erase heading not required.)

Place	Date	Hour	Summary of Events and Information	Remarks and references to Appendices
	9th		Bombardment by all batteries as for 8th inst.	
	10th		Hero day for Fifth Army Operations. 24th Division endeavours to establish a post on T.25.b. Zero hour 4.35 am. All batteries firing barrage until 5 am & afterwards occasional rounds on S.O.S. 24th Division fails to reach objectives. Lt. Col. de SATGÉ D.S.O. and H.Q. 298th A.F.A.B. take over command of D.Group 6 pm. 106th Bde. H.Q. moves to wagon lines. Personnel of A/106 moves to wagon lines.	
	11th		All batteries searching area in T.26. & T.27.	
	12th		D/106 & B/298 bombard ruins of VELDHOEK with gas & smoke shell from 1 pm onwards.	
	13th		All batteries searching area in T.26. & T.27 during day. Gas & smoke bombardment of houses in T.15.C. by night.	
	14th		Personnel of A/106 returns to gun position & personnel of B/106 moves to W.L. All batteries firing on special tasks on back areas & on hostile batteries in T.34 & T.22.	
	15th		Personnel of B/106 returns to gun position. All batteries bombard trenches, tracks etc. in Group zone during day & fire gas & smoke on VELDHOEK during night.	
	16th		All batteries bombard INVERNESS COPSE from 12 noon to 3 pm & areas in T.26. & T.27. during night.	
	17th		All batteries searching areas in T.26. & T.27. during 24 hours.	

Menuhle Lt. Col. R.F.A.
Comdg. 106th Bde. R.F.A.

Army Form C. 2118.

106th Brigade R.F.A. WAR DIARY
or
INTELLIGENCE SUMMARY.

August 1917.

(Erase heading not required.)

Instructions regarding War Diaries and Intelligence Summaries are contained in F.S. Regs., Part II. and the Staff Manual respectively. Title pages will be prepared in manuscript.

Place	Date	Hour	Summary of Events and Information	Remarks and references to Appendices
	18th		All batteries searching areas on T.26. & T.27 during 24 hours.	
	19th		" " " " " " " "	
	20th		Personnel of B/106 returns to gun position & that of C/106 proceeds to Wagon lines.	
			All batteries searching areas East of S.O.S points.	
	21st		Bde H.Q. moves into action (LARCH WOOD TUNNELS) Col. H.F. STREET CMG takes over command of B Group at 4 pm from Lt. Col. de SATGE 298th Army F.A.B. Personnel of C/106 returns to gun position. All batteries searching areas E. of S.O.S. points during 24 hours.	
	22nd		All batteries firing barrage covering operations carried out by Division on our left. Zero hour 4 am. Enemy post T.19.b. 70.05 captured. Day & night firing by all batteries on areas East of S.O.S points.	
	23rd		All batteries searching areas around BASSEVILLEBEEK during day & night.	
	24th		" " " " " " " "	
	25th		Col. H.F. STREET CMG killed in action 9.50 am outside Group H.Q. I.29.c.55.72. Major The Hon R.G.A HAMILTON (Master of Belhaven) assumes command of "B" Group. All batteries searching areas as on 24th	
	26th		A & B/106 & B/298 firing on S.O.S lines in response to S.O.S call 5.30 am. Personnel C/106 returns to gun position & that of A/106 proceeds to wagon line.	

A. Hamilton Major
Lt. Col. R.H.A.
Comdg 106th Bde. R.F.A.

106th Brigade R.F.A. WAR DIARY August 1917.

INTELLIGENCE SUMMARY.

Army Form C. 2118.

Place	Date	Hour	Summary of Events and Information	Remarks and references to Appendices
	August 26th		All batteries firing on special tasks during day & night.	
	27th		All batteries searching areas East of S.O.S. points during 24 hours	
	28th		" " in T.26.b. T.20.d. & T.27. D/295 fires 400	
	29th		rounds gas shell into POLDHOEK WOOD.	
			S.O.S points in Group Zone reallotted, 295th Bde taking Northern half & 106th Bde. Southern half of zone.	
			All batteries firing on special tasks East of S.O.S. points.	
	30th		" " " " " " D/295 fires on	
	31st		special tasks in T.22.a. T.20.d. and T.26.b.	

Mannusik
Lt. Col. R.F.A.
Commanding 106th Bde R.F.A

Army Form C. 2118.

WAR DIARY
or
INTELLIGENCE SUMMARY
(Erase heading not required.)

Vol 25

106 BDE
R.F.A.

Sept 1917

106th BDE R.F.A.   SEPTEMBER 1917
Army Form C. 2118.

WAR DIARY
or
INTELLIGENCE SUMMARY.
(Erase heading not required.)

Place	Date	Hour	Summary of Events and Information	Remarks and references to Appendices
In the Field.	September			
	Saturday 1st		All batteries firing on tracks & approaches East of SOS lines during 24 hours.	
	2nd			
	3rd		298th Bde. passes under command of O.C. "A" Group at 10 a.m. Battery zones of 106th Bde. re-allotted to cover the whole front of B Group. B Battery being superimposed on A & C. Personnel of D/106 relieve personnel of D/298 in action on night 3rd-4th.	
	4th		All batteries searching tracks and approaches in J.26 & J.20 during the 24 hours.	
	5th		All batteries.	
			Also Special Task night firing on trench in J.26.a from 10 p.m. to 5 a.m. One section of each battery of 106th Bde. relieves a section of 4th Australian Bde. and 298th Bde. as follows :—	
			A/106 relieves 10th Australian Battery	
			B/106 " B/298th Bde.	
			C/106 " "	
			D/106 " 104th Australian Battery.	

Hamilton Lt. Col. R.F.A.
Commanding 106th Bde. R.F.A.

106th. BDE. R.F.A. SEPTEMBER 1917

Army Form C. 2118.

WAR DIARY
or
INTELLIGENCE SUMMARY.
(Erase heading not required.)

Place	Date	Hour	Summary of Events and Information	Remarks and references to Appendices
In the Field.	September 5th contd.		The above sections of 106th. Bde. are relieved in their positions by corresponding sections of 186th. Bde.	
	Thurs. 6th.		All batteries continue day & night firing as on 4th inst. Incoming sections register.	
	Night 6/7th		Second sections of batteries of 186. relieve each other as on night 5th/6th.	
	7th		All batteries day & night firing on tracks and approaches as on 6th inst.	
	Night 7/8th		Remaining sections of batteries relieve each other as on night 6/7th. Batteries of 106th Bde. come under command of Lt. Col. Lloyd 4th Australian F.A.B. commanding 'A' group. 106th Bde H.Q. remains in command of 'B' group.	
	8th		Major HERON and Headquarters 186th. Bde. R.J.A. relieve Lt. Col. the Hon R.G.A. HAMILTON & H.Q. 106th. Bde in command of 'B' group. 106th. Bde. H.Q. moves to wagon lines.	
	9th		Lt. Col. the Hon R.G.A. HAMILTON and Headquarters 106th. Bde relieve Lt.Col. LLOYD and H.Q. 4th Australian F.A.B and take over the command of 'A' group 12 noon. 'A' group comprises 106th. Bde. R.F.A, A,B+C Batteries 156th Bde R.J.A. and A+B Batteries 190th. Bde. R.J.A.	
	10th		All batteries of group firing on tracks + approaches East of SOS lines during 24 hours.	

H Hamilton Lt. Col. RFA
Comdg 106th. Bde. R.J.A.

106th BDE. R.F.A.   SEPTEMBER 1917   Army Form C. 2118.

WAR DIARY
or
INTELLIGENCE SUMMARY
(Erase heading not required.)

Place	Date	Hour	Summary of Events and Information	Remarks and references to Appendices
In the Field	September 11th		S.O.S. Lines of 'A' group now run as follows:- J.14.c.90.00 - J.20.a.17.50 - J.20.c.10.25	
			All batteries fire concentration on hostile battery J.Z.31 (J.21.c.95.85) at 5.30 pm and again at 9.30 pm.	
	12th		All batteries searching tracks & approaches East of S.O.S. lines throughout 24 hours. Day & night firing on tracks etc East of S.O.S. lines.	
			One section each of A/106, B/106 & C/106 relieved by the corresponding section of 9th Bde. R.F.A. and one section of D/106 relieved by a section of D/95 Bde. Relieved sections withdrew to Wagon Lines RENINGHELST.	
	13th		All batteries day & night firing as on 12th inst.	
			Lt. Col. B.A.B. BUTLER, R.F.A. and Headquarters 156th Bde. R.F.A. take over command of 'A' group at 6 pm. Remaining sections of 106th Bde relieved by sections of 9th Bde & 95th Bde as on 12th inst. Headquarters and relieved sections of 106th Bde march to wagon lines RENINGHELST.	
			One section per battery 106th Bde. march to billets in BOESCHEPE at 9 am.	
	14th		Bde. H.Q. and remainder of 106th Bde. march to billets in BOESCHEPE via RENINGHELST.	

Hammell Lt. Col. R.F.A.
Commanding 106th Bde. R.F.A.

106th BDE. R.F.A.

SEPTEMBER 1917. Army Form C. 2118.

WAR DIARY
or
INTELLIGENCE SUMMARY.

Place	Date	Hour	Summary of Events and Information	Remarks and references to Appendices
In the Field	SEPTEMBER 14th (cont'd)	6 am	RENINGHELST. Wagon Lines of 106th Bde. taken over by batteries of 21st D.A.	
	15th		In billets in BOESCHEPE.	
	16th		Batteries and Bde. H.Q. march to HOPOUTRE Siding POPERINGHE and entrain. Portions of No 1 Section D.A.C. entrain with each active battery and headquarters. Trains leave at the following times: A/106 1.35pm, B/106 4.45pm, C/106 7.45pm, HQ/106 5.30 am (17th), D/106 9 am (17th).	
	17th		Trains arrive at BAPAUME and batteries march separately to camp just outside the town.	
	18th		In camp BAPAUME	
	19th		"	
	20th		"	
	21st		"	
	22nd		"	
	23rd		"	

Alexander Lt. Col. R.F.A.,
Commanding 106th Bde R.F.A

106th BDE R.F.A.   SEPTEMBER 1917.   Army Form C. 2118.

WAR DIARY
or
INTELLIGENCE SUMMARY.
(Erase heading not required.)

Place	Date	Hour	Summary of Events and Information	Remarks and references to Appendices
In the Field	24th		In camp BAPAUME.	
	25th		Bde. marches to camp near PERONNE via main road BAPAUME – PERONNE at 10am.	
	26th		G.O.C. 24th DIV. and C.R.A. inspected the Bde as it marches through SAILLY SAILLYSEL. Bde. Commanders and Battery Commanders proceed to RIGHT GROUP 34th D.A. to reconnoitre positions preparatory to taking over.	
	27th		In camp PERONNE. One section per Battery 106th Bde. marches to Wagon lines of corresponding Battery of 152nd Bde. A/106 via DOINGT – CARTIGNY, – HANCOURT – BERNE – MONTIGNY FARM, remainder via DOINGT, – TERTRY – CAULAINCOURT. Portions of batteries of 106th Bde. relieve sections of 152nd Bde. in action as follows:– 4 guns A/106 relieve 2 guns A/152 4 " B/106 " 2 " B/152 3 " C/106 " 2 " C/152 3 how. D/106 " 2 how. D/152.	

Hammerton
Lt. Col. R.F.A.
Commanding 106th Bde. R.F.A.

106th Bde. R.F.A.   September 1917

Army Form C. 2118.

WAR DIARY
or
INTELLIGENCE SUMMARY.
(Erase heading not required.)

Place	Date	Hour	Summary of Events and Information	Remarks and references to Appendices
In the Field	September 28th		Incoming guns register.	
	29th		Remainder of 106th Bde. R.F.A. marched by batteries to wagon lines of 152nd Bde and remaining guns moved into action in relief of those of 152nd Bde. Relief complete	
		10 p.m.	Lt. Col. McKeon R.G.A. HAMILTON R.F.A. takes over command of Right Group consisting of A/RHA (Brechin Group) B/106 + D/106. Headquarters situated at K 35 d 5.6. Sheet 62 c. A & C/106 come under command of Centre Group.	
	30th		Registration of zero points etc. by all batteries.	

Hammerton
Lt. Col. R.F.A.
Commanding 106th Bde. R.F.A.

Confidential

Vol 26

War Diary for October 1917
106 Bde R.F.A.

100th Brigade R.F.A.   October 1917.

Army Form C. 2118.

WAR DIARY
or
INTELLIGENCE SUMMARY.
(Erase heading not required.)

Instructions regarding War Diaries and Intelligence Summaries are contained in F. S. Regs., Part II. and the Staff Manual respectively. Title pages will be prepared in manuscript.

Place	Date	Hour	Summary of Events and Information	Remarks and references to Appendices
Field	Sunday 1st		Reference Sheet 62 B.	
	Monday 2nd		Nothing of importance.	
	Tuesday 3rd		" " "	
	Wednesday 4th		" " "	
	Thursday 5th		In co-operation with Centre & Left Groups D/106 fires a concentration on BOISSON	
	Friday 6th		GAULAINE FARM 12/100m.	
	Saturday 7th		Nothing of importance.	
			" " "	
	Sunday 8th		A/RHA & B/106 night firing on dumps in G.28.a. (Sheet 62 B)	
	Monday 9th		Nothing of importance.	
	Tuesday 10th		In co-operation with Centre & Left Groups D/106 fires a concentration on trenches in G.14.C. at 2.30 pm.	
	Wednesday 11th		Major A. DUDLEY A/RHA takes over command of Right Group from Lt. Col. The Hon. R.G.A. HAMILTON proceeding on leave to U.K.	
			293rd Army F.A.B. (Left Group) withdraws to Reserve.	
			24th D.A. front is redistributed into two Groups (Right & Left).	

Hamilton Lt. Col. R.F.A.
Commanding 106th Brigade R.F.A.

106th Brigade R.H.A. WAR DIARY – October 1917.

Army Form C. 2118.

INTELLIGENCE SUMMARY.

(Erase heading not required.)

Place	Date	Hour	Summary of Events and Information	Remarks and references to Appendices
	Wednesday 11th		Right Group now consists of A/RHA, B/106, D/106 & A/106.	
	Thursday 12th		One Section of A/106 moves from positions occupied on 27th September, & relieves one Section A/RHA in action. Relieved Section of A/RHA withdraws to Wagon Lines. Group zones are re-allotted will effect from 7 p.m. Right Group now consists of A/RHA, A/106, B/106, & D/106 (less 1 Section D/106.) One Section D/106 moves to position evacuated by D/293 & comes under the orders of O.C. D/107 (Left Group) forming an 8 gun Battery.	
	Friday 13th		Remaining Sections A/106 relieve Sections A/RHA in action. Command passes on completion of relief at 10 p.m. Relieved Sections withdraw to Wagon Lines. Major H. HOBDAY M.C. B/106 R.F.A. takes over command of Right Group from Major A. DUDLEY A/RHA on completion of relief of A/RHA by A/106.	
	Saturday 14th		All batteries night firing on CANAL CROSSINGS & approaches to BELLENGLISE (suspected enemy relief)	
	Sunday 15th		Nothing of importance.	
	Monday 16th		All batteries night firing on tracks etc in G.33. & G.34.	

Hannaford Lt. Col. R.H.A.
Commanding 106th Brigade R.H.A.

106th Brigade R.F.A. WAR DIARY October 1917

Army Form C. 2118.

INTELLIGENCE SUMMARY.

(Erase heading not required.)

Instructions regarding War Diaries and Intelligence Summaries are contained in F. S. Regs., Part II. and the Staff Manual respectively. Title pages will be prepared in manuscript.

Place	Date	Hour	Summary of Events and Information	Remarks and references to Appendices
	Tuesday 17th		Group zone is extended Northwards to cover new front occupied by Right Inf. Bde.	
	Wednesday 18th		All batteries night firing on tracks & bridges WEST of BELLENGLISE.	
	Thursday 19th		All batteries night firing on tracks & roads in G.21 & G.27.	
	Friday 20th		Nothing of importance.	
	Saturday 21st		" " "	
	Sunday 22nd		" " "	
	Monday 23rd		Headquarters Right Group closes at K.35.B.5.6. at 3.p.m. & re-opens at same time at R.8.a.4.9.	
	Tuesday 24th		In co-operation with H.A. all Batteries fire a concentration on new work in enemy trenches G.28.c. & d. 3.15 p.m. Lt. Col. the Hon. R.G.A. HAMILTON returns from leave & takes over Command of Right Group.	
	Wednesday 25th		Nothing of importance.	
	Thursday 26th		1.30.a.m. A/106, B/106, & D/106 fire in conjunction with a said by 72nd I.B. (Left Group Zone)	
	Friday 27th		Nothing of importance.	
	Saturday 28th		All Batteries night firing on dump in G.34.d.	

Alexander
Lt. Col. R.F.A.
Commanding 106th Brigade R.F.A.

106th Brigade R.H.A. WAR DIARY October 1917.

Army Form C. 2118.

INTELLIGENCE SUMMARY.
(Erase heading not required.)

Instructions regarding War Diaries and Intelligence Summaries are contained in F. S. Regs., Part II. and the Staff Manual respectively. Title pages will be prepared in manuscript.

Place	Date	Hour	Summary of Events and Information	Remarks and references to Appendices
	Sunday 29th		Nothing of importance.	
	Monday 30th		All batteries night firing on Coy H.Q. in G.33.b.	
	Tuesday 31st		Nothing of importance.	

Hammond
Lt. Col. R.H.A.
Commanding 106th Brigade R.H.A.

WO 27

24 Div

WAR DIARY.

106th BDE R.F.A.

From Nov 1st to Nov 30th

1917.

15

SECRET

106th Brigade R.F.A.   November, 1917.

Army Form C. 2118.

WAR DIARY
INTELLIGENCE SUMMARY.
(Erase heading not required.)

Place	Date	Hour	Summary of Events and Information	Remarks and references to Appendices
	November 1917.			
	Thursday 1st.		Nothing of importance.	
	Friday 2nd.		One Section A/106 moves from R.10.c. to the position vacated by B/293 (L.2.c.6.3) coming under the orders of Left Group. C/106 and 4 guns B/106 pass under command of O.C. Left Group for S.O.S purposes. Right Group zone re-allotted to 2 guns B/106 and 4 howrs D/106. Remainder of A/106 covers zone of 2 guns B/106 during the move.	
	Saturday 3rd.		Second Section A/106 moves to position in L.2.c.6.3. One section B/106 moves to new position R.6.c.00.29.	
	Sunday 4th.		Third Section A/106 moves to position in L.2.c.6.3. The Section B/106 vi R.6.c. take over S.O.S points etc. from A/106. All batteries Night firing on LA BARAQUE.	
	Monday 5th.		Nothing of importance.	
	Tuesday 6th.		All batteries Night firing on SWAN REDOUBT G.27.d.	
	Wednesday 7th.		17th I.B. carry out raid on SQUARE COPSE 10pm. All batteries stand to 9.45 pm. but Artillery assistance not required.	

Lt. Col. R.F.A.
Commanding 106th Brigade R.F.A.

Army Form C. 2118.

106th Brigade. R.F.A. WAR DIARY November, 1917.

INTELLIGENCE SUMMARY.
(Erase heading not required.)

Instructions regarding War Diaries and Intelligence Summaries are contained in F. S. Regs., Part II. and the Staff Manual respectively. Title pages will be prepared in manuscript.

Place	Date	Hour	Summary of Events and Information	Remarks and references to Appendices
	1917. November			
Wednesday	7th (contd)		Major H. HOBDAY, M.C. B/106, takes over command of Right Group from Lt. Col. The Hon. R.G.A. HAMILTON proceeding to England on a course.	
Thursday	8th		Nothing of importance.	
Friday	9th		All batteries Night firing. Canal crossing in G.34.d.	
Saturday	10th		Nothing of importance.	
Sunday	11th		All batteries Night firing on Tracks etc. in G.22.c.5.d.	
Monday	12th		Liaison duties with Infantry Battalions temporarily suspended owing to shortage of Officers.	
Tuesday	13th		Nothing of importance.	
Wednesday	14th		do	
Thursday	15th		do	
Friday	16th		do	
Saturday	17th		4 guns B/106 are withdrawn from position in R.10.a. at dusk and handed over to B/107 at wagon lines in HAMELET. Personnel B/106 (less detached Section) take over the 4 guns of B/107 in action in relief of personnel B/107, and become part of Left Group.	

RHamilton Lt.Col., R.F.A.
Commanding 106th. Brigade. R.F.A.

106th Brigade, R.F.A.   WAR DIARY   November, 1917.   Army Form C. 2118.

INTELLIGENCE SUMMARY.
(Erase heading not required.)

Place	Date	Hour	Summary of Events and Information	Remarks and references to Appendices
	1917. November			
Sunday	18th		Working party 5 O.R's 106th Bde. report to D.T.M.O., 55th Division 12.noon. B/106 passes temporarily under command of Left Group 6 p.m.	
Monday	19th		One Section D/106 moves at dusk from R.11.a. to a prepared position in L.5.c.9.7. and comes under orders of Left Group. Remaining Section D/106 moves at same time to a position in L.35.d.45.25. All three Sections D/106 come under the orders of the VII Corps. R.A. for Counter Battery work.	
Tuesday	20th		Zero day for Operations by 55th Division on our left. Zero hour 6.20 a.m. 2 guns B/106 fire on trenches in neighbourhood of SQUARE COPSE in support of a minor operation being carried out by the 17th I.B. during the attack by 55th Division. Batteries of Groupe Michel, 5th French Divisional Artillery, co-operate. Personnel of B/106 are relieved by B/107 at dusk, take over their own guns, and return to original position R.10.a. Section of D/106 withdrawn from L.35.d. to R.11.a. All batteries searching approaches etc. during the night.	

Ahwulir
Lt. Col. R.B.A.
Commanding 106th Brigade R.F.A.

106th Brigade R.F.A.   November, 1917.

Army Form C. 2118.

WAR DIARY
of
INTELLIGENCE SUMMARY.
(Erase heading not required.)

Instructions regarding War Diaries and Intelligence
Summaries are contained in F. S. Regs., Part II.
and the Staff Manual respectively. Title pages
will be prepared in manuscript.

Place	Date	Hour	Summary of Events and Information	Remarks and references to Appendices
	1917. November			
	Wednesday 21st.		Steady bombardment of enemy trenches from 5 a.m. followed by hurricane bombardment at 6.30 a.m. No Infantry attack.	
			All batteries searching approaches etc. during the night.	
	Thursday 22nd.		Another feint bombardment carried out commencing at 5 a.m. ending at 6.45 a.m.	
			All batteries searching approaches etc. during the night.	
	Friday 23rd.		All batteries searching approaches etc. during the night.	
	Saturday 24th.		B/106 moves 1 gun to G.31.d.4.9. and C/106 moves 1 gun to L.23.b.2.4., for wire cutting.	
			All batteries searching approaches etc. during the night.	
	Sunday 25th.		B/106 wire cutting Square Copse.	
			C/106 " " G.14.c.6.5.	
			All batteries searching approaches etc. during the night.	
	Monday 26th.		B/106 & C/106 wire cutting. Night firing as on night 24th/25th.	
	Tuesday 27th.		do	
	Wednesday 28th.		do	

Hamilton Lt. Col., R.F.A.,
Commanding 106th Brigade R.F.A.

106th Bde. R.G.A.

Army Form C. 2118.

WAR DIARY
INTELLIGENCE SUMMARY

November, 1917

(Erase heading not required.)

Instructions regarding War Diaries and Intelligence Summaries are contained in F. S. Regs., Part II. and the Staff Manual respectively. Title pages will be prepared in manuscript.

Place	Date November, 1917.	Hour	Summary of Events and Information	Remarks and references to Appendices
	Thursday 29th		Wire cutting guns withdrawn to original positions.	
			Night firing on approaches etc.	
			Lt. Col. The Hon. R.G.A. HAMILTON returns from course and takes over command of Right Group.	
	Friday 30th		All batteries night firing on approaches etc.	

Hamilton Lt. Col. R.G.A.
Commanding 106th Bde. R.G.A.

106th Brigade R.F.A. December 1917. Army Form C. 2118.

WAR DIARY
or
INTELLIGENCE SUMMARY.
(Erase heading not required.)

Place	Date	Hour	Summary of Events and Information	Remarks and references to Appendices
In the Field	1st		All batteries night firing on CANAL CROSSINGS	
	2nd		Nothing of importance	
	3rd		C/106 at disposal of LEFT GROUP fires on quarries in G17 co-operation with R.E. discharging gas bom.bs. All Batteries night firing on backs & roads	
	4th		Nothing of importance	
	5th		One section C/106 on relief by one section D/107 returns to Right Group & old position. Remaining section moves to about L.8.B. and comes under R.F.A. Group. Normal SOS lines of C/106 & B/106 (4 guns) are lard on right flank of 2nd I.B. in R11a.	
	6th		Night firing by all batteries on CANAL CROSSINGS etc BELLENGLISE	
	7th		17th I.B. makes demonstrations in front of BIG BILL & SQUARE COPSE D/106 (4 guns) & B/106 (2 guns) co-operate by firing on Boy HQ etc Trench Artillery co-operate.	
	8th	10am	Lt.Col.G.R. WAINEWRIGHT R.H.A. & Headquarters 5th Bde. R.H.A. relieve Lt Col the Hon. R.G.A HAMILTON R.F.A. & Headquarters 106th Bde R.F.A on command of Right Group. Lt. Col. the Hon. R.G.A. Hamilton R.F.A. & Headquarters 106 Bde. R.F.A. withdrawn	
	9th		to F./106. Wagon Line	

Hamilton
Lt. Col. R.F.A.
Commanding 106 Bde. R.F.A.

(2) 106th Brigade R.F.A. WAR DIARY or INTELLIGENCE SUMMARY. Army Form C. 2118.

December 1917.

Place	Date	Hour	Summary of Events and Information	Remarks and references to Appendices
	10th		15/106 moves to positions L.15.c. & B.	
	11th		Nothing of importance	
	12th		—do—	
	13th		—do—	
	14th		—do—	
	15th		D/106 (4 hours), B/106 (3 guns) night firing in accordance with suspected enemy relief.	
	16th		D/106 & B/106 as on 15th. One section D/106 relieved by one section D/311 Army Brigade R.F.A. Relieved section of D/106 withdraws to wagon lines.	
	17th		Nothing of importance.	
	18th		Fifth Army assumes command of front held by Cavalry Corps & VII Corps at noon. Fifth Army HQ at VILLERS BRETONNEUX.	
	19th		Lt. Col. The Hon. R. Hamilton & Headquarters 105th Brigade R.F.A. relieve Lt. Col. D.W.L. SPILLER, D.S.O. & Headquarters 107th Brigade R.F.A. at Centre Group H.Q. and Wagon Lines in HERVILLY. Command of Centre Group passes at 6.p.m.	

Hamilton
Lt. Col. R.F.A.
Commanding 106th Bde. R.F.A.

(3).

106th Brigade R.F.A. WAR DIARY or INTELLIGENCE SUMMARY. December 1917. Army Form C. 2118.

Instructions regarding War Diaries and Intelligence Summaries are contained in F. S. Regs., Part II. and the Staff Manual respectively. Title pages will be prepared in manuscript.

(Erase heading not required.)

Place	Date	Hour	Summary of Events and Information	Remarks and references to Appendices
	20th		Nothing of importance	
	21st		do	
	22nd		do	
	23rd	4.15pm	D/107 fires on enemy positions in SKIN TRENCH in co-operation with French Heavy Artillery and Trench Mortars.	
	24th		Nothing of importance	
	25th		do	
	26th		S.O.S. lines of Centre Group are allotted as from 10.a.m.	
	27th		Nothing of importance.	
	28th		do	
	29th		Major R.P. GALLOWAY R.H.A. and Headquarters 107th Brigade R.F.A. relieve Lt. Col. The Hon. R.G.A. HAMILTON R.F.A. & Headquarters 106 Bde. in command of Centre Group 24th Divn. Arty. at 12 noon. Lt. Col. The Hon. R.G.A. HAMILTON R.F.A. & H.Q./106 Bde withdraw to new Headquarters in HERVILLY (K.23.d.5.8)	
	30th		Owing to re-grouping of Artillery on the Cav. Corps Front the 106 Bde.	

Bennett
Lt. Col. R.F.A.
Commanding 106 Bde. R.F.A.

106th Brigade R.F.A.   December 1917   Army Form C. 2118.

WAR DIARY
INTELLIGENCE SUMMARY

Place	Date	Hour	Summary of Events and Information	Remarks and references to Appendices
	30th (cont)		(Less 4 hows 3/106) passes under command of Lt. Col. A. WAINEWRIGHT R.H.A. CRA, CAV. DIV. ARTY. Lt. Col. The Hon. R.G.A. HAMILTON, RFA & HQ/106 Bde. R.F.A. assume command of Left Group. Cav. Div. Arty. at 10. a.m. Left Group consists of HAMILTON'S SUB-GROUP (A,B, & C/106 Bde. R.H.A) and SCARLETT'S SUB-GROUP (G.C., Y K/RHA) and covers the front of the 2nd Divn Cav. Divn.	
	31st		Nothing of importance.	

Hamilton
Lt. Col. R.F.A.
Commanding 106th Brigade R.F.A.

WAR DIARY or INTELLIGENCE SUMMARY.

(Erase heading not required.)

106th BRIGADE.   **JANUARY 1918.**

Instructions regarding War Diaries and Intelligence Summaries are contained in F.S. Regs., Part II. and the Staff Manual respectively. Title pages will be prepared in manuscript.

Place	Date	Hour	Summary of Events and Information
Jan.	1st		Nothing of importance.
	2nd		do.
	3rd		do.
	4th		do.
	5th		do.
	6th		E.A. dropped bombs in neighbourhood of ROISEL.
	7th		Nothing of importance.
	8th		do.
	9th		do.
	10th		Night firing by detached gun A/106, section E/106, and detached gun C/R.H.A. on tracks in G.14. probably German relief taking place on night 10/1.
	11th		Wagon Lines of Headquarters from MOISLGNY and E/106, C/106 and D/106 from CAULAINCOURT move to Wagon Lines at ROWCLY vacated by 3rd Bde. R.H.A. Amm. Col. and E/R.H.A and J/R.H.A.
	12th		Nothing of importance.
	13th		do
	14th		do
	15th		do
	16th		On night 16th/17th Section of D/106 relieved by Section of D/311, Section of D/106 comes under Left Group.
	17th		Cav. Div. Arty. "A" night. Night 17 to/18th "B" Night no action taken by 105th Bde. R.F.A. Nothing of importance.
	18th		Nothing of importance.
	19th		do
	20th		Left Group Cav. Div. Arty. fired in support of a raid by 3rd Battalion Rifle Bde. on enemy trenches in A.25.d. Zero hour 6.45. am.
	21st		Nothing of importance.
	22nd		Night 22nd/23rd. "C" Night. 3 guns A/106 relieved 3 guns I/R.H.A. 3 guns C/106 relieved 3 guns V/R.H.A.
	23rd		From noon 23rd January 1918 S.O.S. Signal on Cav.

106th Brigade R.F.A.

January 1917 **WAR DIARY** or **INTELLIGENCE SUMMARY.**

(Erase heading not required.)

Instructions regarding War Diaries and Intelligence Summaries are contained in F.S. Regs., Part II. and the Staff Manual respectively. Title pages will be prepared in manuscript.

Place	Date	Hour	Summary of Events and Information
Jan.	23rd		and VII Corps front will be a Rifle Grenade bursting into two RED and two GREEN STARS instead of Two GREEN and Two WHITE. Night 23rd/24th "D" Night. 3 guns A/106 relieve 3 guns I/R.H.A., 3 guns C/106 relieve 3 guns Y/R.H.A. A/106 takes over tasks from H/R.H.A., C/106 takes over tasks from Y/R.H.A. B/106 remains in position and hands over tasks to Y/R.H.A. on arrival at their new position. B/106 then takes over tasks from I/R.H.A. Lt.Col. R.HAMILTON,R.F.A. and H.Q. of 106th Bde. R.F.A. relieve Lt.Col. W.CLARKE. R.H.A. and H.Q. of 7th Bde.R.H.A. at GEORGES COPSE, near TEMPLEUX LE GUERARD. L.Col. HAMILTON R.F.A. assumes command of Left Group 24th D.A. from Lt.Col. W.CLARKE, R.H.A.
	24th		Nothing of importance.
	25th		do
	26th		do
	27th		From 12 noon Section D/106 now under Left Group is attached to D/107 forming an 8 gun battery under O.C. D/107. A/106 and C/106 fired into QUENNET COPSE at 11.15. pm to assist infantry patrol.
	28th		A/106, B/106, and C/106 fired on enemy tracks at 12 midnight 27th/28th in conjuction with all M.G's and Lewis guns. Daily allotment to Left Group 24th D.A.. 250 rounds 18-pdr. 40 rounds 4.5" How.
	29th		Nothing of importance.
	30th		do
	31st		A/106 moved three guns into position near GEORGES COPSE.

Lt.Colonel, R.F.A.
Commanding 106th Bde. R.F.A.

WAR DIARY
or
INTELLIGENCE SUMMARY

106TH BRIGADE R.F.A.

Instructions regarding War Diaries and Intelligence Summaries are contained in F.S. Regs., Part II. and the Staff Manual respectively. Title pages will be prepared in manuscript.

(Erase heading not required.)

Place	Date	Hour	Summary of Events and Information
	FEBRY.1918		
	1st		D/R.H.A. delivered one 13 pdr. Q.F.Gun & Limber to Wagon Lines at BOUZLY; above gun is placed in position as Anti-Tank Gun at F.21.d.30.70 (S.E. of RONSSOY) and manned by detachment from A/106. A/106 move 3 guns to position near GEORGES COPSE.
	2nd.		Nothing of importance.
	3rd.		Night of 3rd/4th B, C, & D/106 carry out night firing on enemy tracks during suspected Battalion relief. C/106 place one 18-pdr. in position at F.22.c.90.00. as Anti-Tank Gun.
	4th.		S.O.S. on Right Battalion front at about 5 pm, lasted about an hour. No enemy left their trenches.
	5th. 6th. 7th.		Nothing of importance.
	8th.		Three guns of C/106 move from position in TEMPLEUX LE GUERARD to position about L.1.d.2.2. Night 8th/9th - Night firing carried out by B & C/106.
	9th.		Nothing of importance.
	10th.		S.O.S. on right half of Divisional front at 5 pm. Lasted till about 5-30 pm. No attempt made by enemy to leave his trenches. It was reported that the enemy's coloured lights were mistaken for our S.O.S.Signal.
	11th.		Captn.Coates, M.C., R.F.A., from D/106, takes command of A/106 vice Major F.L.Farrer, R.F.A. Night 11th/12th Royal Canadian Dragoons carried out a successful raid on the right of 24th (contd.)

Hewitt
Lt-Col. R.F.A.

WAR DIARY

INTELLIGENCE SUMMARY.
(Erase heading not required.)

106TH. BRIGADE, R.F.A.

Instructions regarding War Diaries and Intelligence Summaries are contained in F. S. Regs., Part II. and the Staff Manual respectively. Title pages will be prepared in manuscript.

Place	Date	Hour	Summary of Events and Information
	Feby.1918.		
	11th(cont)		Division. 1 Officer & 13 O.R. captured. Our casualties - 1 man killed, 1 man wounded.
	12th 13th		Nothing of importance.
	14th.		Defensive Barrage "DEFEND HARGICOURT" for A, C, & D/106 comes into force.
	15th.		Nothing of importance.
	16th.		C/106 establish a forward sniping gun at F.28.b.60.30. (near TOINE WOOD). Considerable E.A. activity. Section D/106 at L.8.b.7.6. joins forward Section D/107 at L.9.a.6.1.
	17th.		Considerable E.A. activity.
	18th.		E.A. dropped bombs on back areas on night 18th/19th.
	19th.		Nothing of importance.
	20th.		Concentration by 24th D.A. and Cav.Corps H.A. on RUBY WOOD at 3-30 pm. Slight retaliation.
	21st.		S.O.S. on Divisional front on our left at 5 am., our batteries fired at slow rates until S.O.S. was confirmed to be on the next division only.
	22nd. 23rd.		Nothing of importance.
	24th.		Group H.Q. shelled at 10-30 pm. About 15 - 10 cm. shells H.E. and Gas. No damage.

Lt.-Col. R.F.A.
Comdg. 106 Brigade R.F.A.

WAR DIARY
INTELLIGENCE SUMMARY.

106TH. BRIGADE, R.F.A.

Instructions regarding War Diaries and Intelligence Summaries are contained in F. S. Regs., Part II. and the Staff Manual respectively. Title pages will be prepared in manuscript.

(Erase heading not required.)

Place	Date	Hour	Summary of Events and Information
	Feby.1918.		
	25th.		Hostile Artillery active on back areas round L.15 and TEMPLEUX-ROISEL road. C.R.A., 66th Division inspects battery positions preparatory to taking over.
	26th.		Major Dixon, Cmdg.331st Bde.,R.F.A. 66th Div., inspects battery positions preparatory to taking over. Midnight 26th/27th S.O.S. on right of Group front. Batteries fired on S.O.S. until receipt of information that Group front was not involved.
	27th.		Nothing of importance.
	28th.		One 18 pdr. drawn by A/106 from D.A.D.O.S., 24th Division, and placed in action as an Anti-Tank gun in place of the 13 pdr. which is returned to D/R.H.A. Information received points to probable enemy attack on this front. Ammunition dumps increased to 500 rds. per gun and batteries ordered to "stand to" at dawn 28th/1st. Considerably increased hostile artillery activity throughout the day and continued up to midnight.

[signature]

Lt.-Col. R.F.A.
Comdg. 106 Brigade R.F.A.

106th Brigade, R.F.A.　　WAR DIARY　　　　March 1918

Place	Date	Summary of events and information
GEORGES COPSE near TEMPLEUX	1st	Nothing of importance
	2nd	do do
	3rd	1 Section per Battery 331st Brigade, relieves 1 Section per Battery 106th Brigade in action. Relieved Sections withdraw to Wagon lines.
	4th	Headquarters and remainder of Batteries 331st Bde. R.F.A. relieve H.Q. and Batteries 106th Bde. in action. Command passes 7.0. pm. H.Q. and Batteries 106th Bde. withdraw to Wagon lines. 1 Section per Battery 106th Bde. marches to camp at MONTECOURT.
MONTECOURT	5th	H.Q. and remainder of Batteries 106th Bde. march to camp at MONTECOURT 10.0. am.
	6th	In rest at MONTECOURT.
	7th	Lt.Col. The Hon. R.G.A.HAMILTON, R.F.A. goes on leave to ENGLAND. Command of 106th Bde. passes to Major. W.M.WELSH, M.C. R.F.A.
	8th	In rest at MONTECOURT.
	9th	do do
	10th	do do
	11th	do do
	12th	do do
TREFCON	13th	106th Bde marches to Wagon lines at TREFCON, 9.30.am.
	Night 13th/14th	A/106th Bde. moves two guns into action at R.4.d. 50.20.(Sheet 62.c.) near VENDELLES, relief of two guns U. Bty. R.H.A. B/106th Bde. moves 6 guns into action at R.4.c. (Sheet 62.c.) near VENDELLES- C/106th Bde. moves 6 guns into action in position at R.8.d.0.5. near VENDELLES, D/106th Bde. moves 4 Hows. into action in position at R.5.c.1.1. near VENDELLES in relief of 1 Section D/311th Bde. R.F.A.
VENDELLES	14th	H.Q. 106th Bde. R.F.A. moves into action at R.8.a.5.9. near VENDELLES. 106th Bde. R.F.A. becomes WELSH'S Sub Group. of the Left Group, 24th D.A. Left Group, commanded by Lt.Col.FREESTON, R.F.A. and H.Q.311th Bde. consists of 311th, 106th Bde, C/23rd. Bde. and 107th Battery.
	Night 14th/15th	A/106th Bde. moves remaining 4 guns into action in position at R.9.c.2.6. (Sheet 62.c.) in relief of 4 guns U. Bty. R.H.A. D/106th Bde. moves remaining 2 Hows. into action in position at R.5.c.10.10. (Sheet 62.c.)
	15th 16th 17th 18th	Nothing of importance.
	19th	H.Q. 106th Bde. moves to new Headquarters in VENDELLES
	20th	Nothing of importance.
	21st	Heavy enemy bombardment all along the line 4.40. am. All Batteries, particularly D/106, heavily shelled with gas and H.E. shell. Infantry attack develops. Forward Sections of B/106 and D/106 and Sniping gun of C/106, which had been subjected to continuous bombardment from 4.40. am. overwhelmed by enemy infantry. Detachments withdrawn, taking some sights and breech blocks. Enemy held on the Red line N. of R. OMIGNON but gets through on the South. B/106 and C/106 withdraw to Brown line to positions near SOYECOURT. Major. S.W.BEVIS, D/106, Lt. R.BUCHANAN D/106 and 2/Lt. J.H.RENTELL, A/106 Wounded. Capt. C.H.HARPER, posted temporarily to command D/106

COMMANDING 106 Bde R.F.A

106th Brigade, R.F.A.   WAR DIARY   March 1918.

Place	Date	Summary of events and information.
VENDELLES.	22nd	Enemy attack resumed. 24th Division threatened on both flanks. 10.0. am., A/106 and D/106 and Bde. H.Q. withdraw to Brown line positions near SOYECOURT. 1 How. D/106 damaged by hostile fire destroyed by battery before withdrawing. 2 other Hows. D/106 out of action due to hostile fire withdrawn to Wagon lines. 2.0. pm., Bde. H.Q. and Batteries withdraw to Green line positions near BOUVINCOURT. 8.0. pm. Bde. H.Q. and Batteries withdraw to positions near PRUSLE Night 22nd/23rd B/106 withdraws across canal to Wood West of BRIOST. 1 How. D/106 with detachment team and wagons, attached to D/107th Bde. Remainder of personell D/106 attached to D.A.C. 24th Division.
BRIOST	23rd.	8.0. am. A/106 and C/106 and Bde. H.Q. withdraw to Wood West of BRIOST covering 8th Division and Canal crossings at BRIE and St. CHRIST. Our Infantry withdraw across Canal. Bridges at BRIE and St. CHRIST blown up about 2.0. pm. X
	24th	Bde. H.Q. and Batteries 106th remain in action in Wood West of BRIOST. Enemy cross Canal South of St. CHRIST.
	25th	Enemy reported in LICOURT and advancing towards St. CHRIST. B/106, C/106, A/106 (less 1 Section) and H.Q. 106 withdraw to DENICOURT. 1 Section A/106 left behind to cover St. CHRIST BRIDGE, surprised and captured by enemy, who had advanced Northwards between the guns and the 23rd I.B.
MEHARICOURT	Night 25th) 26th)	106th Bde. marches via ESTREES- SOYECOURT - VERMANDOVILLERS- FOUCOCOURT - RAINVILLE - ROSIERES thence H.Q. to MEHARICOURT, Batteries to MAUCOURT (20 miles)
	26th	8.0. am. Bde. H.Q. and Batteries of 106 withdraw via ROSIERES - CAIX - to positions near Mill W. of WARVILLERS. D/107 withdraws to position near BEAUFORT and is attached to 106th Bde. B/106 and C/106 move to Wood 1300 yards S. of CAIX.
	27th	A/106 shelled. 2/Lt. W.HARMAN and 1 O.R. killed. A/106 withdraws to about 500 yards N.W. of the Mill C/106 moves up to a position about 1000 yards W. of the Mill. H.Q. moves to a position near B/106 Lt. Col. The Hon. R.G.A.HAMILTON, returns from leave
	28th	B/106 retires to position amongst the stables S.E. of the Wood E. of BEAUCOURT. C/106 Bty. and Gun teams shelled. Lt. H.F.SLATTERY wounded. A/106. C/106 and D/107, move to Wood E. of BEAUCOURT. B/106 moves two guns up to crest and engages enemy with open sights. C/106 moves via CASTEL BRIDGE to position 1000 yards West of BOIS de SENECAT. B/106 retires via BEAUCOURT to MAISON BLANCHE N.,of MEZIERES thence to position in Wood N. of VILLERS-O-AERABLES. H.Q. and A/106 retire to same position coming under heavy fire on road entering MEZIERES.
	Night 28th) 29th)	At 9.0. pm. H.Q. A, and B/106 retire across country to CASTEL BRIDGE, cross the river AVRE and come into action W. of the BOIS-DE-SENECAT.
ROUVREL	29th	H.Q. moves to ROUVREL. B/106 moves across River NOYE to near ESTREES-SUR-NOYE. A/106 and B/106 move to Wood 2000 yards W. of MOREUIL.
	30th	Bde. remains in action in same position as on 29th inst. covering MOREUIL crossings.
	31st.	B/106 shelled. Lt.Col. The Hon. R.G.A. HAMILTON, killed near B/106 battery position. Major W.M. WELSH, M.C. R.F.A. assumes command of the Bde.

106th Brigade, R.F.A.   WAR DIARY   March 1918.

Place	date	Summary of events and information.
ROUVREL	31st	A, and B/106 move to positions W. of BOIS DE SENECAT. C/106 moves forward to position W. of the BOIS DE SENECAT.

12/4/18.

Commanding 106th Bde. R.F.A.

24th Div.

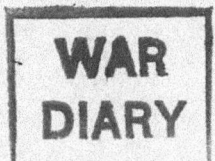

Headquarters,

106th BRIGADE, R.F.A.

A P R I L

1 9 1 8

106TH BRIGADE R.F.A. WAR DIARY
INTELLIGENCE SUMMARY
APRIL 1918

Place	Date	Hour	Summary of Events and Information
ROUVREL	1/4/18		Nothing of importance.
	2nd		HQ/106 Bde.march from ROUVREL and batteries 106 Bde from positions near BOIS DE SENECAT to positions East of FOUENCAMPS Village.
FOUENCAMPS	3rd		Assisting French troops in front of CASTEL. H.Q.move from house East side of Village to School-house 9 a.m. and later to House near Church.
	4th		Assisting French Troops in front of CASTEL.
	5th		do
	6th		H.Q.move to House west of Railway. Batteries assist French Troops in front of CASTEL.
ST.FUSCIEN	7th		311th A.F.A.Bde.relieve 106th Bde.9 pm. H.Q.& Batteries 106th Bde.march from FOUENCAMPS to ST.FUSCIEN via BOVES 9 pm.
REVELLES	8th	1 pm.	H.Q. & Batteries 106th Bde. march to REVELLES via AMIENS and SALOUEL.
ANDAINVILLE	9th	8 a.m.	H.Q. & Batteries 106th Bde. march to ANDAINVILLE via HORNOY.
	10th		Nothing of importance.
SOREL	11th	11am.	H.Q. & Batteries 106th Bde.march to SOREL via HALLEN-COURT. Lt.Col.J.C.WALCH,D.S.O. takes over command 106th Bde.R.F.A.from Major W.M.WELSH,M.C. Major W.M.WELSH resumes command of "C" Battery,106th Bde.
	12th		
	13th		
	14th		Nothing of importance.
	15th		
	16th		
BELLANCOURT	17th		H.Q. & Batteries 106th Bde.march to BELLANCOURT via PONT REMY. H.Q.,A,& B Batteries billet in BELLANCOURT, C & D Batteries billet in MONTHLIERS.
BEAUVOIR-RIVIERE	18th		H.Q. and Batteries 106th Bde march to BEAUVOIR RIVIERE via DOMLEGER

Lt.Colonel,R.F.A.
Commanding 106th Bde.R.F.A.

106th Brigade, R.F.A.   April 1918   WAR DIARY
or
INTELLIGENCE SUMMARY.

(Erase heading not required.)

Instructions regarding War Diaries and Intelligence
Summaries are contained in F. S. Regs., Part II.
and the Staff Manual respectively. Title pages
will be prepared in manuscript.

Place	Date	Hour	Summary of Events and Information
HERNICOURT	19th		
do.	20th		H.Q. and Batteries 106th Bde. march to HERNICOURT via PREVENT AND ST. POL.
ETREE WAMIN	21st		Nothing of importance. H.Q. and Batteries 106th Brigade, R.F.A. march to ETREE WAMIN via EUNEVILLE.
do	22nd		
	23rd		
	24th		
	25th		
	26th		
	27th		Nothing of importance, Brigade in training.
	28th		
	29th		
	30th		

Lt.Colonel, R.F.A.
Commanding 106th Bde, R.F.A.

Army Form C. 2118.

WAR DIARY 106TH BDE. R.F.A.

INTELLIGENCE SUMMARY
(Erase heading not required.)

Instructions regarding War Diaries and Intelligence Summaries are contained in F.S. Regs., Part II. and the Staff Manual respectively. Title pages will be prepared in manuscript.

Place	Date	Hour	Summary of Events and Information	Remarks and references to Appendices
ETRÉE WAMIN	1.5.18		Brigade at rest in Etrée Wamin	
ETRÉE WAMIN	2.5.18		Lt.Col. J.C. WALCH D.S.O. and Battery Commanders of the 106th Brigade visit positions of 242nd A.F.A. Brigade in LENS sector. Re. Lens sheet 36 S.W.1.	
ETRÉE WAMIN	3.5.18		Personnel of one section for Battery of 106th Bde. relieve personnel of one section for Battery of 242nd Bde. at the following positions A/106 at M.11.c.97.77 and M.11.c.35.90, M.11.a.02.54, B/106 M.11.c.97.77, C/106 M.10.d.35.90, D/106 M,22b.23. 3.0.0	
	4.5.18		H.Q and personnel of remaining two sections for Battery of 106th Bde. relieve H.Q & personnel of remaining two sections of 242 Bde. A.F.A. at the following positions - H.Q. Hoxton Post at M.15.b.10.90, A/6 M.11.c.50 M.10.a.47.47, B/6 M.10.c.25.65, C/6 M.22.b 60.78, D/6 M.17.c.10x54.0 A detachment A/6 relieve detachment A/242 at Anti-tank gun at M.6.d.56. C/6 take over Anti-tank gun at M.3.d 29 from C/242 A.F.A. Bde. 106th Bde. take over in positions of 242 Bde A.F.A. Bde. excepting one How. D/242 2nd Relief of few positions complete at 3.p.m. Remainder of 106th Bde. march at 9 a.m. under Capt S.P. Leisant from Etrée Wamin to New Wagon lines at SAINS GOHELLE via, LIENCOURT, AVESNES, AUBIGNY,- Relief of Wagon lines complete at dusk.	
HOXTON POST M.15.b.10.90	5+6/5/18		Harrassing fire programme on approaches carried out	
	7.5.18		Finding re-adjustment of 24th Divl. front into 3 Inf. Brigades, 106th Bde became a sub group under Lt Col. Stallard C.M.G. D.S.O. Commanding Lt. Group with H.Q. at G.34.d.95.30 covering 73rd Inf. Bde. Usual harassing fire programme carried out	
	8+9/5/18		Night 8th-9th 48th A.F.A Bde came into action with H.Q. at M.2.C.12.15, one 18/pr. Batty. at M.2.d.6756, one 18/pr. M.2b.2358, one 18/pr at G.32.b.8520 & one 4.5 Hour Batty at G.32.d.85.75 & allotted S.O.S lines two 18/pr Batteries Superimposed upon S.O.S. lines of batteries of 126 Bde & one 18/pr S.O.S. line H.32.b.62 to H.33.c.01 Superimposed on Batteries of 106th Bde. On night 8th-9th 92nd A.F.A. Bde. Came into action with H.Q. at M.16.a.07 A/92nd M.15.C.83 B/92nd M.15.d.47, C/92nd M.15.a.71 & S.O.S. lines allotted one 18/pr and one 4.5 How. battery superimposed upon S.O.S. lines of Batteries of 106th Bde as follows H.33 C01 to N.2.d.grep for 18hr Battery & H.32.b.62 to H.33.c.01 to N.2.d.grep for How Battery	
	10+11/5/18 12+13/5/18		Harrassing fire programme carried out on approaches etc. 92nd Bde. R.F.A. transferred to 20th Div in exchange with the 8th A.F.A. Bde. C.F.A.	
	13+14/5/18		24th Divisional front re-adjusted with 3 Inf. Bdes in the line, centre Bde 17th I.B. (H.Q. M.3.b.26) Covered by Centre Sp. 24th Divl. Arty under Command of Lt.Col. Walch D.S.O. 106th Bde, R.F.A. & Consisting of 106th Bde. reinforced by 8th C.F.A. Lt. Col. Walch D.S.O. Establishes his H.Q at 17 I.B. H.Q. Major M.M. Welsh M.C. C/106 take over Command of 106 Bde.	
	13/5/18		D/6 move one Hour to forward posn. at M.17.b.9080	

Lt.Col. R.F.A.
Comdg. 106 Brigade

Army Form C. 2118.

WAR DIARY 106 BDE R.F.A. (cont.)

INTELLIGENCE SUMMARY

(Erase heading not required.)

Instructions regarding War Diaries and Intelligence Summaries are contained in F.S. Regs., Part II. and the Staff Manual respectively. Title pages will be prepared in manuscript.

Place	Date	Hour	Summary of Events and Information	Remarks and references to Appendices
	15.5.18		Harassing fire programme on approaches carried out	
	16 "		" " " " " "	
	17 "		Night 17th–18th B/6 move 2 guns to position at M.10.a. 67. Usual harassing fire carried out	
	17 "		Harassing fire on approaches carried out	
	18 "		" " " "	
	19 "		" " " "	
	20 "		" " " "	
	21 "		" " " "	
	22 "		" " " "	
	23 "		" " " "	
	24 "		Night 24th–25th A/6, B/6, C/6 & D/6 support Rt Grp in raid. Usual harassing fire carried out	
	25 "		Harassing fire carried out.	
	26 "		" " " "	
	27 "		" " " "	
	28 "		Night 28th–29th A/6, B/6 & D/6 assist in Gas bombardment	
	29 "		On night 29th–30th C/106 & D/106 assist in Gas bombardment of Hostile Batteries on Corps front	
	30 "		Harassing fire carried out on approaches	
	31 "		" " " "	

Lt.-Col R.F.A.
Comdg 106 Brigade R.F.A.

Ref. GRAND TRUNK. LOG MAP
106 Bde RFA
651 34

106TH BRIGADE R.F.A. WAR DIARY   JUNE 1918.

INTELLIGENCE SUMMARY

(Erase heading not required)

Place	Date	Hour	Summary of Events and Information	Remarks and references to Appendices
MAROC	1st		Forward section A/6 & B/6 snipe at movement in Carvin Road – during night forward sections of all Batteries 106th Brigade carry out harassing fire on roads, tracks, and trenches in N.3. 4, 5, 6, & H.33, 34, & H.35. Ammunition expended in harassing fire 580 rounds.	
	2nd		Forward sections snipe at movement in Carvin Road and Rotten Row – during night expenditure 600 rounds in harassing roads, tracks, trenches etc., in N.3., 4, 5, & 6., H.33., 34, & 35. At 12 midnight 2 guns of A, B, C, & D/106 assist in raid on Right Group front.	
	3rd		Forward sections engage movement in N.5.c. & d., M.6.a., & c. During night expenditure 600 rounds in harassing roads trenches etc., in usual places.	
	4th		Forward sections snipe at movement at H.34.d.1.5. and in Carvin Road at night. 580 rounds expended in harassing fire on selected targets. – H.Q.106 Bde.R.F.A. move from Honton Post to new Headquarters IMXMXX at M.3.6.00.45. MAROC. B/106 assist in raid on Right Group front. Major W.M. Welsh M.C. resumes command of C/106. Lt.Col.J.C.Walch R.F.A. resumes command of 106th Brigade R.F.A. 637 rounds harassing roads and tracks etc.	
	5th		Forward sections engage movement in M.10.b. & M.11. & 12 during day and at night. Expenditure in harassing fire. Hostile artillery shelled our support trenches.	
	6th		Forward sections snipe at movement at H.34.d.1.5. and in Carvin Road – at night 600 rounds expended at night harass roads and tracks etc. – at frequent moving targets at Fosse 21 and in fields near Carvin Road – telephone communication suspended for 24 hours test.	
	7th		Forward sections snipe at movement in N.5.c. & d. – 600 rounds expended harassing roads and tracks during night.	
	8th		Forward d sections engage movement on tramway Rotten Row, and at N.5.c. During night 580 rounds expended in harassing fire.	
	9th		Forward sections snipe at movement in N.3. b.90.10. and M.4.a.80.20. Harassing fire at night carried out on roads, targets and trenches, 600 rounds expended.	
	10th		Forward sections A, B, & D Batteries 106th Brigade snipe at movement in the vicinity of Carvin Road – roads and tracks harassed during night. 510 rounds expended – at midnight hostile artillery heavily bombarded our front line for 5 minutes.	
	11th		Forward sections engage several moving targets in Carvin Road and Rotten Row, and during night expend 560 rounds in harassing fire.	
	12th		All forward sections engage movement during the day and at night. – expend 580 rounds harassing roads, tracks, and trenches.	
	13th		Forward sections engage movement in Carvin, and at Fosse 21 – hostile artillery shelled trenches in N.8.a. heavily, also CITE ST.PIERRE – battery position of A/106 was shelled by 4.2" How.	
	14th		During night forward sections expended 610 rounds harassing roads and tracks.	

Comdg 106 Brigade RFA

Sheet 2   106TH BRIGADE R.F.A.   WAR DIARY   JUNE 1918.   Army Form C. 2118.

or

INTELLIGENCE-SUMMARY.
(Erase heading not required.)

Place	Date	Hour	Summary of Events and Information	Remarks and references to Appendices
	15th		Forward sections snipe at movement in Carvin Road. C/106 register 2 targets with balloon observation. D/6 cut wire at H.32.d.76.42.& 16.24. - 520 rounds expended in harassing fire during the night.	
	16th		Forward sections engage movement in Carvin Road - N.11.a.,N.5.a.,N.6.a. - A/106 register targets with balloon observation - 580 rounds expended harassing roads,bridges,tracks etc. Enemy artillery inactive throughout the 24 hours.	
	17th		Forward s sections snipe at movement in Carvin Road.C/6 carry out instructional shoots at 6.pm. A,& B/106 assist in dummy raid in support of raid carried out on Left Group front - 520 rounds expended in harassing roads and tracks. Hostile artillery shelled heavily trenches in N.7.b.	
	18th		Forward sections engage numerous moving targets in N.5.d., N.10.c., M.4.c. - D/6 fire 50 rounds on hostile T.Ms at H.26.a.65.04. - 560 rounds expended in harassing fire.	
	19th		Forward sections shoot at movement in N.3.c.& N.4.c. - D/6 register target N.10.c.66.18. by balloon observation. Lt.Col.J.C.Walch attends conference held by C.R.A.at HQ of 48th Army Bde R.F.A., to decide new line of resistance - 540 rounds expended in harassing fire during night.	
	20th		Forward sections engage several fleeting targets in vicinity of N.4.d.95.40.,N.5.d.80.40., M.6.d.50.30.and expend 580 rounds in harassing fire during night - hostile artillery very active on our trenches all day.	
	21st	t	Forward guns shoot at movement at N.10.b.,N.11.b.,& N.5.d.and expend 540 rounds in harassing fire during the night. Lt.Col.J.C.Walch attends a tank demonstration. Enemy artillery very quiet throughout the day.	
	22nd		Forward sections engage movement by forward guns - 540 rounds expended harassing roads,and tracks during the night. Hostile shelling more severe than usual - mostly on forward trenches.	
	23rd		Forward sections engage movement in N.5.a.,N.6.a.and during night expend 580 rounds in harassing fire.	
	24th		Forward sections engage numerous moving targets at Fosse 21, N.5.c., & N.6.d.During night expend 480 rounds ins harassing fire.	
	25th		Lt.Col.J.C.Walch D.S.O goes on leave to England - Major W.M.Welch M.C. C/106 takes over the command of Centre Group. Forward sections engage movement on the Carvin Road during the day and expend 550 rounds in harassing fire by night. Enemy artillery shell the battery position of D/106 with 10.5 How, and 15 cm How.200 rounds fell near them and did no damage.	
	26th		Forward s sections shoot at movement in Carvin Road, and during night expend 500 rounds in H.F.	
	27th		Forward sections engage movement round Fosse 21 during day,and expend 520 rounds in H.F.by night. At 8.am.106 Bde.assist 1B raid carried out by 1st Battn.Royal Fusiliers.	
	28th		Forward sections engage movement at N.10.d.,N.11.a.,N.5.d.,& N.6.d.and during night expend 600 rounds in Harassing fire.Hostile artillery activity considerable on trenches at N.2.c.	

Sheet 3

106TH BRIGADE R.F.A.   WAR DIARY.   JUNE 1918.

INTELLIGENCE SUMMARY.

(Erase heading not required.)

Army Form C. 2118.

Instructions regarding War Diaries and Intelligence Summaries are contained in F. S. Regs., Part II. and the Staff Manual respectively. Title pages will be prepared in manuscript.

Place	Date	Hour	Summary of Events and Information	Remarks and references to Appendices
	29th		Forward sections shoot at movement round N.5.d., & N.6.c. 580 rds expended on harassing fire by night.	
	30th		Forward sections engage usual movement and expend 540 rds in harassing fire by night. New dispositions known as Black Line come into force, and S.O.S. lines allotted to Batteries.	

Lt.Col.R.F.A.
Commanding 106th Brigade R.F.A.

CONFIDENTIAL

WAR DIARY

of

106th. BRIGADE, R.F.A.

From 1st JULY, 1918.   To 31st JULY, 1918.

Army Form C. 2118.
Sheet 1.
Ref: Grand Trunk
Log. Map. (3rd Edition)

WAR DIARY JULY 1918
INTELLIGENCE SUMMARY. 106TH BDE. R.F.A.
(Erase heading not required.)

Instructions regarding War Diaries and Intelligence Summaries are contained in F. S. Regs., Part II. and the Staff Manual respectively. Title pages will be prepared in manuscript.

Place	Date	Hour	Summary of Events and Information	Remarks and references to Appendices
MAROC	July 1st	Night 1-2	Fwd. Sects. B/106 engage movement at N.3.b.2080, N.3.d.9540, N.6.d.3050. A/106 snipe at movement in N.3.c, N.6.c, N.9.a. Fwd. Sects. A.B. C/106 expend 360 rounds in harassing roads, tracks in back areas. Hostile arty. active during the forenoon on NOGGIN, HYTHE, NETLEY & CATAPULT trenches 77mm fire & 10.5cm how. used A/106 move one gun from fwd. posn. M.11.c.9249. 6 man. pos. at M.11.c.30. D/6 move 4 hows. from fwd. posn. M.17.c to a new pos. in area round M.3.d.0362. During night enemy bombard with gas & shrapnel Batty. posn. A + B/106 snipe at movement in N.3.d.8000, N.3.c.55 + N.5.d.76. D/106 move fwd. sect. to new pos. at M.10.a.6.38 DOUBLE CRASSIER	
	2nd		Fwd. Sects. expend 480 rounds in harassing fire during night. Enemy action slight throughout.	
	3rd		Fwd. Sects. snipe at moving target in CARVIN RD. N.3.c, N.4.c. D/6 register from new fwd. posn. During night Fwd. Sects. expend 620 in harassing fire on tracks buildings etc.	
	4th		Fwd. Sects. engage small movement at N.3.d.76, N.6.d, + N.3.b. C/6 register target. with balloon observation N.11.a.48 at 11pm. Fwd. Sects. engage 3 small movement B.C, D/6 assist in organised shoot "SMASH" ST. AUGUSTE" during night expend 540 rounds in harassing fire. Enemy arty. very active all day	
	5th		Gun posn. A/106 shelled by 15cm how. from midday until 4 pm. about 300 rounds fell. No damage done. A.S. + C/106 fwd. Sects. engage movement at N.6.c.05.90, N.6.a. N.5.d. During night fwd. Sects. expend 490 rounds in harassing fire. Hostile arty. again active. A/6 posn. was shelled 60 rounds 10.5cm shells fell near and did no damage	
	6th		A + B/106 Fwd. Sects. snipe at movement in N.11.a.3050, N.5.d.3068, N.11.a.3060. N.5.d.76 + during night expend 490 in harassing fire. Hostile arty. not so active today.	
	7th		Individual movement at N.4.a.8.0. N.5.d.76. H.33.d + H.34.c engaged by fwd. Sects. During night Harassing fire increased on account of suspected relief taking place. 1020 rounds fired on roads tracks etc. at 11pm. A.B.C + D/106 fwd. Sects. assist in organised shoot "SMASH CONDÉ". Silent day on telephone	
	8th		Fwd. Sects. engage movement on CARVIN RD. during day & at night expend 720 rounds in harassing fire.	
	9th		Fwd. Sects. expend 70 rounds in sniping at movement round N.10.b.d + N.6.c at night expend 520 rounds in harassing fire. D/106 move two hows. 6 pos. in M.17.c in order to take part in Gas Bombardment of Hostile Batteries.	
	10th		Fwd. Sects. shoot at movement N.4.c.98, N.10.b, N.6.c. Hostile arty. carry out Counter battery shoot on sect. of 6" Hows. in M.3.b.90. about 300 shells fell mostly 15cm. some gas shells also used. Fwd. Sects.	

Lt.-Col. R.F.A.
Comdg. 106 Brigade R.F.A.

Army Form C. 2118.
Sheet 2.

WAR DIARY JULY 1918
of
INTELLIGENCE SUMMARY. 106 BDE. R.F.A.

(Erase heading not required.)

Instructions regarding War Diaries and Intelligence Summaries are contained in F.S. Regs., Part II. and the Staff Manual respectively. Title pages will be prepared in manuscript.

Place	Date	Hour	Summary of Events and Information	Remarks and references to Appendices
MAROC	July 10th 11th		A/106 Expend 420 rounds in harassing fire. A/106 engage several small parties in neighbourhood of CARVIN RD. D/106 carry out registration - & C/106 several instructional shoots. B/106 harass gun seen firing at N.36.9575. Batteries 106th Bde assist in supporting Raid carried out by 8th Batt. "THE QUEENS" on enemy trenches at N.2d.70.15. at 3 a.m. on night of 11th/12th. A & D/101 assist in Counter battery Gas Bombardment 730 rounds Expended in harassing fire during night. LT. COL. WALCH. D.S.O. returned from England & resumes Command of Centre Group. MAJOR. W.M. WELSH. M.C. resumes Command of C/101. Hostile arty activity slight.	
	12th		Fwd. Sec.s engage much movement during day about CARVIN RD. Extensive harassing fire in connection with discharge of gas 1320 rounds Expended. A/106 more fire from 6 new posn. at M.9.c.9.1.	
	13th		Fwd. Scots engage movement in N.36, N.3d. - Continue with harassing fire. Expending 850 rounds during night. Hostile arty activity very slight. Night 13th-14th one Sect. per Batty. of 52nd A.F.A. Bde relieve one Sect per Batty of 8th C.F.A. Bde	
	14th		Fwd. Scots Expend 540 rounds in harassing fire. H.Q. & remaining two Sects of 8th C.F.A. Bde. relieve H.Q. & two Secs. per Battery of the 52nd A.F.A. Bde. R.F.A. Commd. passes at 12 midnight	
	15th		Fwd. Scts engage movement on CARVIN RD. & Expend 540 rounds in harassing fire during night. Enemy Activity about normal.	
	16th		LT. COL. J.C. WALCH. D.S.O. having injured his knee, goes down to Wagon lines for medical treatment. MAJOR. W.M. WELSH. M.C. C/106 takes over Command of Centre Gp. Very little individual movement seen. 560 rounds Expended in harassing fire during night. Enemy arty about normal. Movement in H.32.b. Sniped at - During night Fwd Sec.s increased their harassing fire 6/120 rounds Hostile arty showed considerable Activity.	
	17th		Fwd. Scts engage targets in N.36.91. N.3.d.81. N.10.a.1t. + N.6.b.9.5. during night. 560 rounds Expended in harassing fire. Hostile arty active on front line trenches intermittently during the day.	
	18th		Fwd. Sec.s Snipe at movement in N.3d. N.9d. + N.15.b. + N.16.a. C/106 registered N.3d. 35 with Balloon observation. 600 rounds Expended in harassing fire 2 Lt.H. Bugg. killed in action at 7.30 a.m. whilst on duty at Hawk O.P. (N.10.9.88) a direct hit on O.P. of roof causing death.	
	19th		Fwd. Scts engage movement in CARVIN RD. Areas. D/106 Carry out Experimental Shoot with Field Survey Coy's R.E. during night 600 rounds Expended in harassing fire. Hostile arty showed increased activity particularly their T.M.s. - O.C. "D" batteries (106 Bde.) takes in organized Shoot "SMASH MINES".	
	20th			
	21st		Fwd. Sec.s engage several moving targets at N.11.b. N.5.d. + N.10. 600 Expended in harassing fire. Enemy Artillery Confined to T.M. Activity	

Comnds. 106 Brigade R.F.A.

Army Form C. 2118.
Sheet 3.

WAR DIARY JULY 1918
INTELLIGENCE SUMMARY. 106 BDE. R.F.A.
(Erase heading not required.)

Instructions regarding War Diaries and Intelligence Summaries are contained in F.S. Regs., Part II. and the Staff Manual respectively. Title pages will be prepared in manuscript.

Place	Date	Hour	Summary of Events and Information	Remarks and references to Appendices
MAROC	July 22nd		Fwd. Sects. Engage movement at N.3.c.57-N.36.91 - N.6.a, N.5.C. B/106 assist in Raid by 7th Northants by putting down a smoke screen 670 rounds expended in harassing fire during the night. Visibility very low & not much sniping done by fwd. sects. D/106 fwd. sect. assist in organised shoot on hostile T.M's 15+16. During night hostile T.M.s were harassed - 600 rounds in harassing fire. Expended A/106 move two guns fwd. D/106 move two guns fwd. D/106 two hour fwd. in order to support Raid to be made by 3rd R.B.	
	23rd		Fwd. Sects. Engage numerous moving targets. At 3.5 p.m. 106th Bde. assist in supporting Raid by the 3rd Batt. R.B. 6 guns C/106 - 4 guns B/106 - 4 guns A/106 + 4 hows D/106 take part. 660 rounds expended in harassing fire during night. At 12.30 a.m. (24th + 25th) A, B, C, + D Fwd. Sects. assist in Raid by 72nd I.B. Col. J.C. WALCH. D.S.O. resumes Command of Centre Grp. - MAJOR W.M. WELSH. M.C. resumes Command of C/106.	
	24th		Fwd. Sects. Engage movement during day at 6.45 p.m. A & C/106 assist in organised shoot. "SMASH CONDÉ" 660 rounds expended in harassing fire. Enemy artillery active	
	25th		C.R.A. 24th D.A. holds Conference with Front & Brigade Commanders at the HQ 106th Bde in MAROC. COL. J.C. WALCH, D.S.O attends.- Very little sniping by fwd. Sects. Carried out. At 11-2 p.m. 106th Bde. Support 8th Batt. The QUEENS REGIMENT in Raid - 325 rounds expended in harassing fire.	
	26th		Night 26 - 27 June 4 hours of A, B, + D/106 that were moved fwd on 22nd inst. return to their main posn. Visibility low during day & no sniping took place.- A systematic R. programme of wire cutting & bombarding of strong points commence under orders from Div. Arty. in order to join the belief held by the Enemy that an attack by us is imminent. D/106 sends four forward to M.10.b.25.78. C/106 sends four forward to M.6.a.2.3. in order to take part in special bombardment programme. D/106 shoot 200 rounds at organised system of shell hole. H.33.c.15. H.Q.al. H.33.c.11 - T.M.s al. H.33.c.30.31 - 585 rounds expended in harassing fire. Heavy thunderstorm during day.	
	27th		C/106 cut wire at H.32.d expending 150 rounds. D/106 expend 200 rndo ar Special bombardment target A + B/106 l snipt. at movement at M.11.a 3.80 + N.4.b.30.32, 7.1 rnds. had in harassing fire during night. Visibility low during day.	
	28th		C/106 cut wire at H.32.d. D/106 carry out shoot on Trench junction at H.33.a.8406 & at Dump at N.36.7086 as per special bombardment programme. Visibility low & very little sniping took place. 570 rounds expended in harassing fire. E.A. dropped 7 bombs near posn. (M.12.a) B/106. D/106 retaliate on T.M.s al. 10.20 p.m & 12.20 a.m. Corks commander presents.	
	29th			
	30th		E, C, & D/106 assist in organised shoot "SMASH MINES" at 10.20 a.m. Corks commander presents.	

Copy to 106 Brigade R.F.A.

Army Form C. 2118.
Sheet. A.

WAR DIARY
JULY 1918
INTELLIGENCE SUMMARY. 106th Bde R.F.A.

(Erase heading not required.)

Place	Date	Hour	Summary of Events and Information	Remarks and references to Appendices
MAROC	July 30th		decorations to Officers, N.C.O's & men of 106th Bde. R.F.A. C/106 & D/106 continue with shooting according to programme laid down, expending 530 rnds. Fwd. Sect. expend 600 rnds in harassing fire. Visibility low during day.	
	31st "		C/ & D/106 continue shooting according to programme for Special bombardment 400 rounds expended. Fwd. Sects. 106th Bde support Raid at 11p.m. made by the 72nd I.B. During night 650 rounds expended in harassing fire.	

Lt.-Col. R.F.A.
Comdg. 106 Brigade R.F.A.

CONFIDENTIAL.

WAR DIARY.

OF

106th Brigade, Royal Field Artillery.

From:- 1st August 1918.   To:- 30th August 1918.

106TH BRIGADE R.F.A. WAR DIARY

INTELLIGENCE SUMMARY

AUGUST, 1918.

(Erase heading not required.)

Ref. Log Map. GRAND TRUNK 1/10,000

Instructions regarding War Diaries and Intelligence Summaries are contained in F.S. Regs., Part II. and the Staff Manual respectively. Title pages will be prepared in manuscript.

Army Form C. 2118.

Place	Date	Hour	Summary of Events and Information	Remarks and references to Appendices
Ma roc.	1 Aug		Hostile Artillery silent during hours of daylight. A/106 engaged several small parties in N.4.c and M.10.b. B/106 engage movement round houses in H.34.c.90.50. C and D/106 continue shooting under special Bombardment programme cutting wire at H.32.d. and Tramway from N.3d.b.0.1 to M.3.b.5.2. Forward Sections harass roads and tracks during night expending 630 rounds.	
	2 "		Visibility low and no sniping took place C and D/106 expend 380 rounds shooting on special Bombardment targets. During night 580 rounds expended on Harassing fire targets.	
	3 "		A/106 snipe at movement in N.5.c. B/106 at movement in N.5.b.70.60 and N.5.c.35.10. C/106 at movement in N.10.a.2.6. Forward Sections expend 440 rounds in harassing fire. Night 3rd/4th Forward Sections of A/106 and D/106 withdraw guns and personnel to Wagon lines at SANS en GOHELLE on relief by 122nd Battery and D 52nd A.F.A. Bde. R.F.A.	
	4 "		Forward Sections—snipeB/106 snipe at movement N.5.c.35.10. and C/106 Forward Section at movement in N.3.a.1.5. C/106 cut wire in N.32.d. Forward Sections B and C/106 and section of 122nd Battery and section D/52 expend 520 rounds in harassing fire. On nights— 4th/5th 122nd Battery less 1 section move to position in M.2.b.23.58½, and 122nd Battery and D/52nd A.F.A. take over S.O.S. Zones etc. of B/106 and D/106 respectively. Personnel of main positions of B/106 and D/106 withdraw to Wagon lines. Centre Group is then readjusted as follows:- 106 Bde. R.F.A. (less personnel at Wagon lines) 122nd Battery and D/52nd; A/52nd and C/52nd pass under command Left Group.	
	5 "		Enemy Artillery very active during day mostly near the forward section of B/106 shelling started at 12.30 pm. continuing intermittently until 6 pm. No damage was done. 590 rounds expended in harassing fire during night.	
	6 "		Lt.Col MARRYAT D.S.O. R.F.A. and H.Qs 52 A.F.A.Bde.R.F.A. relieve Lt.Col J.C.WALCH,D.S.O.R.F.A. and H.Qs 106 Bde. R.F.A. in command of Centre Group at M.3.b.00.45. H.Qs.106 Bde. R.F.A. with- draw to Wagon lines and establish H.Qs. at Fosse 10.	
FOS SE 10.SANS en-GOHELLE	7 "		A/106 and D/106 commence training A/106 carry out Scheme under Brigade Orders	
	8 "		24th Divisional Horse Show at Guay SERVINS takes place.	
	9 "		A and D/106 carry out training programme under Battery arrangements	
	10 "		do do do do.	
	11 "		do do do do.	
	12 "		D/106 carry out Scheme in open warfare.	
	13 "		A/106 do do do do	
	14 "		D/106 carry out Scheme in open warfare training.	
	16 "		A and D/106 carry out usual training parades under Battery arrangements. Night 16th/17th personnel and 2 guns A/106 and D/106 go up into action and re-occupy positions vacated on night 3rd/4th. Personnel and forward guns B/106 withdraw to Wagon lines for training.	

Army Form C. 2118.

106TH BRIGADE.R.F.A. WAR DIARY August 1918.
or
INTELLIGENCE-SUMMARY.
(Erase heading not required.)

Instructions regarding War Diaries and Intelligence Summaries are contained in F. S. Regs., Part II. and the Staff Manual respectively. Title pages will be prepared in manuscript.

Place	Date	Hour	Summary of Events and Information	Remarks and references to Appendices
FOSSE 10 SANS-en-GOHELLE Maroc	17 Aug.		B/1 06 commence training programme.	
	18 "		Lt.Col.J.C.WALCH.D.S.O., and H.Qs. 106 Bde. relieve Lt.Col.MARRYAT D.S.O. and H.Qs.52nd A.F.A.Bde in command of CENTRE GROUP. Command passes at 10 am. Enemy Artillery very quiet.Fwd Sections 106 Bde. and 122nd B battery expend 1022 rounds in harassing fire.D/106 in addition to harassing fire expend 100 rounds of gas shell under D.A.orders. Night 18th/19th.Personnel and 2 guns of Section of B/106 relieve guns and personnel of section of 122nd Battery at forward position at M.12.a.27.27. 52nd A.F.A. Bde.,withdraw from Centre Group.to Wagon lines. Centre Group npw consists of 106th Bde. R.F.A. (personnel of 2 sections B/106 and 1 gun B/106 being at W.L.),122nd Battery and D/52	
	19 "		Hostile 15 cm.How. and gun shelled eastern outskirts of Maroc from 8am. till 2.45.pm.During night fo rward section A.B.C. and D/106 carry out harassing fire expending 500 rounds.	
	20 "		Enemy Artillery very quiet.Forward Sections 106th Bde expend 605 rounds during night in harassing fire.	
	21 "		Hostile Artillery quiet. Forward Sections expend 550 rounds in harassing fire during night. Forward sec tions support raid by 3rd Battalion The Rifle Brigade at 4.45am. on Enemy post at N.8.b.35.90	
	22 "		Enemy carry out destructive shoot on forward position of B/106 using 15 cm. How. H.E. and Gas. No damage to gun or personnel.Night 22nd/23rd Forward Section B/106 move guns to position at M.11.c.97.45. under orders from D.A. No harassing fire takes place.	
	23 "		Enemy Artillery active on trenches in N.1.a.,N.2.a.,N.1.b.and H.32.c.Forward Sections expend 605 rounds in harassing fire.	
	24 "		Hostile Artillery quiet Forward Sections expend 550 rounds in harassing fire.	
	25 "		Forward sections carry out harassing fire expending 606 rounds.C/106 engage movement at M.5.c.2.9. A/106 movement at N.4.a.80.60.Hostile Artillery very quiet.	
	26 "		Hostile 15 cm How. shelled vicinity of H.Q.106 Bde.R.F.A. from 1.30.pm. to 7.pm.Forward sections 106 Bde. expend 605 rounds in harassing fire.Night 26th/27th personnel 2 sections B/106 return to action from Wagon lines.Personnel of one section B/106 go down to Wagon lines for rest and training,one gun B/106 remain at Wagon lines.	
	27 "		Enemy Artillery quiet.Forward Sections harass roads and tracks during night expending 600 rounds.	
	28 "		Hostile Artillery quiet during day.106 Bde assist in organised shoot "SMASH MINES" at 10./30.pm. usual harassing fire carried out,605 rounds expended.Night 28th/29thDivisional Boundary re-adjusted on account of the 8th Corps side slipping one Infantry Bde.front Southwards.Centre Group become Left Group.Forward Sections assist in organised shoot "SMASH ST.AUGUST".	

Lt.-Col. R.F.A.
Comdg, 106 Brigade R.F.A.

Army Form C. 2118.

WAR DIARY August 1918.

106TH BRIGADE R.F.A.

INTELLIGENCE SUMMARY.

(Erase heading not required.)

Place	Date	Hour	Summary of Events and Information	Remarks and references to Appendices
MAROC	29 Aug		Hostile Artillery quiet during the day, at night enemy harass Maroc Sector. Silent night on Divisional front and no harassing fire carried out.	
	30 "		Enemy Artillery quiet during day, at night more active. A.B and D/106 assist Right Group in support of raid at 12.45.am.by Centre Brigade on enemy trenches at N.8.d. C/106 personnel and 2 guns withdraw to Wagon lines for rest and training. Forward Sections A.B. and D/106 expend 440 rounds in Harassing fire.	
	31 "		Lt.Col Walch,D.S.O. with Battery Commanders makes a reconnaissance of forward positions in anticipation of enemy retirement. Enemy Artillery quiet. Forward Section expend 440 rounds in H.F.	

Lt.-Col. R.F.A.
Comdg. 106 Brigade R.F.A.

Army Form C. 2118.

106TH BRIGADE R.F.A. WAR DIARY SEPTEMBER 1918
or
INTELLIGENCE SUMMARY.
(Erase heading not required.)

Instructions regarding War Diaries and Intelligence Summaries are contained in F. S. Regs., Part II. and the Staff Manual respectively. Title pages will be prepared in manuscript.

VR 37

Place	Date	Hour	Summary of Events and Information	Remarks and references to Appendices
MAROC	1st Sept		Front quiet - A,B,& D/106 Forward Sections engage small working parties, and during night expend 940 rounds in harassing fire. Night 1st/2nd Group front extended on left in consequence of adjustment of Divisional front.	
	2nd		Front quiet - D/106 shoot at movement in N.4.c.75.20. A & B/106 fwd.sects.expend 550 rnds in harassing fire during night. D/106 fwd.sects.move to position at M.6.a.75.80.	
	2nd 3rd		Enemy artillery activity slight - A,B,& D/106 engage movement in N.5.c.40.20. N.6.c.50.20.and M.10.b.70.20. At 2.30.pm.106th Brigade called upon to assist Right Group,enemy having attacked one of their forward posts. A,B,and D/106 fwd.sects.fire for 15 minutes, 480 rounds expended in HarassingFire during night.	
	4th		Enemy inactive during the day, at night more lively - Right Battn.H.Q.were harassed with 10.5.cm. H.E.& Gas - Forward Sec.D/106 assist in organised shoot "Gas Ovens" commencing at 11.30.pm.in retaliation - Forward sections support raid made by the 15th Division at 4.45.am.,on enemy trenches at H.25.b.67.17.to H.25.b.43.78. Forward Sections expend 480 rds in H.F.during the night.	
	5th		Enemy quiet both by day and night - A, B,& D/6 fowd.sects.,engaged movement in N.6.d.,N.5.d.- and N.4.a.,at night between 8.30.pm.and 5.30.am.,expend 440 rds in harassing fire.	
	6th		Enemy artillery quite inactive during daylight. D/106 shoot at movement at N.3.c.45.25.and disperse small working party. A/106 disperse working party at N.5.c.40.00.,forward sections expend 480 rds in H.F.	
	7th		Hostile Arty continues to be inactive during daylight hours - D/106 engage frequent movement in N.11.b.and N.12.b.During night forward sections expend 420 rounds in H.F.	
	8th		Hostile Artillery again quiet by day - At night roads around LOOS and Double Crassier harassed by enemy. Our forward sections engage movement in Fosse 21 and N.5.d.H.F.expenditure 490 rnds. Forward sections D/10 6 cut wire at N.2.b.60.30.,day wet and stormy.	
	9th		Enemy artillery quiet by day - some harassing fire by night. Forward sections engage many moving targets,and during night expend 440 rounds in H.F. D/106 cut wire at N.2.b.	
	10th	h	A,B,& D/106 forward sections assist in support of raid by 1st Battn.R.F. on enemy trenches in N.2.d.,and N.3.c. Enemy artillery very quiet throughout the day. Our ford sects expend 450 rds in H.F.	
	11th		Forward sections engage movement N.5.c.,N.5.d.,and N.6.d.D/106 expend 130 rds in wire cutting. - 490 rds expended in H.F.	
	12th		Hostile artillery very quiet. Forward sections A/6 shoot at movement in N.5.c.D/106 cut wire and fire on B.T.M.emplacements in H.32.b.,N.3.a. - 490 rds expended in H.F.Heavy rains during the day.	
	13th		Enemy 15.cm.how shelled area immediately West of Double Crassier off and on during the day, otherwise day quiet. B/1 06 engage many moving targets,mostly on and in neighbourhood of Carvin Road. D/106 cut wire in N.3.a. Forward sections expend 500 rds in H.F.	Commanding 106 Brigade R.F.A. Lt Col R.F.A.

Sheet 2

106TH BRIGADE R.F.A. WAR DIARY SEPTEMBER 1918
or
INTELLIGENCE-SUMMARY.
(Erase heading not required.)

Army Form C. 2118.

Place	Date	Hour	Summary of Events and Information	Remarks and references to Appendices
	14th		Enemy artillery fire practically nil - D/106 shoot at movement in N.11.b.,430 rds expended in H.F.during the night. Night 14th/15th A/106 Battery personnel and guns withdraw to wagon lines and personnel and guns of C/106 return from rest and training.D/106 cut wire in N.3.a.	
	15th		Enemy artillery activity practically nil during the day,and individual movement much below normal.Forward section carry out usual night firing programme,D/106 cut wire in N.3.a.	
	16th		Enemy artillery fire showed a marked increase both by day and night. Several sharp and short organised shoots took place on our trenches N.6.b.N.7.b.,and H.31.d. B/106 engaged several parties in the CARVIN ROAD area. Usual H.F.carried out by the forward section.	
	17th		Enemy artillery quiet - C/106 engaged a party of 30 men attempting to cross from OVAL STACKS to NEGRO TR.at 4.pm.Forward sections 106 Brigade R.F.A.assist 15th Division in raid on enemy's trenches at H.25.b.,H.26.a.,H.19.d.	
	18th		Enemy artillery showed much more activity than for the past few days, trenches in N.1.b.,N.2.c., and roads in M.3.c.were harassed - C/106 forward section engaged movement in N.11.c.,and N.9.a.,7.5. D/106 expend 156 rds in wire cutting in N.3.b. During night forward sections expend 470 rds in H.F. Very little hostile shelling - B/106 engage much movement in and near CARVIN ROAD - D/106 continue wirecutting in N.3.b. Forward sections expend 450 rds in wire cutting during the night.	
	19th			
	20th		Day quiet and visibility poor. D/106 cut wire, and at night assist in an organised shoot "GAS COMBE" - 470 rds expended in H.F.during the night.	
	21st		Very little artillery fire - more individual movement than usual. The forward sections of B,C,and D/106 engage movement at N.6.a.,N.5.d.,N.3.b.,and N.3.c.and during night harass roads and tracks, expending 450 rds - D/106 cut wire in N.3.b.,Officers A/106 carry out scheme in open warfare under Lt.Col.J.C.WALCH D.S.O.	
	22nd		Enemy fire very slight during the day - at night our outpost line heavily shelled.D/106 shoot at movement in N.12.a.and cut wire in N.3.b.visibility poor during the greater part of the day. A/106 carry out scheme in open warfare under Lt.Col.J.C.WALCH D.S.O.	
	23rd		The day was quiet and very little artillery action. D/106 cut wire at N.3.a.and M.3.a. - C/106 sniped at movement in N.2.d.90.90.and M.9.a.95.87. Forward sections expend 450 rds in H.F. during the night.	
	24th		Enemy artillery very active in our trenches in H.32.c.from 11.am.to 2.30.pm.D/106 cut wire in H.32.d. During the night forward sections expend 440 rds in H.F.	
	25th		Enemy artillery again fairly active on trenches in H.32.c.,N.2.d.,and N.2.b. - B/106 shoot at movement in N.5.d.,N.6.c. - A/106 carry out scheme in open warfare under Lt.Col.J.C.WALCH D.S.O. No harassing fire carried out,the night being silent on the Divisional front.	

Commanding 106 Brigade R.F.A.

Army Form C. 2118.

WAR DIARY
or
INTELLIGENCE-SUMMARY.

(Erase heading not required.)

106TH BRIGADE R.F.A. SEPTEMBER 1918

Place	Date	Hour	Summary of Events and Information	Remarks and references to Appendices
	26th		Enemy artillery very active on our forward trenches - he carried out two short sharp shoots on N.3.c.with 77.mm.gun,and using gas shell. During night forward sections carried out usual programme of H.F. 5.5.am.B,C,and D/106 assist in demonstration on Divisional front,the guns at main battery positions being taken to forward positions for the night.	
	27th		Enemy artillery quiet. B/106 engage numerous fleeting targets in N.6. A/106 carry out scheme in open warfare training under Lt.Col.J.C.WALCH D.S.O. - wirecutting programme continued by D/106.	
	28t.	h	Situation quiet throughout the day. Hostile artillery fire practically nil. D/106 cut wire in N.3.c. Several small working parties engaged by B,and D/106 in vicinity of CARVIN ROAD. B/106 personnel and guns withdraw to wagon lines for rest and training - A/106 return to action after period of rest and training at wagon lines - usual harassing fire carried out by A,D,and C/106.	
	29th		Enemy artillery active. Forward section of D/106 shelled twice during the day by 4.2". How - A/106 registers zero line. D/106 cut wire in H.3.c.usual harassing fire carried out during night.	
	30th	h	At 6.15.am.forward sections A, C, and D/106 assist 15th Division in raid on enemy's trenches. D/106 shoot at movement in N.5.c. The day was quiet and little individual movement seen. Usual H.F.carried out by night.	

Lt.Col.R.F.A.
Commanding 106th Brigade R.F.A.

Appx 38

WAR DIARY.   106th Brigade, R.F.A.

October, 1918.

MAROC	1st. Oct.	Enemy artillery very quiet, only one important shoot. 2 – 5.9" Hows. carry out destructive shoot on avens in M.5.a.& c. and M.5.central about 200 rounds fired. Forward Sections of D/106 engage small parties in N.11.a. D/106 cut wire in H.33.c. & N.3aa. During night 470 rounds were expended in Harassing fire.
QUARRIES M.6.a.80.30.	2nd. "	24th Divisional Infantry relieved by 58th Division. 106th Brigade,R.F.A. now support 174th Infantry Bde. Enemy reported to have fallen back from their forward positions. At 1430 hours H.Q. move forward to QUARRIES in M.6.a.8.3. Night 2nd & 3rd. A/106 move guns forward to M.1.c.6.5.; B/106 move 6 guns to M.1.c. 90.20.—C/106 to M.6.b.10.35.— D/106 move 4 Hows. to M.1.d.10.32. 2 Hows. D/106 remain in position at M.6.a.63.90.
HYTHE TUNNELS	3rd. "	At 0545 hours All Batteries, 106th Brigade,R.F.A. assist 174th Infantry Brigade to establish themselves on second bound viz:— line of railway from H.29.d.2.3. Southwards to N.5.a.5.3. Line established at 1100 hours H.Q./106 move forward to HYTHE TUNNELS at H.32.c.6.5. Night 3rd/4th. C/106 move 6 guns forward N.2.a.32.20. D/106 move 2 Hows. from N.6.a.53.90. to about N.2.a.3.2. All Batteries harass enemy M.Gs., Roads & tracks during the night.
"	4th. "	106th Brigade harass enemy M.Gs. roads and tracks by day and night. Brigade O.P. established in N.29.d.15.30 B/106 move section forward to H.33.d.1.9. H.Q. & Battery wagon lines move forward to MAROC.
"	5th. "	A/106 move section forward to N.3.a.85.50. D/106 move forward section from N.2.a.?.2. to GRAVEL PT. at H. 32.d.
"	6th. "	Enemy artillery quiet — A, B, C & D/106 assist in demonstration on 15th Divisional front. During night A, C & D/106th Brigade & B/48 A.F.A. Brigade expend 600 rounds in Harassing fire. B/106 personnel and guns withdraw to wagon line for rest and training on relief by B/48 A.F.A.
"	7th. "	Day quiet, little hostile artillery fire. Batteries 106th Brigade carry out several destructive shoots on houses where M.Gs. are reported to be active, and during night harass roads and tracks.
"	8th. "	Enemy artillery very quiet. Our artillery during the day carry out destructive shoots on houses in ANNAY and at night harass M.Gs.,tracks,roads etc. 175th Infantry Brigade relieve 174th Infantry Brigade.
"	9th. "	Day quiet as far as hostile fire is concerned. Our artillery continue aggressive destructive shoots on houses sheltering hostile M.Gs. From 1745 hours to 1830hours Batteries 106th Brigade assist Centre Group in small attack on LOISON. LT.COL.J.C.WALCH, D.S.O. attends C.R.A's Conference at H.Q. Centre Group. All Batteries carry out vigorous harassing fire on roads, tracks and M.Gs. throughout the night. O.P. established at H.27.c.55.10. On night 9th/10th. A/106 move one section from their main position to forward position at N.3.a.9.4. One section D/106 move forward from main position to GRAVEL PITS at H.32.d.3.4.
"	10th. "	Situation Quiet: little hostile artillery fire during the day. At night, enemy harass roads and tracks in N.3.a & b. During night D/106 cut wire in H.33.a. C & D/106 assist Centre Group by firing on N.12.a & b. During night. A, C & D/106 harass roads and tracks. B/106 personnel and guns return from rest and training and occupy positions in H.33.c.10.80., 2 sections about N.3.d.4.3.
"	11th. "	During day enemy artillery quiet except for slight shelling of DYNAMITE ROAD. 378th and 379th Batteries 169th Brigade,R.F.A. come into action in CITE ST. AUGUSTE and are attached to Left Group under LT.COL.J.C. WALCH, D.S.O.— C/106 fire on Water Tower area in ANNAY. D/106 keep up a vigorous harassing fire on roads and tracks east of ANNAY. Batteries 106th Brigade R.F.A. with 378th and 379th Batteries DYNAMITE ROAD and roads in CITE ST. AUGUSTE continuously throughout the night.

Signed, Lt-Col. 106 Brigade R.F.A.

WAR DIARY.   106th Brigade, R.F.A.

October, 1918.

HYTHE FUNNELS	12TH. Oct.	Infantry move forward taking Canal maze in morning. ANNAY occupied by 10th LONDON REGT. 1700 hours. Responsibility for covering the Left Group front passes to 169th Brigade,R.F.A. under command of LT.COL. HANWAY. Batteries and Brigade H.Q.106th Brigade,R.F.A. move back at dusk to Wagon lines
MAROC.	13th. "	Hostile artillery inactive until evening when VENDIN is heavily shelled. Brigade at wagon lines in MAROC. Situation quiet.
ECURIE.	14th. "	Brigades marches 0635 hours to ECURIE via BULLY GRENAY, AIX NOULETTE, SOUCHEZ, arriving 1030 hours Personnel billeted in huts.
GUEMAPPE.	15th. "	Brigade marches 0715 hours to GUEMAPPE via ST. CATHERINE - ARRAS arriving 1150 hours. Batteries bivouac on sloping ground ½ mile S.E. of village.
CAMBRAI R.	16th. "	Brigade marches 0845 hours to CAMBRAI via main ARRAS - CAMBRAI ROAD arriving 1400 hours. A & B Batteries billeted in RUE DE LA LIBERTE, C & D Batteries and H.Q. in the Cavalry Barracks.

W. [signature]
Lt-Col. R.F.A.
Comdg. 106 Brigade R.F.A.

WAR DIARY.

106th Brigade, R.F.A.

October, 1918.

Cambrai	17.10.18.	106th Brigade, R.F.A. at CAMBRAI in same billets. C.O., Adjt., B.C.'s and one subaltern Officer per battery visit the ST.AUBERT area by lorry to reconnoitre positions, leaving at 1000 and returning at 1530. Fine; very misty.
	18.10.19.	106th Brigade,R.F.A. marches from CAMBRAI to wagon lines at RIEUX, proceeding by the LE CATEAU road for the first 2 miles, then south and east along the SOLESMES road. Order of march "D","A", "B","C",H.Q., "D" battery moving at 0800 and arriving at 1045. Locations (51 A.):- H.W. AVESNES-LES-AUBERT; "C". U28a5055, H.-W.L. U28a7257 ; "A". W.L. U28a7257 ; "B". W.L. U20c2700 ; "C".W.L. U20c2007; "D". W.L. U25b4575. Guns are moved during the afternoon to cover the SELLE river between HAUSSY and SAULZOIR ; "A"V15d25; "B" V15central; "C" V15d32; "D" V15d80. Detachments return to W.L. for the night. Considerable artillery activity on both sides. Ammunition taken up by wagon with assistance from D.A.C. Fine; misty during the morning; "C" Casualties ; "C" - 4 O.Rs. wounded, "D" - 1 O.R. wounded.
AVESNES.	19.10.18.	Ammunition at positions made up to 400 per 18-pr. and 300 per How. Barrage tables and orders issued at conference of B.C.'s at Bde. H.Q. at 1400. At 1700 Bde. H.Q. moves to the Sucrerie U24d87. Battery positions manned in the evening. Artillery very active again on both sides. Misty in morning, clearing later; some fine rain. Casualties ; "B" - 1 OR. killed, 4 ORs.wounded, H.Q.-R. missing.
ST.AUBERT.	20.10.18.	106th Bde. fires in support of attack by 57th. and 58th. Inf. Brigades between 0200 and 0510. Attack successful, and line VERCHAIN - MAISON DRUON reached. C.O. and B.C.'s reconnoitre forward positions during morning and batteries move up to them via HAUSSY at 1400. Locations:- "A" P36a 80; "B" P36d05; "C". P26d78; "D" V6b17; H.Q. established in HAUSSY at 1800. Considerable hostile artillery activity, chiefly 15 cm. on HAUSSY, and field artillery over forward areas. Misty; steady rain during afternoon. Casualties: "H.Q. - 1 O.R. wounded, "A" - 4 O.R.s wounded.
HAUSSY	21.10.18.	No further change in situation. Hostile artillery still very active on same localities. Much rain. O.P. at P30d91. Casualties; "A" Lieut G.W.C.Selwyn wounded; "D" - 1 O.R. wounded.
H.U Y	22.10.18.	Batteries forthwith to be silent except for S.O.S. "B" battery moves Left Section to P3005005 to be under voice control of Liaison Officer at Batt. H.Q. P36a36. "C" Battery moves one gun to P24d9510 for anti-tank purposes. Hostile artillery slightly decreased.Rain. Casualties; "H.Q." 1 O.R. wounded, "A" - 1 O.R. wounded, "D" - 3 O.Rs. wounded.
HAUSSY.	23.10.18.	No change in situation. 106th Bde. takes part in a short creeping barrage for local operation by right Battr. to improve position between 1600 and 1645. Fine,@older,misty.
HAUSSY.	24.10.18.	106th Bde. fires barrage in support of general attack between 0300 and 0730. Line advanced nearly to final objective (3000 yards) on flanks, but held up in centre by M.G. fire from VENDEGIES. Swinging barrage fired between 1645 - 1705 to encircle VENDEGIES. Operation only partly successful. Hostile atillery fire very slight all day. Fine.

WAR DIARY

106th Brigade, R.F.A.
October, 1918.

HAUSSY. 25.10.18.
0830. 106th Bde. detailed for Advanced Guard artillery on information that enemy is retiring. 1000. Batteries begin to move forward. (anti-tank gun and liaison section rejoining their batteries,) and come into action between BERMERAIN and ARTRES at noon, marching via MAISON BLEUE and ST.MARTIN. Locations :- "A" Q10b46 ; "B" Q10b16; "C" Q4d40 ; "D" Q10a43; H.Q. Q15c69. Wagon Lines move forward during afternoon to :- "A" Q15d16; "B" Q.16c58, "C" Q21b70, "D" Q15d 69, "B" Q22a39. 106th Bde. fires barrage 1600 to 1620 in support of local operations between SEPMERIES and ARTRES, to be followed by observed shooting if successful. Darkness prevents completion of operation. Slight hostile field artillery activity, with a few H.V. on BERMERAIN. Fine till evening when fine rain falls.

BERMERAIN. 26.10.18.
No operations. Hostile artillery activity much increased, with salvoes of 77 mm. and deliberate 15 cm. shoots. Fine.

BERMERAIN. 27.10.18.
106th Bde. fires between 0830 and 0900 in support of operation E. of ARTRES. Operation only partly successful. During the morning, observed shooting is carried out on scattered parties of infantry E. of ARTRES, and in and E. of MAROSCHES. Aeroplane S.O.S. in M24 is responded to at 1320. Infantry situation vague during afternoon. Hostile artillery fairly active, especially with 77 mm. In early morning. Fine till 1600, then showers.

BERMERAIN. 28.10.18
"A", "B" and "C" established forward sections at K5c22, K34d63, K24d87 respectively. Hostile artillery activity still considerable, chiefly 15 cm. and H.V. 106th Bde. carries out harassing fire. Fine.

BERMERAIN 29.10.18
"D" established forward section. Hostile artillery activity. Hostile artillery activity, slightly less but several 15 cm. and 24 cm. shoots were carried out and 10 cm. guns were active at night. Fine.Casualties - "D" 1 O.R. Wounded.

BERMERAIN.30.10.18.
No operations. Hostile artillery very active all day and increased at night with 10 cm. guns. 24 cm. how. firing on brigade area located north of JENLAIN.Casualties. "C" - 4 O.Rs. wounded.

ERMERAIN. 31.10.18.
No operations. Hostile artillery shelling slight. Light rain all day with mist. Casualties "A" - 1 O.R. wounded, "B" - 1 .O.R. wounded, "C" - 1 O.R. wounded.

Lt.-Col. R.F.A.
Comdg. 106 Brigade R.F.A.

106TH BRIGADE, R.F.A.

WAR DIARY

INTELLIGENCE SUMMARY.

NOVEMBER, 1918.

Army Form C. 2118.

Place	Date	Hour	Summary of Events and Information	Remarks and references to Appendices
BERMERAIN	1st		106th Bde.,R.F.A.,88th Bde.,R.F.A., and 107th Bde.,R.F.A., constitute Left Group,61st D.A.,under command of Brig.Gen. H.G.LLOYD. From 0515 to 0825 hours 106 Bde.R.F.A. fire barrage supporting 182nd and 183rd Inf.Bdes.of 61st Divn. in attack for capture of villages of MARESCHES and PRESEAU and the high ground in L.20 and L.26 central (Ref.Sheet 51A 1/40,000). All objectives reach at 1045 hours. Counter attack developes. Enemy use tanks. 106th Bde.R.F.A.fire S.O.S.for an hour on the final protective barrage. Our Infantry slightly pressed back. At 1700 hours line runs L.19.c., L.19.a.,K.18.d.,(Ref.Sheet 51A 1/40,000). At 1800 hours Lt.Col. J.C.WALCH,D.S.O.,with H.Q.106th Bde.R.F.A. takes over command of Left Group from Brig.Gen. H.G.LLOYD & H.Q. 24th D.A. at Q.4.c.7.4. (Sheet 51A 1/40,000), in sunken road at LA JUSTICE. From 1930 to 2030 hours Left Group fire barrage to retake lost ground South of PRESEAU. Operation only partially successful. Casualties (106th Bde. R.F.A.) during day – 2 O.Rs.killed – 5 O.Rs.wounded.	
LA JUSTICE	2nd		At 0530 hours the Artillery covering 61st Divnl.Front is re-grouped. Lt.Col. J.C.WALCH,D.S.O., with H.Q.106th Bde.R.F.A. takes command of Main Group consisting of 106th Bde.R.F.A.,107th Bde. R.F.A.,306th Bde.R.F.A.,307th Bde.R.F.A.,86th Bde.R.F.A.,and 87th Bde.R.F.A. At 0630 hours 106th, 107th,and 88th Bdes.R.F.A. repeated the barrage fired from 1930 to 2030 hours on 1st inst.,in support of further attack to retake lost ground. Operation successful. During morning batteries of 106th Bde.move forward to positions near LES MARAIS (co-ordinates given below). Day quiet and no further Infantry action takes place. Hostile artillery activity slight. Batteries of Main Group harass enemy during night. Location of batteries as follows :- A/87 – K.36.a.2.3., B/87 – K.36.c.3.8., C/87 – K.36.a.3.8., D/87 – K.35.d.6.9., A/88 – K.23.c.7.2., B/88 K.23.c.1.4., C/88 – K.23.c.3.8., D/88 – K.29.d.2.8., A/106 – K.36.b.4.5., B/106 – K.36.b.4.7., C/106 – K.36.b.7.2., D/106 – K.36.b.4.8. Batteries of 107th Bde. in vicinity of ARTRES in K.29.b.and K.30.b.& c.(Ref.Sheet 51A 1/40,000). Casualties during day – 2 O.Rs.wounded.	
SEPMERIES	3rd		At 0900 hours 106th Bde.H.Q. moves to Chateau in SEPMERIES Q.6.b.3.5. At 1000 hours 61st Div.Arty. is again re-grouped. Lt.Col. J.C.WALCH,D.S.O.with H.Q.106th Bde.R.F.A. assumes command of Left Group consisting of 106th Bde.R.F.A. and 107th Bde.RFA. The 306th and 307th Bdes.R.F.A.pass to Right Group under Lt.Col. E.W.S.BROOKE, and 86th and 87th Bdes.R.F.A. rejoin 19th Div.Arty. One Section of 122nd Heavy Battery is attached to Left Group. 24th Divisional Infantry relieve 61st Divisional Infantry. Casualties during day – 2 O.Rs.wounded.	
JENLAIN.	4th		At 0500 hours H.Q.106th Bde.R.F.A.moves forward and joins the 73rd Inf.Bde.H.Q. in village of MARESCHES at L.26.c.2.6. At 0600 hours H.Q.106th Bde.R.F.A. move forward with 73rd Inf.Bde.H.Q. to sunken road in L.21.c.6.0. Batteries 106th Bde.R.F.A.move forward and take up positions before dawn as follows ;- A/106 & B/106 in L.27.c.central., C/106 in L.26.c.7.3., and D/106 in L.27.c.c.2. (Ref.Sheet 51A 1/40,000). At 0500 hours 107th Bde.R.F.A. leave Left Group and come/under direct orders of 24th Div.Arty.	

Army Form C. 2118.

WAR DIARY
106TH BRIGADE, R.F.A.
or
INTELLIGENCE SUMMARY
NOVEMBER, 1918.

(Erase heading not required.)

Instructions regarding War Diaries and Intelligence Summaries are contained in F.S. Regs., Part II. and the Staff Manual respectively. Title pages will be prepared in manuscript.

Place	Date	Hour	Summary of Events and Information	Remarks and references to Appendices
JENLAIN	4th (cont)		At 0630 hours 73rd Inf.Bde.commences advance from the main JENLAIN – LE QUESNOY Road. 106th Bde. in close support. All Batteries 106th Bde.R.F.A.(less Forward Sections attached to Battalions) fire barrage in support of Infantry attack. At 0715 hours our Infantry established on GREEN LINE approx; G.14.c.8.0.– G.2 O.a.8.0.– G.20.d.6.0.– G.27.d.0.0. At 0800 hours batteries of 106th Bde. R.F.A. advance to positions of observation, A/106 in Xxxxxxxxx L.29.c.3.5., B/106 in L.28.b.7.0., C/106 in L.28.d.5.3., D/106 in L.29.c.7.5. At 0815 hours H.Q.106th Bde.R.F.A.move forward with H.Q.73rd Inf.Bde. to L.29.a.2.2. Detached Sections of A/106, B/106, & D/106 take up positions about L.22.c.& L.28.c.before dawn and come under direct orders of the Battn.Commanders of the 73rd I.B. moving forward in close touch with the advancing infantry to positions near BRICKSTACKS in G.19.d. At 1200 hours Infantry reported to be rapidly advancing towards 3rd objective (RED LINE) G.22.b.4.5.– G.28.b.8.0.– G.29.c.3.0. 306th & 307th Bdes.R.F.A.under command of Lt.Col.E.W.S.BROOKE form Main Group of Artillery supporting 73rd I.B. and keep in touch with H.Q.106th Bde.R.F.A. & 73rd I.B. At 1600 hours H.Q.106th Bde.R.F.A.advance to JENLAIN and establish H.Q.at L.17.d.5.2. At 1800 hours our Infantry reach 3rd objective (RED LINE) including WARGNIES-LE-GRAND and WARGNIES-LE-PETIT. Casualties 106th Bde.R.F.A.during day – Lieut.(A/Major)H.HOBDAY,D.S.O.,M.C.,B/106,slight wound, remains at duty – Lieut.J.R.TUFFLEY,B/106,slight wound,remains at duty – 2/Lt.A.G.ALLAN,B/106, wounded and goes to hospital – 1 O.R.killed – 21 O.Rs.wounded. D/106, D/c06, and Section of 122nd Heavy Battery harass roads during night.	
LA BOIS CRETTE R	5th		At 0500 hours 17th I.B.relieve 73rd I.B.as Advance Guard, and continue to advance. At 0500 hours H.Q.106th Bde.R.F.A.move forward to join the H.Q.17th I.B.at house on main JENLAIN – BAVAY Road at L.20.b.5.0.(Ref.Sheet 51A 1/40,000). 307th Bde.move to positions about G.19.d.before dawn and 106th & 306th Bdes.follow to G.25.b.& G.26.c.respectively immediately after. Forward Sections A, B, & D/106 advance in close touch with the 8th Queens' & 1st Royal Fusiliers to G.25.b.& G.29.a. and later to the following positions:– A/106 H.20.c.3.1. – B/106 H.19.d.8.3. – D/106 H.25.c. Enemy continue to withdraw. At 1100 hours H.Q.106th Bde.& H.Q.17th I.B.advance along main BAVAI Road to the Halt at G.22.d.0.2. Batteries 106th Bde. move to positions in G.29.a.& b. Main Group follows. At 1230 hours H.Q.106th Bde.R.F.A.advances with H.Q.17th I.B. to LA BOIS CRETTE and opens H.Q.at G.30.a.9.4.(Sheet 51A 1/40,000). C/106 and D/106 advance to positions at G.29.d.5.8. and G.30.central respectively. A/106 located at G.29.a.3.5., B/106 at G.29.c.3.2.(Sheet 51A 1/40,000). At 1415 to 1425 hours all Batteries 106th Bde.R.F.A. fire barrage in support of Infantry attack on high ground in H.21.a.and H.15.c. At 1530 C/106 send Sections to relieve Forward Sections of A.& B/106 at H.20.c.3.1.& H.19.d.8.3., remaining subsection of C/106 in action is attached to B/106. At 1530 hours A,B,& D/106 move forward to positions at H.19.c.6.2. – H.25.c.5.5.– & H.25.c.4.7. respectively. Main Group advances to positions of observation. Section of 122nd Heavy Battery comes	

Army Form C. 2118.

WAR DIARY

106 TH BRIGADE, R.F.A.

NOVEMBER, 1918.

of

INTELLIGENCE SUMMARY.

(Erase heading not required.)

Instructions regarding War Diaries and Intelligence Summaries are contained in F. S. Regs., Part II. and the Staff Manual respectively. Title pages will be prepared in manuscript.

Place	Date	Hour	Summary of Events and Information	Remarks and references to Appendices
LA BOIS CRETTE.	5th		into action at G.29.b.1.6. At 2000 hours 106th, 306th,& 307th Bdes.R.F.A. fire barrage in support of Infantry attack on high ground in H.28.a.& c. Attack successful. During night 106th, 306th,& 307th Bdes.R.F.A. harass roads. Casualties in 106th Bde.R.F.A. - 8 O.Rs.wounded.	
LA BOIS CRETTE.	6th		At 0600 1st Battn.R.F. attack high ground in H.17.& H.23. 106th, 306th,& 307th Bdes.R.F.A.support attack by creeping barrage from 0600 to 0639 hours. Section 122nd Heavy Battery assists by firing on main BAVAY Road, the slopes north of it, and the Railway running through H.22.d.and H.29.a.& b. Objectives not reached. Our Infantry reported to have crossed River HOGNEAU in G.16.c. at 1100 hours. Detached Sections of C/106 move forward in close support of Inf.Battn. to H.21.a.2.3.& H.27.d.7.3. and engage enemy parties on high ground E. of River HOGNEAU. At 1130 hours H.Q.106th Bde.R.F.A. move forward to H.20.d.8.8.on Main BAVAY Road near Railway Crossing. At 1230 hours B & D/106 fire for 20 minutes on area H.16.b.5.5.- H.17.a.5.5.- H.23.a.0.5.- H.22.b.5.5.in support of local advance. During afternoon H.Q.and Batteries 107th Bde.R.F.A. moves into action preparatory to taking over from 106th Bde.R.F.A.as Brigade in close support. Whilst relief is in progress orders received for 106th Brigade R.F.A.to remain in action preparatory to firing barrage in support of attack next morning. H.Q.107th Bde.R.F.A.takes over command of Adv.Guard Artillery at 1730 hours. Forward Sections C/106 withdraw at dusk and come into action as a 4-gun battery at H.25.c.3.3. At 1800 hours H.Q.106th Bde. R.F.A. move to G.24.c.1.4. Enemy shelling heavy throughout day on H.20.& H.21. Casualties 106th Bde. R.F.A. - 12 O.Rs.wounded.	
LA BOIS	7th		At 0600 to 0740 hours all batteries 106th Bde.R.F.A.fire creeping barrage in support of Infantry attack on high ground East of the HOGNEAU river. Attack successful - all objectives reached. On completion of the barrage the 107th Bde.R.F.A.becomes the Brigade in close support, of the Advance Guard. Batteries of 106th Bde.R.F.A. withdraw to rest in their Wagon Lines. Casualties - 1 O.R.wounded.	
LE LOUVION	8th		At 1230 hours H.Q.& Batteries 106th Bde.R.F.A.march to Billets in LE LOUVION as follows:- H.Q.106th Bde.R.F.A.at I.22.d.7.6. - A/106 at I.22.c.2.4. - B/106 at I.29.b.2.8. - C/106 at I.22.d.2.7.- D/106 at I.22.d.9.5. Casualties - 1 O.R.wounded.	
LES GUEULARDS (FEIGNIES)	9th		106th Bde.R.F.A. is detailed to take over duties of Bde.in close support of Advance Guard and joins 73rd Inf.Bde.H.Q.in LA LONGUEVILLE (I.36.a.9.9.)at 0600 hours. At 0730 hours H.Q.73rd Inf.Bde.and H.Q.,106th Bde.R.F.A.move forward to J.20.central. At 0730 C/106 send forward two sections in close support of Infantry - one section is attached to 7th Northants Regt, and the other to the 9th Royal Sussex. Remainder of batteries 106th Bde.R.F.A.move out of billets in LE LOUVION and rendezvous 0800 hours with head of column at cross roads at J.25.c.6.9. Advance continues at 0800 hours the final objective being the line of the MONS - MAUBERGE Road and the high ground immediately East of it. At 0830 A, B, & D/106 move to positions of readiness about J.15.c. At 0900 H.Q.106th Bde.R.P.A. move forward with 73rd Inf. Bde.H.Q.to LES VENTS (J.36.a.6.7.). Battery Commanders of A,B,& D/106	

Army Form C. 2118.

WAR DIARY - NOVEMBER, 1918.
INTELLIGENCE SUMMARY.

106TH BRIGADE, R.F.A.

Instructions regarding War Diaries and Intelligence Summaries are contained in F. S. Regs., Part II. and the Staff Manual respectively. Title pages will be prepared in manuscript.

(Erase heading not required.)

Place	Date	Hour	Summary of Events and Information	Remarks and references to Appendices
LES GUEULARDS (FEIGNIES)	9th (cont.)		reconnoitre positions about K.13. At 1200 hours our Infantry reach MONS-MAUBERGE Road in K.3-9-15-21-27. Patrols push out further East of this line, but no further general advance takes place. At 1300 hours A, B, & D/106 come into action at K.13.a.8.8.- K.13.b.0.7.4 K.7.c.8.0.- all in vicinity of ROTELEUX FME. At 1300 hours H.Q.106th Bde.,R.F.A.moves to LES GUEULARDS (J.17.b.7.1.) Right Section C/106 in close support of Infantry follow up retreating enemy, and come into action at 1300 hours in K.2.d.2.7. At 1530 hours move forward to position at K.5.b.3.5. and fire on enemy in E.18.c. Left Section C/106 follow up Infantry and come into action at FORT SIHERON (K.14.a.) and engage enemy party and Machine Guns on MONS-MAUBERGE Road. Later advance to position at FORT des SART (K.9.d.) and fire on enemy in OUVRAGE de la SALMAGNE.	
LEVEAU (FEIGNIES)	10th		At 1800 hours H.Q.106th Brigade moves to LEVEAU (J.30.a.7.3.). All Bde.,R.F.A.remain in positions of yesterday. No Infantry action takes place and Batteries 106th Bde.,R.F.A.remain silent throughout the day. Right Section C/106 in close support of Infantry fire on enemy in E.18.c.	
LEVEAU (FEIGNIES)	11th		At 0915 hours official information received that an armistice had been signed between the Allies and enemy, and orders to "cease fire" at 1100 hours to-day. Batteries stand fast in present positions. At 1600 20th Divisional Infantry relieve 24th Divisional Infantry. Artillery covering 20th Divisional Front re-grouped as follows:- Left Group - 20th D.A. Right Group - 24th D.A. 19th and 61st D.As.in "positions of readiness" in rear. Forward Sections of C/106 withdraw and come into action as a Battery in J.16.b.	
FEIGNES. (GUISIAN BRAY)	12th	h	Lt.Col. J.C.WALCH,D.S.O.proceeds on leave to England. Major W.K.WELSH,M.C., C/106 takes command of 106th Brigade,R.F.A. At 1600 hours,H.Q.106th Bde.R.F.A.moves to GUISIAN BRAY (FEIGNIES) J.22.a.8.8.	
= do = = do = = do = = do = ETH	13th) 14th) 15th) 16th) 17th	h	Situation quiet and nothing of importance happened.	
ESCAUDAIN.	18th.		At 0945 hours H.Q.and Batteries 106th Bde.R.F.A.withdraw from action and march to ETH via BAVAY - St.WAAST-LES-BAVAY - LA FLAMENGRIE and BRY. At 1430 hours H.Q.106th Bde.R.F.A.established in Chateau at ETH.	
LEWARDE.	19th.		At 0745 H.Q.and Batteries 106th Bde.R.F.A.march to ESCAUDAIN via MARLEY - VALENCIENNTS - LA SENTINELLE - ROUVIGNIES - and DENAIN. H.Q.106th Bde.R.F.A.established in ESCAUDAIN at 1230 hours. At 0900 H.Q.and Batteries 106th Brigade R.F.A.march to LEWARDE via ABSCON - AMICHE and AUBERCHICOURT. H.Q.106th Bde.R.F.A.established in LEWARDE at 1230 hours.	
LEWARDE. = do = = do =	20th.) 21st.) 22nd.)		H.Q.and Batteries 106th Bde.,R.F.A. at rest in Billets in LEWARDE.	

Army Form C. 2118.

106TH BRIGADE, R.F.A.

WAR DIARY — NOVEMBER, 1918.

or INTELLIGENCE SUMMARY.

(Erase heading not required.)

Instructions regarding War Diaries and Intelligence Summaries are contained in F. S. Regs., Part II. and the Staff Manual respectively. Title pages will be prepared in manuscript.

Place	Date	Hour	Summary of Events and Information	Remarks and references to Appendices
LEWARDE.	23rd)			
- do -	24th)			
- do -	25th)	d	H.Q.and Batteries 106th Bde.,R.F.A. at rest in Billets in LEWARDE.	
- do -	26th)			
BERTINQUESME 27th (ROSULT)			At 0745 hours H.Q.and Batteries 106th Bde.R.F.A. march from Billets in LEWARDE to Billets in BERTINQUESME and RUE BALORY area via MONTIGNY - PEQUENCOURT - MARCHIENNES (VILLE) - BOUVIGNY - BEUVRY and ROSULT arriving at 1230 hours (Ref.Sheet 12 VALENCIENNE 1/100,000). H.Q.and Batteries 106th Bde.R.F.A.take over Billets vacated by H.Q.and Batteries of 62nd Bde.R.F.A. located as follows:— H.Q.at I.33.a.3.8.— A/106 I.26.d.8.2.— B/106 H.36.c.6.2.— C/106 H.36.c.5.5.— D/106 I.32.b.3.7. (Ref.Sheet 44 1/40,000).	
- do -	28th)			
- do -	29th)		H.Q.and Batteries 106th Bde.R.F.A. in rest billets. Nothing of importance happens.	
- do -	30th)			

Capt & Adj
Major.R.F.A.
Commanding, 106th Brigade, R.F.A.

Army Form C. 2118.

WAR DIARY
or
INTELLIGENCE SUMMARY
(Erase heading not required.)

106TH. BRIGADE, R.F.A.   **DECEMBER 1918.**

Instructions regarding War Diaries and Intelligence Summaries are contained in F.S. Regs., Part II. and the Staff Manual respectively. Title Pages will be prepared in manuscript.

Vol 40

Place	Date	Hour	Summary of Events and Information	Remarks and references to Appendices
BERTINQUESME ROSULT.	1		H.Q. and Batteries 106th Bde., R.F.A. in rest billets. Nothing of importance happens.	
	2		Batteries assist farmers in carrying crops.	
	3		do.	
	4		do.	
	5		do.	
	6		do.	
	7		Col. J.C. WALCH, D.S.O., leaves for England to attend Senior Officer's Course. Command 106th. Bde., R.F.A. passes to Major H. MOBDAY, D.S.O., M.C.; of B/106.	
	8		H.Q. and Batteries of 106th Bde., R.F.A. in rest billets. Nothing of importance happens.	
	9		Batteries assist farmers in carrying crops.	
	10		H.Q. and Batteries in rest billets. Partial demobilization commences. First draft of miners leave for England. Batteries continue to assist farmers.	
	11		Nothing of importance happens. Assistance to farmers continues.	
	12		do.	
	13		do.	
	14		do.	
	15		do.	
	16		Major W.M. WELSH, M.C., takes over Command of 106th Bde. Major H. MOBDAY, D.S.O., M.C., resumes Command B/106. Assistance to farmers continues.	
	17		Nothing of importance happens. Farming work continues.	
	18		At 1000 hours H.Q. & Batteries 106th. Bde., R.F.A. march from billets in BERTINQUESME and RUE BALORY area (ROSULT) to permanent billets in ANTOING (near TOURNAI), via RUMEGIES, RONGY, and MOLLAIN. Major W.M. WELSH, M.C. goes on leave - Major H. MOBDAY, D.S.O., M.C., takes over Command 106th Bde., R.F.A.	
	19		Nothing of importance happens.	
	20/24		Batteries engaged in training and assisting farmers in carrying in crops.	
	25		Christmas dinners arranged by all batteries for men. Nothing of importance happens.	
	26/29		Batteries engaged in training and assisting farmers in carrying in crops.	
	30		Col. J.C. WALCH, D.S.O. returns from England. Major H. MOBDAY, D.S.O., M.C., resumes command B/106. Training and farming work continues.	
	31		Batteries engaged in training and farming work.	

Lieut.-Colonel, R.F.A.,
Commanding 106th Brigade, R.F.A.,

Army Form C. 2118.

WAR DIARY
or
INTELLIGENCE SUMMARY
(Erase heading not required.)

106TH BRIGADE, R.F.A.
JANUARY, 1919.

Place	Date	Hour	Summary of Events and Information	Remarks and references to Appendices
ANTOING.	1st		H.Q. and Batteries 106th Bde.,R.F.A. in billets. Nothing of Importance happens.	
	2nd			
	3rd			
	4th		Batteries assist farmers by lending their animals.	
	5th		Lt.R.P.BAXTER,R.F.A. appointed Adjutant vice A/Capt.R.WILMOT, to England for Ordnance Course.	
	6th			
	7th			
	8th		Batteries engaged in helping farmers, and training.	
	9th			
	10th			
	11th			
	12th		Numbers despatched for demobilization - 1 Other Rank.	
	13th		Usual Routine.	
	14th			
	15th		Numbers despatched for demobilization - 3 Other Ranks.	
	16th		93 Mules proceeded to COURTRAI for sale.	
	17th		Usual routine.	
	18th		Numbers despatched for demobilization - 7 Other Ranks.	
	19th		- do - - do - - do - - 14 - do - 11	
	20th		- do - - do - - do - - 1 Officer and 10 Other Ranks.	
	21st		Usual routine.	
	22nd			
	23rd			
	24th		Numbers despatched for demobilization - 21 Other Ranks.	
	25th	h	- do - - do - - do - - 13 Other Ranks.	
	26th		- do - - do - - do - - 17 Other Ranks.	
	27th		- do - - do - - do - - 1 Officer and 22 Other Ranks.	
	28th			
	29th		Usual Routine.	
	30th			
	31st			

Lt.Col.,R.F.A.,
Commanding, 106th Brigade, R.F.A.

APPENDIX TO WAR DIARY OF 106TH BRIGADE, R.F.A., FOR MONTH ENDING 31ST JANUARY, 1919.

The 106th Brigade, R.F.A. Inter-Section Football Competition was played off during the month. The draw and results are given below:-

First Round.	Second Round	Semi-Finals.	Finals.	Winners.
Centre Sectn. C/106.				
Bye.	Centre Sectn. C/106. versus	Centre Sectn. C/106.		
Centre Sectn. A/106 versus Left Sectn. D/106.	Left Sectn. D/106.			
Right Sectn. D/106. versus Right Sectn. B/106.	Right Sectn. B/106 versus Left Sectn. B/106	Left Sectn. B/106.	Left Sectn. B/106.	
Brigade Headquarters versus Left Sectn. B/106.				Left Section. B/106th Bde. RFA.
Left Sectn. C/106.			versus	
Bye	Left Sectn. C/106. versus Right Sectn. C/106.	Left Sectn. C/106.		
Centre Sectn. D/106. versus Right Sectn. C/106.			Left Sectn. A/106.	
Right Sectn. A/106. versus Left Sectn. A/106.	Left Sectn. A/106. versus Centre Sectn. B/106.	Left Sectn. A/106.		
Centre Sectn. B/106.				
Bye.				

APPENDIX TO WAR DIARY OF 106TH BRIGADE, R.F.A. FOR MONTH OF JANUARY, 1919.

The 24th Divisional Artillery Football Competition was commenced during the month, and the following matches were played by Batteries of the 106th Brigade, R.F.A.

Teams.	Scores.
A/106 versus B/106th Bde., R.F.A.	2 - 2.
A/106 versus A/48th Army Bde., R.F.A.	1 - 1.
A/106 versus No.1 Section, 24th D.A.C.	0 - 6.
B/106 versus No.1 Section, 24th D.A.C.	3 - 0.
B/106 versus No.3 Section, 24th D.A.C.	5 - 4.
B/106 versus A/48th Bde., R.F.A.	6 - 2.
C/106 versus B/107th Bde., R.F.A.	1 - 1.
C/106th V C/48th Army Bde., R.F.A.	0 - 3.
C/106 versus No.2 Section, 24th D.A.C.	1 - 3.
C/106 versus D/107th Bde., R.F.A.	1 - 1.
C/106 versus 194th Coy., A.S.C.	1 - 3.
D/106 versus 24th Divisional Artillery H.Q.	0 - 2.
D/106 versus No.3 Section, 24th D.A.C.	1 - 3.
D/106 versus B/48th Army Bde., R.F.A.	2 - 0.
D/106 versus 194th Coy., A.S.C.	0 - 0.

Army Form C. 2118.

WAR DIARY 106TH BRIGADE R.F.A.

INTELLIGENCE SUMMARY

FEBRUARY 1919

(Erase heading not required.)

Instructions regarding War Diaries and Intelligence Summaries are contained in F.S. Regs., Part II. and the Staff Manual respectively. Title pages will be prepared in manuscript.

Place	Date	Hour	Summary of Events and Information	Remarks and references to Appendices
ANTOING	1st		Brigade in billets at ANTOING	
	2nd		Allotments for demobilization 16 O.Rs. }	
	3rd		" " " 10 Officer 18 O.Rs } Usual Routine.	
			" " " 21 O.Rs. }	
	4th		49 Z Horses for sale at PONT au MARCQ	
	5th		Usual Routine	
	6th		Allotment for demobilization 1 Officer 23 O.Rs	
	7th		" " " 10 O.Rs.	
	8th		" " " 9 O.Rs. 50 Y Horses to Base.	
	9th		Usual Routine	
	10th		" "	
	11th		" "	
	12th		" "	
	13th		" "	
	14th		" "	
	15th		" "	
	16th		" "	
	17th		" "	
	18th		" "	
	19th		" "	
	20th		" "	
	21st		" " 42 Y Horses to Base.	
	22nd		" "	
	23rd		" "	
	24th		" "	
	25th		21 Y Horses to Base	
	26th		31 Z Horses for sale at TOURNAI.	
	27th		Usual Routine	
	28th		Lt.Col.J.C.WALCH D.S.O.,proceeded on leave to U.K. Major W.M.M.O'D WELSH D.S.O.,M.C. assumed Command of Brigade.	

R.P.Bart Capt ?
Major R.F.A.
Commanding 106th Brigade R.F.A.

Army Form C. 2118.

106TH BRIGADE R.F.A. WAR DIARY MARCH 1919.

INTELLIGENCE-SUMMARY.

(Erase heading not required.)

Instructions regarding War Diaries and Intelligence Summaries are contained in F. S. Regs., Part II. and the Staff Manual respectively. Title pages will be prepared in manuscript.

Place	Date	Hour	Summary of Events and Information	Remarks and references to Appendices
ANTOING			Demobilization continued throughout the month as follows :-	
"	1/3/19		Nil.	
"	2/3/19		Nil.	
"	3/3/19		Nil.	
"	4/3/19		Nil.	
"	5/3/19		16. "Z" Horses to Animal Collecting Camp DOUAI.	
"	6/3/19		Nil.	
"	7/3/19		19. "X" Horses to Animal Collecting Camp DOUAI.	
"	8/3/19		5. Other Ranks to Concentration Camp TOURNAI for Demobilization.	
"	9/3/19		Nil.	
"	10/3/19		89. "Z" Horses to No.4 Base Remount Depot BOULOGNE.	
"	11/3/19		Nil.	
"	12/3/19		19. "X" Horses to 108th Brigade (Army) R.F.A.	
"	12/3/19		1. Other Rank to Concentration Camp TOURNAI for Demobilization.	
"	13/3/19		3. "Y" Horses to LA ROSERIE for purchase.	
"	13/3/19		2. Other Ranks to Concentration Camp TOURNAI for Demobilization.	
"	14/3/19		A/106 sent 6, 18pdr. Guns and 14 Vehicles to 24th Divisional Vehicle Park BAISIEUX.	
"	14/3/19		1. Other Rank to Concentration Camp TOURNAI for Demobilization.	
"	15/3/19		Lieut. R.Smalley M.C. and 3 other ranks to Concentration Camp TOURNAI for Demobilization.	
"	16/3/19		B/106 sent 6, 18pdr. Guns and 14 Vehicles to 24th Divisional Vehicle Park BAISIEUX.	
"	16/3/19		C/106 sent 6, 18pdr. Guns and 14 Vehicles to 24th Divisional Vehicle Park BAISIEUX.	
"	17/3/19		H.Q./106 sent 2 Vehicles to 24th Divisional Vehicle Park BAISIEUX.	
"	17/3/19		2/Lieut. A.Manley and 3 other ranks to Concentration Camp TOURNAI for Demobilization.	
"	18/3/19		50. "X" Horses to Base Remount Depot HAVRE.	
"	18/3/19		D/106 sent 6, 4.5" Howitzers and 14 Vehicles to 24th Divisional Vehicle Park BAISIEUX.	
"	19/3/19		Nil.	
"	20/3/19		Nil.	
"	21/3/19		18. "Z" Horses to No.7 Vetinary Hospital GORGES-LES-EAUX.	
"	22/3/19		Nil.	
"	23/3/19		5. "Y" Horses to No.1 V.E.S. LE POSTERIE.	
"	24/3/19		Lieut. T.H.S.Hacker and 1.other rank to Concentration Camp TOURNAI for Demobilization.	
"	25/3/19		106th Brigade moved from ANTOING to billets at TEMPLEUVE, BELGIUM.	
TEMPLEUVE	26/3/19		2. "X" Horses to Base Remount Depot ROUEN.	
"	27/3/19–31/3/19		Nothing of importance.	

Lt.Col.R.F.A.
Commanding 106th Brigade R.F.A.

Army Form C. 2118.

WAR DIARY or INTELLIGENCE SUMMARY

106th. BRIGADE R.F.A.

APRIL 1919.

(Erase heading not required.)

Place	Date	Hour	Summary of Events and Information	Remarks and references to Appendices
TEMPLEUVE (Belgium)	1st. 2nd. 3rd. 4th. 5th. 6th. 7th. 8th.	))))))))	Brigade in billets at TEMPLEUVE.	
	9th.		Usual Routine.	
	10th.		Major W.M.M.O'Donnell WELSH left Brigade on posting to 2nd.Horse Squadron. Lieut. R.PLISSONNEAU and Lieut.C.B.O.CAMPBELL-JOHNSTON and 39 Other Ranks left Brigade on posting to Army of Occupation, 2nd.Army Reinforcement Camp.	
	11th. 12th. 13th. 14th.	))))	Usual Routine.	
	15th.		Lieut. C.B. INGHAM left Brigade on posting to 107th.Brigade R.F.A. 12 Other Ranks left Brigade on posting to 24th.D.A.C.	
	16th.		Major W.M.M.O'Donnell WELSH rejoined on posting to 2nd.Horse Squadron being cancelled.	
	17th. 18th.	))	Usual Routine.	
	19th.		Major W.M.M.O'Donnell WELSH proceeded to U.K. for posting abroad.	
	20th. 21st. 22nd. 23rd.	))))	Usual Routine.	
	24th.		Lieut.A.H.HAMILTON-GORDON left Brigade to join Army of Occupation. 3 Other Ranks left Brigade for dispersal stations.	
	25th. 26th. 27th. 28th. 29th. 30th.	))))))	Usual Routine.	

Lt.Col. R.F.A.
Commanding 106th.Brigade R.F.A.

Army Form C. 2118.

WAR DIARY

106th. BRIGADE R.F.A.

~~INTELLIGENCE SUMMARY~~

MAY 1919.

Instructions regarding War Diaries and Intelligence Summaries are contained in F. S. Regs., Part II. and the Staff Manual respectively. Title pages will be prepared in manuscript.

(Erase heading not required.)

Place	Date	Hour	Summary of Events and Information	Remarks and references to Appendices
TEMPLEUVE. (Belgium)	1st.		Brigade in Billets at Templeuve, Belgium. Usual Routine.	
	2nd.		-do-	
	3rd.			
	4th.		Captain W.C.de C.WALSH, struck of strength, awaiting Repatriation. Usual Routine.	
	5th.		-do-	
	6th.		-do-	
	7th.		-do-	
	8th.		-do-	
	9th.		Lt.Col.J.C.WALCH proceeded on leave to Paris. Major C.H.Harper assumed Command of Brigade.	
	9th.		Lieut. H.L.LENNOX and 10 Other Ranks proceeded to Concentration Camp for demobilization.	
	10th.		Usual Routine.	
	11th.		-do-	
	12th.		-do-	
	13th.		-do-	
	14th.		-do-	
	15th.		25 Other Ranks proceeded to Concentration Camp for demobilization.	
	16th.		Lt.Col.J.C.WALCH assumed Command of Brigade on return from Leave.	
	17th.		Usual Routine.	
	18th.		-do-	
	19th.		-do-	
	20th.		10 Other Ranks proceeded to Concentration Camp for demobilization.	
	21st.		Usual Routine.	
	22nd.		9 Other Ranks proceeded to Concentration Camp for demobilization.	
	23rd.		Usual Routine.	
	24th.		-do-	
	25th.		-do-	
	26th.		-do-	
	27th.		-do-	
	28th.		-do-	
	29th.		-do-	
	30th.		-do-	
	31st.		-do-	

Lt.Col.R.F.A.
Commanding 106th Brigade R.F.A.

www.ingramcontent.com/pod-product-compliance
Lightning Source LLC
Chambersburg PA
CBHW080848230426
43662CB00013B/2046